VOLITION'S FACE

ReFormations: Medieval and Early Modern

Series Editors: David Aers, Sara Beckwith, and James Simpson

Recent Titles in the Series

Against All England: Regional Identity and Cheshire Writing, 1195–1656 (2009)
Robert W. Barrett, Jr.

The Maudlin Impression: English Literary Images of Mary Magdalene, 1550–1700 (2009)
Patricia Badir

The Embodied Word: Female Spiritualities, Contested Orthodoxies, and English Religious Cultures, 1350–1700 (2010)
Nancy Bradley Warren

The Island Garden: England's Language of Nation from Gildas to Marvell (2012)
Lynn Staley

Miserere Mei: The Penitential Psalms in Late Medieval and Early Modern England (2012)
Clare Costley King'oo

The English Martyr from Reformation to Revolution (2012)
Alice Dailey

Transforming Work: Early Modern Pastoral and Late Medieval Poetry (2013)
Katherine C. Little

Writing Faith and Telling Tales: Literature, Politics, and Religion in the Work of Thomas More (2013)
Thomas Betteridge

Unwritten Verities: The Making of England's Vernacular Legal Culture, 1463–1549 (2015)
Sebastian Sobecki

Mysticism and Reform, 1400–1750 (2015)
Sara S. Poor and Nigel Smith, eds.

The Civic Cycles: Artisan Drama and Identity in Premodern England (2015)
Nicole R. Rice and Margaret Aziza Pappano

Tropologies: Ethics and Invention in England, c. 1350–1600 (2016)
Ryan McDermott

VOLITION'S FACE

PERSONIFICATION AND THE WILL IN RENAISSANCE LITERATURE

ANDREW ESCOBEDO

University of Notre Dame Press

Notre Dame, Indiana

University of Notre Dame Press
Notre Dame, Indiana 46556
www.undpress.nd.edu
All Rights Reserved

Copyright © 2017 by University of Notre Dame

Published in the United States of America

Library of Congress Control Number: 2016058504

∞ *This paper meets the requirements of*
ANSI/NISO Z39.48-1992 (Permanence of Paper).

For Garey and Ford, whose faces are always before me

CONTENTS

ILLUSTRATIONS

PREFACE

I have modernized the poetry and prose quoted in this book except for the verse of Edmund Spenser, in accordance with the long-standing view that he seeks to produce the impression of archaic language.

A prefatory comment about terminology and usage is in order. I employ *prosopopoeia* as a close synonym for *personification*, despite the many centuries that separate the emergence of these two terms, and I do not italicize the former. Regarding the plural form of *prosopopoeia*: in an effort to avoid the pedantry of *prosopopoeiae* and the archaism of *prosopopoeias*, I use this single term both as a mass noun (like *advice* or *evidence*) and as an uninflected count noun (like *series* or *sheep*). Thus prosopopoeia always adds a face where there was none before, but some prosopopoeia add voices as well as faces.

As for the adjectival form, many historical options present themselves: *prosopopoeial*, *prosopopoeic*, and *prosopopoeical*, among others. I have opted for *prosopopoetic*, since we already have a modern analogue in the English word *onomatopoetic*. I briefly considered employing a separate adverbial form, but reason prevailed.

Brief sections of chapter 5 appeared in two previously published essays: "The Sincerity of Rapture," *Spenser Studies* 24 (2009): 185–208, and "Daemon Lovers: Will, Personification, and Character," *Spenser Studies* 22 (2007): 203–25. Likewise, portions of chapter 6 appeared previously in "Allegorical Agency and the Sins of Angels," *English Literary History* 75, no. 4 (2008): 787–818. My thanks to AMS Press and the Johns Hopkins University Press for permission to reproduce those sections in this book.

I DID MUCH of the early research for this book during a 2009–10 residency at the National Humanities Center, and I remain very

xi

grateful to the staff who provided me with so much assistance, as well as to the fellows who provided intellectual comradeship. Friends and colleagues have supported this project the entire way through. I cannot name them all, but the following people commented on whole chapters: Neil Bernstein, Rüdiger Bittner, John Curran Jr., Jeff Dolven, Mary Floyd-Wilson, Genevieve Guenther, Theresa Krier, Jennifer Lewin, Susannah Brietz Monta, Melissa Sanchez, and Jennifer Waldron. This book is far better than it would be if these kind readers had not shown such generosity. My coeditors at *Spenser Studies*, Anne Lake Prescott and Bill Oram, have for years offered nourishing food for thought about Spenserian personification. I am also deeply grateful to the three series editors at the University of Notre Dame Press—David Aers, Sarah Beckwith, James Simpson—for their interest in this project and their criticisms of the initial typescript, as well as to the two anonymous outside readers who offered helpful suggestions for improvements. My wife, Beth Quitslund, has been a sympathetic and acute reader throughout the process, even as she worked to meet her own obligations and deadlines.

Our books are always in a sense like children, but this book sometimes robbed my sons, Garey and Ford, of time that could have been spent sword fighting, reading together, playing games, or practicing our sarcasm. I am thankful for their forbearance and dedicate this book to them.

INTRODUCTION

Personifications have become almost spooky in the modern literary imagination. Critics have compared them to zombies, freaks, sadists, automatons, death-dealers, fanatics, robots, and clinical compulsives. Personifications, it seems, travel on a trajectory toward fully realized characterhood but do not quite arrive. They are failed persons. When modern critics think of personification, they implicitly start with a notion of a psychologically deep, mimetically probable literary character and then subtract from this character until all that remains is a narrow strip of that character, a strip that cannot feel, think, or choose. For us, by and large, personification transforms subjectivity into objecthood.

This perception goes beyond the assessment of fictional character. Modern feminist philosophers, such as Jennifer Saul, explore the degree to which pornography personifies women, thereby reducing actual women to the single function of providing sexual satisfaction for men.[1] Modern ethicists, such as Ian Ashman and Diana Winstanley, explore the degree to which business corporations personify people, thereby compromising the moral responsibility of actual individuals.[2] For a deconstructionist critic such as Paul de Man, personifications signal the haunting potential of language to undo the category of the human: "They can dismember the texture of reality and reassemble it in the most capricious of ways, pairing man with woman or human being with beast in the most unnatural shapes.

Something monstrous lurks in the most innocent of catachreses: when one speaks of the legs of the table or the face of the mountain, catachresis is already turning into prosopopeia, and one begins to perceive a world of potential ghosts and monsters."[3]

Not all modern assessments of the dehumanizing effect of personification find it reductive or haunted, however. Some recent commentators see a productive dimension in the prosopopoetic confusion of people and things. The sociologist Bruno Latour has celebrated the degree to which prosopopoeia give agency to nonhuman objects under the rubric of the "Parliament of Things."[4] Heather Keenleyside suggests that the poetry of James Thomson, by imbuing the features of the landscape with personified agency, "works to conceive of a social order that would include everything under the sun, and to imagine an ethics that could serve such an expanded system."[5] Sheryl Hamilton has surveyed examples of modern personifications in legal discourse—corporations, computer bots, genetic clones, property—and she concludes that such instances help us see that personhood is "an always incomplete normative project" and that personification supplements the naturalized *person* with the socially constructed *persona,* toward which "we can productively refocus our gaze."[6]

The modern response to personification, then, is not univocal: it ranges from accusations of moral obfuscation and bad literary taste to praise for its beneficial decentering of the human. All these assessments, however, tend to share the assumption that personification is a derivation of or foil to the person. The person is the full, autonomous, and morally responsible agent, and personification—by dint of its refusal to respect the boundary between humans and things—produces a distortion within this agent.[7] This distortion may be decried as a corporate legal evasion or as a caricature of literary character, or it may be welcomed as a talisman against the illusion of autonomous human agency or unmediated consciousness. Yet either way, in the modern view, personification has the effect of leading us away from the realm of the person and toward the realm of nonhuman things.

This impression reflects a vast sea change in literary sensibilities. In the premodern world, personification works in the reverse direction: it starts with ostensibly inanimate things, such as passions, ideas, and rivers, and imbues them with animation and vitality. Nearly all the ancient and early modern commentators claim that prosopopoeia creates force, energy, and emotional intensification. Like de Man, these commentators understand personification to enact a commerce between living and the nonliving, but unlike him, as we will see in chapter 1, they emphasize the movement from death to life, from stasis to animation. And personifications maintain this energy in premodern literary narratives, racing across the landscape in pursuit of their single-minded projects, drawing affect and action out of otherwise insentient or motionless things. The fact that the term *personification* is an eighteenth-century coinage suggests the degree to which the dialectic between *personi*fication and personhood is a peculiarly modern one. In premodern fictions, by contrast, personifications are not trying (and failing) to resemble real human beings or psychologically complex literary characters. Instead, they are channeling energy.

It is not the point of this book to argue that the premoderns got personification right and the moderns got it wrong. Literary art does what a given culture or era needs it to do. Rather, the point is to see what happens if we suspend the anachronistic imposition of the modern template onto premodern literary personification and try to get a clearer picture of what premodern writers and readers thought personification was doing.

Volition's Face argues that the energy characteristic of premodern literary personification is best understood, not as a derivation of personhood, but rather as an expression of will. Figures such as Joy, Fear, Rumor, and War emerge from the agent or from the landscape and take action in the world. They dramatize the transformation of affect or concept into volition: as a character exercises reason or feels fear, Reason and Fear extend from that character into the landscape, augmenting the scope of her agency. By the same token, however, by becoming partly independent of the agent, personifications deny that agent complete control of her will. Personifications are trajectories of volitional energy that have taken on a life of their own.

Literary prosopopoeia thus captures a distinctly premodern intuition about the human will, namely, that the will is both mover and moved, the origin of our actions and the effect of prior determinisms. It will be the burden of chapter 2 to make this interpretation of premodern volition, but at the outset I can say that the medieval and Renaissance understanding of the will offered especially fertile ground for prosopopoetic representation. As the will emerges as an isolatable faculty in the Christian Middle Ages, commentators come to see it as the instrument of human agency but also as partly independent of other human capacities, such as intellect and moral character. Renaissance accounts of the will amplify this independence, conceiving of volition both as the means to self-creation and as the faculty by which people lose control of themselves. The will does not express the self in some fundamental way but rather is a faculty that sometimes undermines the self.

Personification is the literary device that uniquely expresses the activity of this executive yet potentially wayward will. Prosopopoeia give life to the capacities and faculties within us, transforming passions into action, but as a consequence, they also assert their independence, sometimes even doing things to us without our consent. Yet it is not quite right to say in such cases that these faculties are "alienated" from us. When characters in a personification fiction are surrounding by figures named Conscience, Despair, Love, or Sin, such scenarios do not imply pathological or alienated states of self but instead anatomize the typical protocols of premodern agency—protocols that assume a gap between self and volition. Wayward independence remains an ordinary and ongoing potential of literary prosopopoeia, much as the premodern faculty of will remained partially out of the control of the cognitive machinery of judgment and affect. As we will see, this is partly what premodern people meant when they called the will "free."

Interpreting literary personifications as an expression of will also involves noting their striking resemblance to the classical daemon, that semidivine figure that populated the landscape and mind-scape of the ancient Greco-Roman world. Daemons, bearing names such as Health, Ambition, and Madness, seem to anticipate medieval and Renaissance personifications in manifold ways. Modern critics have tended to read this association as a sign of personification's fixation: just as an ancient daemon might force a human agent to behave in a certain way, so a personification obsessively performs a narrow set of actions. Perhaps most famously, Angus Fletcher associated the daemonic dimension of personification with clinical compulsion, and this view has been highly influential in scholarly accounts. Yet, as this book argues, such a view mistakes the primary function of daemonism, namely, to indicate the interior capacities of the human agent in constant interaction with the energies of the external landscape, a complex mixture of activity and passivity. Daemonism, although predating the historical formulation of an isolatable faculty of will, nonetheless underwrites the unpredictable independence of premodern volition: my will is mine, but not identical with me.

Once modernity makes this identity a standard feature of volition—once my will's autonomy becomes synonymous with my autonomy—personification no longer adequately represents human agency. It ends up threatening the human agent (or realistic literary character) as an uncanny double, or, on the flip side of the same coin, it secures human agency by offering a contrasting image of imperfect personhood. Steven Knapp has remarked how often in post-Renaissance personification literature one encounters the scenario of a fictional character coolly observing a personification as it fanatically abandons itself to extreme or pathological behavior—the observer's contrasting impassivity is the assurance of his agency and autonomy.[8] This is *not* the typical scenario of premodern personification, since there was practically no expectation that premodern agents exerted their volition in isolation from the forces of the external landscape. Until the faculty model of the human psyche passes away, over the course of the eighteenth and nineteenth centuries, prosopopoeia offers a rich and powerful expression of the human will's fitful energy. This book explores the link between personification and volition in a range of English Renaissance literature, arguing that Spenser, Marlowe, Milton, and many of their literary contemporaries understand acts of will as a discharge of prosopopoetic energy.

These writers personify certain human affects or concepts—such as despair, erotic passion, and sin—in ways that reflect both the executive and the wayward dimensions of premodern volition. Marlowe's *Doctor Faustus*, placing the protagonist in a vaguely predestinarian world, makes it impossible to be sure if the prosopopoetic good and bad angels *express* Faustus's will or *control* it. Spenser's Britomart, seeking a means to free Amoret from Busirane's torture, has an encounter with a daemonic statue of Cupid that either co-opts her will to the service of Petrarchan desire or inspires her to boldly rewrite Busirane's version of that desire. Milton's Satan, conspiring with his fellows in heaven, gives cephalic birth to the allegorical figure of Sin, rendering his choice to rebel either one of absolute autonomy or one of involuntary reflex. In all these cases, personification is not merely a figure of stasis or constraint; rather, it signals immensely powerful exertions of the will. Yet personification does not represent undiluted self-mastery either: its independence implies that an act of will imposes itself on the agent as much as it channels that agent's power.

In selecting literary examples that best showcase the book's thesis, I have chosen texts in which critics have found personification to constrain the agency and vitality of the characters involved. Hence, it has been suggested that the Tudor interlude plays, often written by Calvinist ministers, employ prosopopoeia to depict the powerless human will in the grip of external forces. Likewise, the scarcity of traditional personification in *Doctor Faustus* is often understood as Marlowe's effort to imbue his protagonist with tragic agency. This kind of view has Spenser offering personification as a cautionary tale about the risk of fixated literalism and has Milton using Satan's birthing of a personification to show the diminished ontological status of the rebel angel.

Once we relinquish the assumption that personification amounts to flat character, psychological compulsion, or tropological stasis, however, fresh possibilities for interpretation emerge. We are able to see that the Protestant Tudor interludes use personification to provide a figurative framework that coordinates the sinner's will to repent with God's grace. Likewise, Marlowe's *Doctor Faustus* minimizes personification to demonstrate the impoverishment of Faustus's will, indicating how thoroughly isolated from the landscape he is as he despairs. Spenser's heroes generally assert their wills and achieve their goals by more closely resembling personification, identifying with the virtue that they represent. And the birth of the personification Sin, in *Paradise Lost*, suggests that a radically free will would become *too* free, behaving randomly and no longer under the agent's control. Repeatedly, these texts turn to personification in order to express the struggles, conundrums, and exertions of the premodern will.

Although I understand my interpretation of personification as a corrective to the received view—or, at least, to a number of received views—I have also gratefully relied on the labor and insights of previous studies. One of these, James Paxson's *The Poetics of Personification*, deserves mention up front, since it is among the few books in English devoted entirely to literary personification rather than more broadly to a topic such as allegory or rhetorical figure. I admire this book a great deal but confess that I engage it only lightly in the pages that follow, since our views of what constitutes the study of personification diverge rather widely. Paxson approaches personification primarily as a rhetorical and textual discourse, one that tends to undo itself in a deconstructionist fashion.[9] By contrast, I take literary personification to distinguish itself from rhetorical device through the performance of action in a narrative, including the act of speech. For Paxson, personification represents the uncanny juncture at which words appear to resemble people; for me, personification undertakes a literary translation of a premodern philosophy of action.

Chapter 1 will offer some preliminary arguments and evidence in support of the view of personification maintained in this book.

Before that, however, I need to say something about the literary-historical scope of this study, along with its implications for literary periodization. It has been argued—probably rightly—that the impulse to personify is part of the psycholinguistic structure of the mind or brain. This study takes as a main departure point the suggestion of George Lakoff and Mark Turner that personification relies on a core metaphor: events are actions.[10] Personification transforms occurrences, states of mind, and moral qualities into actions willed by agents. As a psycholinguistic phenomenon, personification has been around for as long as human beings have been around, and from this view it would be difficult to demonstrate that the figure has changed in any fundamental way. My study, by contrast, has a more specific target: literary personifications that appear as characters in fictional narratives. (Lakoff and Turner are silent about such cases.) The assessment of personifications in this regard has manifestly changed since the Renaissance: modern fiction rarely allows prosopopoeia to appear as characters in its plots. Since this study's interests are primarily literary, it relies on a view of personification that spans the rise and fall of its literary popularity—roughly, between the fifth and seventeenth centuries.

This view does not, of course, deny that literary personification both pre- and postdates this period. Literary prosopopoeia frequently occur in the ancient world, characters with names such as Health, Rumor, Pleasure, Virtue, and Peace. Yet, as chapter 1 discusses, many classicists argue that such characters are in fact daemons, not personifications in the postclassical sense of the figure. Even if one holds (as I do) that the distinction between daemon and personification often blurs and even collapses in narrative, one cannot reasonably deny that characters with names such as Health, Rumor, and Peace appear in Christian literature far more than they do in ancient literature. The Christian Middle Ages sponsors a full-scale tradition of personification literature to a degree that the ancient world did not. One reason for this development, as this book argues, involves the medieval formation of an isolatable faculty of will.

If the long view of personification underwrites this study, then why focus on the Renaissance? One reason is that scholars have, rightly or wrongly, long seen in this era the emergence of modern notions of self and agency and so have been pressed to explain what role conspicuously artificial figures such as personifications played in this emergence. It may be significant that Renaissance scholars, unlike medievalists, need to account for personification under the shadow of Hamlet, Cleopatra, Quixote, Satan, and Eve. If a new style of literary character is emerging in such figures, then the Renaissance period poses important questions for literary prosopopoeia. Why does personification continue to flourish in imaginative literature of the period? And what kind of relationship did Renaissance writers and readers understand personified figures to have with other types of literary character?

Furthermore, as I demonstrate in the pages that follow, the Renaissance inherits its notion of will from a set of intellectual debates that grew in complexity over the centuries. In the final era of its existence as a piece of faculty psychology—before it turns into the expression of an ego or "true self"—the will runs into various kinds of trouble. For one, Reformation theology takes the long-standing view of the will's bondage to sin—which medieval writers treated as important but negotiable—and makes this idea the centerpiece of its moral psychology. For another, seventeenth-century writers begin to deny the legitimacy of the faculty psychology model of human agents, making it more difficult to specify the nature of the will's freedom from other cognitive machinery. Finally, in the literary sphere, a newly robust discourse about ancient daemons, cultivated especially by Renaissance Platonism, creates an ambiguity about the literal/figurative status of the personifications that seek to impose themselves on the wills of the other fictional characters.

The literary personifications examined in this book all respond to these problems in various ways. Conscience and Despair take action within a theological and devotional scenario in which the faculty of conscience is no longer understood to prompt the will directly and in which the state of despair cannot be managed by the sinner's volition. Milton's Sin references a seventeenth-century debate about whether evil human choices result from the semi-independent faculty of will or from the cause and effect of natural determinism. Spenser's Love responds to an ambiguity within Renaissance Platonism about whether the personage of Cupid was to be understood entirely figuratively, as a metaphor for erotic love, or partly literally, as a daemonic spirit that assaults agents from without and co-opts their will.

This book focuses on Renaissance literature, then, not because the nature of personifications changed at that time but because the medieval faculty of the will faced new pressures that some writers engaged by means of literary prosopopoeia. That these writers found it natural to do so underscores the fact that personification had long served as a figure of agency. As a result of these various developments, the authors that this book studies tend to be self-conscious about the link between personification and the will. But this self-consciousness differs from medieval literary practice in degree rather in kind. The problems of the will that these authors confront are Renaissance ones, but their primary tool—personification—remains thoroughly medieval. This book thus draws generously from earlier literary examples.

Indeed, an important implication of this book is that the Renaissance invented new templates for neither the human will nor literary personification. These templates had already been drawn up by medieval writers. Renaissance writers, although putting them to new uses, did not fundamentally change them. Given that scholarly studies have long entertained a notion of the "Renaissance will," it seems worth emphasizing the extent to which this study argues for a strong continuity between medieval and Renaissance conceptions. Despite the efforts of philosophers such as Descartes and Hobbes, the faculty model of the will persists through the seventeenth century and arguably beyond. Despite the presence of seemingly novelistic literary characters such as Faustus, the Duchess of Malfi, and Satan, personifications continue to flourish in literary fictions. To study these phenomena, then, a scholar must give attention to the medieval formulations from which they derive. That is one reason this book employs the term *Renaissance* rather than *early modern*. Early modern people are necessarily looking forward, inviting the inclination to treat them through a deliberately modern lens. Renaissance people, although dubiously imagined as "reborn," nonetheless are looking back to where they came from.

Personification remains the dominant literary figure of agency through the seventeenth century. Even the late Renaissance tendency toward literary verisimilitude, prompted by neoclassicism and by the rediscovery of Aristotle's *Poetics*, did not diminish the widespread popularity of prosopopoeia.[11] This suggests that changes in literary taste cannot alone explain the gradual decline of personification's fortunes in the centuries following the Renaissance. In any case, it is not until the eighteenth century that commentators such as Jean-Baptiste Dubos, Samuel Johnson, and Lord Kames begin to complain about the artificiality and improbability of personified figures, particularly when they appear as agents.[12] These complaints only grow louder in the nineteenth century.[13] As the North Atlantic world sheds earlier assumptions about faculty psychology and the nonidentity of self and will, personification increasingly seems to freeze human agency rather than mobilizing it.

None of this is to imply, I hasten to add, that literary personification simply vanishes after the Renaissance or that it ceases to be interesting. Prosopopoeia continue to populate eighteenth-century poetry, and full-scale personification allegories can be found into the twentieth century.[14] Furthermore, literary character of the eighteenth century remains sufficiently various to resist any clear teleology toward the novelistic self. Dramatic characters in this period, for example, show less concern for verisimilitude than do their cousins in novels.[15] Writers of the eighteenth and nineteenth centuries experiment with innovative prosopopoetic forms, such as "it-narratives" that tell a story from the point of view of inanimate domestic items like overcoats and pens.[16] These examples of post-Renaissance character and personification certainly broach rich questions of agency, animation, and objectification. Yet they all occur alongside a chorus of complaints that personification fails to reach the lived experience of human action. Thus, without denying

the variety of the figure, we should note how often in modern literature personification is a *foil* for human agency.[17] By contrast,
premodern personification was first and foremost an *expression* of
agency, human or nonhuman, albeit a complex one.

Such, in brief, is the view of personification that this study proposes. Before we move to the arguments for this view in chapter 1,
it is worth saying a few words about what this study does not do. It
does not focus on nonliterary examples of personifications, such
as illustrations in emblem books and statues on the facade of the
Amiens Cathedral. These phenomena are important, and I consult
them in relation to literary examples, but this study assumes that
prosopopoeia most resemble agents when they do things in a fiction. It is also important to note that this investigation does not
single out texts that personify the faculty of will, such as the wifely
Will in the thirteenth-century personification allegory "Sawles
Warde," or Will the dreamer in *Piers Plowman*, or Free Will the sinner in the Tudor interlude *Hick Scorner*. Rather, the argument is that
all premodern literary personification—be it Reason, Rage, Winter,
or Rome—expresses volition, whether of a human agent or of the
natural landscape.

Furthermore, this study does not undertake a survey of personification literature, tracing (for example) the development of the
figure from Prudentius to Blake. My interests are theoretically
broader and textually narrower than such a survey could accommodate. This book tries, as it were, to decipher literary personification's genetic code, explaining why it works as it does and describing
its relationship to its ancestors and descendants.

The book begins with a chapter makes a case for the basic thesis, engaging the modern scholarly consensus that literary prosopopoeia signals constraint or lifelessness by arguing that such a view
relies on mistaken assumptions about daemonism and premodern
literary character. Chapter 1 also offers an account of personification's dual identity as sign and character in relation to allegorical
narrative. Chapter 2 then undertakes a sketch of the history of the
will, from antiquity to the Renaissance, in order to suggest why a
full-scale tradition of personification literature did not flourish until

the Christian era. It describes the distinctive aspects of the Renaissance will—particularly through the lens of Reformation theology and seventeenth-century philosophy—while still maintaining that this view of volition comes largely from the Middle Ages. In other words, the continuity of a certain model of will roughly matches the duration of the flourishing of literary prosopopoeia.

Chapters 3 through 6 each focus on a single passion or quality personified in English Renaissance literature. Each chapter generally begins with a brief précis of the history of its passion or quality in personification literature and then grounds its discussion in a particular text or set of texts: Conscience in the Tudor interludes (chapter 3), Despair in *Doctor Faustus* and book 1 of *The Faerie Queene* (chapter 4), Love in books 3 and 4 of *The Faerie Queene* (chapter 5), and Sin in *Paradise Lost* (chapter 6).

The selection of these four personified qualities, beyond their popularity in Renaissance literature, allows me to show the range of modes by which personification expresses volition. Conscience, for example, highlights the degree to which personification makes internal faculties external to the agent, thereby capturing the sense of conscience as a censuring voice that both belongs to us and comes from someone else. The personification of Despair alternately enjoys a full command of will—he deliberately inflicts despair on others—and suffers a lapse of self-control by falling into despair himself. Love, as mythical Cupid or Platonic Eros, carries out a daemonic possession of his victims that skirts the line between voluntary self-surrender and involuntary self-dispossession. Finally, the personification of Sin raises fundamental questions about the origin of our will: Does the appearance of Sin cause the agent to sin, or does Sin signal that act of evil already willed by the agent? These various cases all develop this study's basic insight: to account for the difference between premodern personification and modern literary character, we must attend to the difference between premodern and modern notions of will.

Without appreciating prosopopoeia's link to volitional energy, and the notion of self that this link assumes, it is hard for us to resist treating personifications as diminished versions of literary characters. We find ourselves sorely tempted to read the fate of Spenser's Malbecco—who metamorphoses from jealous husband to a personification named Gelosy—as an allegory of what really happens with all personification. This comic cuckold, who "forgot he was a man," transforms from person to monster, confined to a dark cave and feeding on toads, his humanity lost to cold abstraction.[18] Yet even here personification animates the state of jealousy into a set of actions in the world. Malbecco, both coveting and loathing his miserable condition, illustrates the way jealousy works in human beings: it mocks the meat it feeds on. Malbecco does not lose his humanity by becoming a personification. He loses his humanity by becoming a personification of *jealousy*. This book seeks to recover a distinction that Spenser's readers found intuitive.

PERSONIFICATION, ENERGY, AND ALLEGORY

Literary personification nearly always produces a transition from the order of being to the order of doing. Now, it does this in a way that potentially produces a reverse movement, whereby doing lapses into states of being. This is the movement on which modern criticism about personification most often dwells, but for the moment let us stay with the transition into action. Literary personification marshals inanimate things, such as passions, abstract ideas, and rivers, and makes them perform actions in the landscape of the narrative. Conscience chides the sinner, Resistance repels the lover, and Rome reproaches Caesar as he crosses the Rubicon. In such cases, states of being and feeling—the aversion of the beloved or the outrage of Roman citizens—metamorphose into active agency. These personifications indicate, not simply desires, but desires tending toward action. Personification is an expression of will.

PROSOPOPOEIA AND ENERGY

Premodern writers offer scant theorizing about personification, and most of that pertains to the rhetorical function of prosopopoeia in oration.[1] But the orators and rhetoricians, almost without exception, characterize the trope as a kind of energy. The third-century

BC treatise *On Style*, usually attributed to Demetrius of Phaleron, introduces *prosōpopoiia* as a figure "which may be used to produce force," and it offers as an example Plato's invocation of the future offspring of Athenian citizens in the *Manexenus*. "The *prosōpon* makes the passage much more lively and forceful, or rather it really turns into a drama," the author of *On Style* concludes.[2]

Quintilian's first-century *Institutio oratoria* distinguishes prosopopoeia from the general category of figures that intensify emotion, such as *exclamatio*, by indicating that the former is "bolder" and needs "stronger lungs."[3] By means of personification, a lawyer can make a judge think that he is directly hearing "the voice of the afflicted," thereby enhancing the power of the case, "just as the same voice and delivery of the stage actor produces a greater emotional impact because he speaks behind a mask."[4] Like all classical commentators, Quintilian understands prosopopoeia as a tool a speaker might use in a speech, but he also associates it with personified abstractions in poetry, such as Rumor, Pleasure, Virtue, Death, and Life. He further indicates that prosopopoeia can appear in narratives, as when Livy describes cities maturing and doing things as if they were human agents.[5]

The idea of personification as a kind of emotional intensification persists into Renaissance rhetorical theory. But an important development occurs, since Renaissance commentators now often explicitly see prosopopoeia as one of the building blocks of literary fiction. Abraham Fraunce, for example, calls it "an excellent figure, much used of Poets."[6] There is thus a merging of poetic and rhetorical theory, although an incomplete one, since commentators "are still not sure if they are writing treatises on oratory with literary examples or treatises about how to read and write literature," as Gavin Alexander has suggested.[7] Nonetheless, in these Renaissance accounts any given discussion about the rhetorical value of prosopopoeia potentially implies the figure's literary value. The energy that ancient theory mostly confined to rhetorical address begins to seep into an implicit theory of fictional character.

Erasmus, in his influential *De copia* (1512–34), locates prosopopoeia under the scheme of *enargeia*, a visualizing device used for "the sake of amplifying, adorning, or pleasing," although he prefers to place personified figures such as Rumor, Mischief, and Malice under the heading of *prosopographia*.[8] English writers likewise emphasize the act of animation, the vitalization of nonliving or nonreasoning things with living attributes and personhood. George Puttenham writes in the *Arte of English Poesie* (1589) that poets use prosopopoeia when they "attribute any human quality, as reason or speech, to dumb creatures or insensible things, and do study (as one may say) to give them a human person."[9] Henry Peacham in *The Garden of Eloquence* (1593) likewise describes the trope as "when to a thing senseless and dumb we fain a fit person," attributing to it "speech, reason, and affection." By means of prosopopoeia, Peacham explains, the poet temporarily reverses the effects of mortality: "Sometime[s] he raiseth again as it were the dead to life, and bringeth them forth complaining or witnessing what they knew."[10] Indeed, he insists prosopopoeia is the last, best defense of a besieged orator, "not unlike to a champion, having broken his weapons in the force of his conflict, calleth for new of his friends . . . or to an army having their number diminished, or their strength enfeebled, do crave and call for new supply."[11] John Hoskyns concurs, distinguishing apostrophe, which adds "life and luster" to a speech, from prosopopoeia proper, which he credits with the capacity to "animate and give life."[12]

Renaissance writers also affirm the intensifying power of personification outside of formal discussions about rhetorical taxonomy. Martin Luther's commentary on Galatians uses the term to explain Paul's opposition between Christ and the law: "And to make the matter more delectable and more apparent, he is wont to set forth the law by a figure called prosopopoeia, as a certain mighty person which had condemned and killed Christ."[13] Commenting on the rousing effect of Paul's questions, "O Death, where is thy sting, O grave, where is thy victory?" in 1 Corinthians, Anthony Tuckney instructs his readers, "As to the strength and elegancy of the expression, take notice of . . . his rhetorical prosopopoeia."[14] Philip Sidney confirms the force of personification when he argues for the poetic dimension of the Bible by adducing David's "notable prosopo-poeias," which "maketh you, as it were, see God coming in His majesty."[15]

When premodern commentators talk about personification, then, their talk nearly always has to do with amplification, intensification, and energy. Literary personification—that is, personified figures who perform actions as characters in a narrative—partakes of this rhetorical dynamism. In leaping into the landscape as agents who do things, seeking to influence the other characters of the fiction, personifications resemble the ancient figure of the daemon. The connection between personification and daemons has been well documented, but I would like to review this material in the hope of isolating distinctive elements that have not been prominent in previous critical discussions.

PREMODERN DAEMONISM

Daemons, as Plato's Diotima explains in the *Symposium*, are spirits intermediate between gods and men, immortal though susceptible to passions, "the envoys and interpreters that ply between heaven and earth, flying upward with our worship and our prayers, and descending with the heavenly answers and commandments."[16] The Greek concept of the daemon was often confused with and sometimes merged into the Roman figure of Genius, which substantially expanded its range of significance beginning in late antiquity.[17] The discourse about daemons, who often have names such as Health, Love, and Discord, stretches from Hesiod to Renaissance Platonism, and it conceives of them in a variety of ways. Some writers, such as Plutarch, Bernardus Silvestris, and Ficino, emphasize the mediatory function that Diotima described; they imagine daemons linking together the various levels of the cosmos and, sometimes, the levels of the self.[18] Other writers, such as Plato (in his story of Er), Apuleius, and Plotinus, describe guardian daemons or genii allotted to us by fate, guiding our actions but also expressing our character.[19] (This is probably what Heraclitus means when he says that a man's character [*ēthos*] is his fate [*daimōn*].) Still others, such as Euripides, Porphyry, and Leone Hebreo, imagine daemons as the conduit whereby the energies of the landscape transact with the energies of the self.[20] Daemons invade your soul from the outside, but you don't simply absorb them: they always retain a degree of externality.

In all these characterizations, two themes stand out. First, daemons channel energy: they prompt, possess, attack, protect, and intercede. Second, daemons provide the means by which our interior lives communicate with the outside world. In a daemonic dispensation, the self is not sealed off from the environment but instead maintains a transaction with the elements of the external landscape. We are not the helpless playthings of these inhabiting spirits—our agency partly comes from them—but neither can we make ourselves invulnerable to them. Daemonism involves a mixture of passivity and activity. (In the *Iliad*, Achilles is certainly susceptible to the influence of Ate, but think how curious it would be to claim that Achilles is the passive victim of Ate.) Daemonism, then, posits a fundamental way in which human beings exert their will in the world.

Certainly, there were skeptics in the premodern period. Cicero's Cotta ridicules the tendency of the Stoics to ascribe daemonic agency to every little movement of the environment. If the sun is a daemon, what about the rainbow? And the clouds? And the seasons and storms? "Either this process will go on indefinitely, or we shall admit none of these," Cotta concludes.[21] Likewise, Christian theologians could not accept the daemon as the ancients conceived of it. Augustine reserves his sharpest vitriol for Apuleius's popular description of these guardian spirits, which he takes to be devils in disguise.[22] Renaissance writers were also perfectly willing to make fun of pagan superstition. Sir John Harington wonders mischievously—If a daemon is assigned to every human function, then which daemon has charge over using the privy?[23]

There is no denying the presence of these philosophical and theological doubts; indeed, the volitional energy of literary personification partly depends, as we will see, on an ambiguity between real and fictional, or (to put it in slightly different terms) between literal and figurative. For the moment, however, let us note that the transactional relationship between self and cosmos posited by the Greco-Roman daemon is the relationship that obtains generally throughout the pre- and early modern Christian world. The advent of Christianity did not lead to the modern, freestanding ego any more than Paul's demotic claim that we are all one in Christ led to modern democracy. A strong continuity persists between the ancient and the premodern Christian notion of the self, which exerts its agency in constant interaction with the external energies of the world. This claim about premodern selfhood does, without a doubt, take so broad a view that it lets slip many fine differences and distinctions. But for my purposes there is no getting away from the broad view: literary personification flourished for over a millennium.

In any case, a range of studies over the last several decades from classicists, philosophers, intellectual and cultural historians, and literary critics has been approaching a rough consensus on certain aspects of premodern selfhood. Ruth Padel has discussed Athenian tragedy as a paradigmatic Greek view of a self constantly susceptible to daemonic forces, a view that fundamentally blurs the distinction between inside and outside.[24] Charles Taylor has recently distinguished between the modern ego, isolated from its environment, and the premodern "porous self" that both was vulnerable to and drew energy from nonhuman forces in the external landscape.[25] Timothy Reiss describes this porousness with the concept of "passibility," whereby the agency of the entangled self does not rely on a firm line between active and passive; instead, the agent takes action in the midst of "concentric circles" of social, sacred, and natural forces surrounding the self.[26] Similarly, Gail Kern Paster and others have used a Galenic model of self and body to describe human interaction with, and management of, the surrounding environment.[27]

Some of these accounts tend to underestimate the executive role of the will in the early modern world (bear in mind that the "executive" does not imply isolation from the deliberative or affective), and chapter 2 will take up this issue in more detail. Nonetheless, all of these accounts imply a relation between self and landscape that

I am calling *transactional*. Why *transactional* rather than another term? For one thing, this term has the word *action* in it, and my study is anxious to analyze the relation between a certain sense of selfhood and expressions of will. I am interested in the self in action. Furthermore, *transactional* connotes at least a minimal degree of assent between the agent and the forces impinging on the agent: transactions are more willed than compulsive. The term's implication of activeness, in fact, suits the purposes of this study more than Taylor's nomenclature of "porousness," suggestive though that nomenclature is. Finally, the term's prefix underscores the extent to which acts of will, in the premodern imagination, take place across the boundary (a comparatively fuzzy one) between self and nonself.

DAEMONIC PERSONIFICATION

Medieval and Renaissance personification is the literary translation of the conception of action implied by daemonism. Like the daemon, personification signals our intuition of the primitive energies inside us by which we exert our wills over against the external landscape and by which we remain susceptible to that landscape's influences. As a character in its own right, a personification has been possessed by a daemon, whose power it now channels. As an influencer of other characters, a personification is the daemon who possesses other agents and imbues them with intensified purpose. For the premodern era, one could scarcely imagine a more apt trope for figuring the self's agentive relation to the world. Personification offers a concentrated, even exaggerated image of transactional selfhood. A literary character can sometimes own its choices to the degree that these choices appear to come from the inside and not only the outside; yet a personification's inside already seems as if it came from the outside. A personification has an agency, but one that does not quite appear fully to belong to it.[28]

Personification's extreme transactionalism, its internal commitment to external forces, constitutes the figure's most fundamental energy. It showcases personification's close relation to the dynamic agency of the daemon, which in Greek and Roman literature often magically possessed human beings, foisting upon them a driving sense of purpose, either good or bad. Having an inside so clearly impelled by the outside, manifesting the interior passions of the mind on the external landscape, personifications enjoy a peculiar independence from the constraining effects of the narrative in which they appear. Famously, personifications refuse to function according to scale or probability: they do not modulate their behavior in response to surrounding narrative circumstance, acting out their being in an untrammeled manner.

This is not to deny that narrative circumstances can influence the reader's understanding of a personification's significance, or that a writer using prosopopoeia may be "concerned with context and shades of meaning," as David Aers has suggested.[29] Indeed, the daemonic basis of literary personification complicates the figure's general momentum from stasis to animation. Personification crosses a figurative threshold whereby an inanimate thing becomes, as it were, a living agent, but in a daemonic dispensation nothing is purely inanimate. *Animae* of all sorts literally circulate through the natural landscape and the human psyche. Prosopopoetic energy thus works on a sliding scale from daemon to figure: it poetically imbues a lifeless thing with liveliness, but that thing itself is already potentially inhabited by a daemonic spark.

This means that the metaphorical scenario that personification features can also be understood as magic or enchantment. For example, when Spenser's Sir Guyon sets out to attack Furor with his sword, the Palmer tells him, "He is not, ah, he is not such a foe, /As steele can wound, or strength can overthroe."[30] Furor defies the ordinary protocols of the story, according to which knights fight villains with weapons. Sword blows can't stop Furor. Why not? We might understand Furor to enjoy magical protection from mortal weapons—that is, understand him as daemonic. Or, we might understand Furor as the *idea* of rage cast figuratively into agentive form: he performs as a character in the fiction but retains a dimension of idea-ness that remains at a remove from the fiction. This distance does not simply drag the story into abstraction: it energizes the story by making it temporarily rearrange its usual rules.

As daemon or personification—or, in the terms I argue for, as daemonic personification—Furor enjoys a freedom from narrative rules and circumstances that operate elsewhere in the poem. He is rage untrammeled, the absolute distillation of a passion into an act of will. But Furor doesn't appear to possess "free will" as we understand this concept in modern debates about freedom. Furor doesn't, for example, deliberate about what to do out of a range of equally possible actions. This limitation is a consequence of the kind of agency that Furor enjoys. Personifications are so radically free to do what they are that, viewed from another angle, they appear gripped by a narrow fixation.

We might put the matter in this way: Furor has "no choice" but to act out his wrath—his inner daemon drives him to it—but, by the same token, nothing can stop Furor from raging—not soothing music, not pleading, not even adverse narrative circumstances. Temperance might bind Furor in chains but cannot change Furor's nature. To employ two concepts from modern political theory, an allegorical agent enjoys both negative and positive liberty: it is "free from" the constraining pressures of narrative circumstance, and it is "free to" realize its nature through volitional action, to "be his own master," as Isaiah Berlin put it.[31]

Again, this is certainly a strange kind of freedom, and a number of critics have associated personification's single-mindedness with psychological compulsion. This impression is mistaken, insofar as compulsion forces people to do what they, in some sense, do not want to do. Personifications, by contrast, *want* to do what they do; they are wholehearted about their actions and attitudes. They gravitate toward what Philip Fisher has described as the "vehement passions," those affections such as wrath, fear, and grief that for their duration possess the whole person.[32] Nonetheless, although prosopopoeia are free to do what they want, they can want only one kind of thing. We therefore have to be cautious in associating personifications with agency, especially if we think that agency amounts to autonomy. The modern notion of autonomy implies the capacity of a freestanding ego to privilege certain inclinations, dispositions, and feelings over others while itself remaining mostly independent of said inclinations, dispositions, and feelings—thereby strictly controlling which mental phenomena are expressed in action and which are not.

Clearly, personifications do not have or represent autonomy in this sense. It is better to associate them with the will, the faculty by which an agent acts upon the world, including actions that we would call *willful*. When people behave willfully, they have adopted an attitude such that it is difficult for them to alter their present course of action. Willful people are, in a sense, temporarily *stuck* with their will. The notions of will and willfulness were closer in the Renaissance than they are now. (It is probably not a complete coincidence that the early modern word *will* meant both appetite and intention.) In any case, it is with this understanding that we may say that personifications represent agency: they are trajectories of volitional energy. This is why they often seem to burst onto the stage when they first enter a fiction and why they sometimes resemble numinous deities. They are like daemonic agents who channel energy from afar, interrupting the rules of the literal narrative.

But if literary personifications function as daemonic agents, to what degree is this agency defined by their visual and ornamental dimension? Prosopopoeia is closely tied to a tradition of iconography such as we find in manuscript illustration, emblem books, church statuary, and so on.[33] Guillaume de Lorris's garden of Love features plenty of prosopopoetic agents, but the poet finds it natural to begin his story by describing the personifications painted on the wall surrounding the garden.[34] This visual dimension does potentially limit personifications' scope as agents, since images signify through appearance and ekphrasis, not through actions. This effect is heightened in cases where personified figures appear only briefly in a fictional scene, where their function begins to seem more ornamental (in the strong sense of interpretive elaboration) and less agentive. When Christian in *Pilgrim's Progress* comes upon Simple, Sloth, and Presumption and exchanges less than a sentence with each of them before departing, these personifications do not so much perform actions as they provide a visual tableau of the spiritual dangers facing the protagonist as he proceeds on his journey.[35]

The question of the point at which personification becomes commentary begins to broach the relation between prosopopoeia and allegory, and I will have more to say about this shortly. For the moment, it will suffice to note that agency requires a narrative appearance of some extension and that what counts as momentary versus extended is hard to schematize definitively. Morton Bloomfield distinguishes between what he calls pseudopersonification, such as the animate metaphor in the sentence "The storm is howling outside," and genuine personification, to which multiple animate verbs are attached over some duration in a narrative. James J. Paxson describes simple animate metaphor as "secondary personification," which he ascribes to the level of discourse, whereas "primary personification" is found at the level of story. Barbara Newman distinguishes the epiphanic vividness of what she calls Platonic personification, which emanates from transcendental reality, from the analytical dullness of what she calls Aristotelian personification, which briefly gives a proper name to an abstraction.[36] Personifications, then, do not always function as agents: sometimes they are visual emblems, ornamental commentary, brief animate metaphors, or momentary nominalizations. The point to emphasize here, however, is that when these phenomena occur in literary narrative (the topic of this study) they are potential cases of prosopopoeia waiting to spring into action. When personifications are allowed to take action in a fiction, they truly distinguish themselves, becoming characters who translate the order of being into the order of doing.

Within recent scholarship, the critic who has most clearly seen this quality of prosopopoetic agency is Theresa Krier, whose account of daemonic allegory posits that personification has the potential to express vital energy. Drawing on the concept of elemental motion in Luce Irigaray, Krier suggests that the daemonism of late antiquity functioned as a kind of allegorical cosmology, whereby the will of the gods was translated into a physics imbued with divine energy.[37] This daemonic physics, she suggests, provides the elemental basis of medieval and Renaissance personification. As fluid movement and energy, personification can produce conceptual linking and demonstrate the divine animation of the physical landscape.[38] I understand my view of personification as an expression of transactional agency to run a roughly parallel course to her view of personification as a model of thinking and physical mobility.

PERSONIFICATION AND THE MODERN PERSON

The notion of a transactional self no longer predominates in the modern world (at least, in the North Atlantic world), and this is one of the reasons that personification now seems to us artificial, archaic, or inhuman. It is instructive to notice that the figure of the daemon suffered a similar fate in the post-Renaissance period. Over the course of the Enlightenment, writers increasingly found the daemon incredible or incomprehensible. John Quincy Adams wondered in a letter to Thomas Jefferson if the Greeks understood daemons as more than metaphors. Jefferson responded that, although men are always susceptible to superstition, someone as intelligent as Socrates could not actually have believed in a guardian spirit: by *daemon* Socrates must have meant his conscience or reason.[39]

No doubt, traces of the daemon remain in the modern world. The common phrase "Something got into me" bears witness to our intuition that acts of will sometimes seem to come upon us from the external landscape. But this intuition has long been pushed to the margin by the conviction that human passions and inspirations occur only as mental, interior phenomena. Perhaps the most thorough transformation of the external daemon into internal mental space comes from Immanuel Kant, when he defines artistic genius as "the innate mental predisposition through which nature gives the rule to art." Kant finds it noteworthy that the word for this mental facility "is derived from [the Latin] *genius*, the guardian and guiding spirit that each person is given as his own at birth."[40] Yet what once came from outside the self is now placed entirely inside. Modern genius is a structure of human consciousness, not an invasion by the spirit of inspiration.

Another way to put this is to say that daemonism no longer underwrites the human agent once modernity defines human beings according to the rubric of the "person." Modern personhood tends to distinguish the contingent parts of the self from the real or essential self: whatever else I am, I am first and foremost a person. Whatever its virtues, then, personhood tends to remove the human being from the landscape of nonhuman things surrounding her. As Kant famously explains in the *Groundwork*, "Beings the existence of which rests not on our will but on nature, if they are beings without reason, still have only a relative worth, as means, and are therefore called *things*, whereas rational beings are called *persons* because their nature already marks them out as an end in itself."[41] This description implicitly limits the interaction an agent has with her environment because such transactions might threaten the fundamental distinction between things and persons. Yet blurring that distinction is precisely how literary personification works.

In claiming that modern personhood ends up making literary personifications seem like obstacles to rather than vehicles of human agency, however, I do not wish to deny premodern prosopopoeia any connection whatsoever to a notion of person or whole agent. For one thing, personifications represent the parts of a psyche or landscape in action, and as parts they thus imply the presence of a whole. The degree to which a given narrative realizes this whole varies from case to case. Fictions such as the *Psychomachia* or *The Faerie Queene* feature personifications that illustrate a set of faculties, passions, institutions, vices, and virtues that do not seem to belong to any particular whole. Other fictions, such as *Confessio amantis* and *Piers Plowman*, appear to be "person-shaped," as James Simpson has put it, insofar as the progress of their personification narratives appears to correlate with the integration of a human psyche.[42] In such cases, however, premodern personifications do not compete with or usurp the place of whole agents, as they will come to do in modernity; rather, they anatomize and constitute the energy of whole agents.

Furthermore, my isolation of premodern prosopopoeia from modern personhood is not meant to imply that only modernity has ownership of the concept of the person. The premodern world also possessed concepts of agency and identity such that we might call premodern agents "persons." Alain de Lille's twelfth-century definition of a person as "a *hypostasis* [individual] distinct by reason of dignity" has surprisingly modern overtones.[43] Indeed, Thomas Pfau has recently argued, in a study of human agency and changing conceptions of reason in the West, that it was premodernity, and not modernity, that developed a coherent notion of personhood, namely, "as endowed with the potential for self-awareness and with the ontological fact of its ethical responsibility."[44] Premodern psychology, according to Pfau, understood humans as persons insofar as they enjoyed a teleological stance toward the natural world and toward themselves. In this respect, his book builds on the work of the German philosopher Robert Spaemann, who mines accounts of *persona* and *hypostasis* in early medieval Christian theology to argue that the special status of persons lies in their capacity to take various stances toward their nature, unlike other living creatures, which are simply identical to their nature.[45] Pfau's and Spaemann's accounts thus potentially reverse the story I am telling: for them, personhood flourished in the premodern world and was subsequently lost when modernity relinquished the assumption of natural teleology.

To some degree, we are dealing with a difference of terminology. Pfau's notion of the premodern "person" has substantial overlap with my account of the premodern transactional self. For example, Pfau observes that whereas the modern agent potentially understands his environment "as a neutral inventory of medium-sized dry goods," for the premodern agent "the world has to be understood as a dynamic and profoundly interconnected grid of phenomena toward which we relate in prima facie evaluative form, viz., as focal points of interpretive curiosity and, potentially, as sources of means for our continued flourishing."[46] For Pfau, this teleological orientation of the person to the natural world is imperiled in modern thought, when writers such as Hobbes, Locke, Hume, and Adam

Smith come to treat nature as an inert background to human action and treat human reason as instrumental rather than normative, the tool of the will to power rather than the basis for the virtuous use of power. Although my emphasis is not on teleology, like Pfau I see the premodern agent, who is partly constituted by her surroundings, as eventually superseded by "the modern idea of a disengaged and hermetic self."[47] The difference is that I am calling this modern self a "person."

The reason I do so is that it is important, for the purposes of my study of personification, to emphasize the degree to which modernity has understood itself to have discovered the person by stripping away the inessential or contingent parts of the self in order to reveal the real "I," the first-person marker that is somehow both unique to me and shared by all human beings. Descartes's ego, Locke's self-conscious self, Kant's transcendental self, Henri Bergson's fundamental self, Harry Frankfurt's wholehearted self, Linda Zagzebsky's irreplaceable first-person—these philosophical formulations have all variously contributed to the modern notion of the person, whose consciousness observes but remains buffered from the external landscape. Once human agents are persons, in this sense, then *person*ifications come to seem like pale imitations, either threatening the integrity of the agent or indirectly confirming her autonomy as a contrasting foil.

Nonetheless, Pfau's account of premodern personhood prompts me to underscore that my term *transactional* does not imply that agents lack individuality, intentionality, or self-control. Premodern writers assumed, as we do, that human actors perceive, deliberate, and decide. Yet they understood them to do these things not just in their minds by also by drawing upon the energies and presences that surrounded them in the environment. This is not to say that premodern agents *never* suspended this transactionality. Stoic sagehood implied impassibility, as did certain profound states of Christian despair, as we will discuss in chapter 4. But such instances were exceedingly rare and were usually understood as exceptions that proved the rule that human action involved interaction with the external landscape. Premodern daemonism was an outstanding example of this interaction, and personification was its literary translation.

PERSONIFICATION AND ALLEGORY

Thinking of personifications as daemonic agents helps to specify what kind of characters they are. They are *willful* characters, committed to a narrow set of actions and seemingly inspired or impelled by external energies. But we have also noted that personifications, unlike daemons, have a pronounced figurative quality. They are metaphors, or perhaps catachreses, that enact a transference between the order of things and the order of persons.[48] Matthew Sutcliffe, anxious to deny the Jesuit Robert Parsons an early church tradition of saint worship, appeals to the figurative dimension of personification: "There is an infinite difference between the words of the Fathers and the blasphemous forms of popish prayers. They [the Fathers] by a figure called Prosopopoeia did speak to saints, as orators do to heaven, or earth, or cities, or other things that hear nothing. These [Catholics] pray to them as if they heard them, saw them, and could help them."[49] Whatever their daemonic power, personifications maintain a distance from literal presence, qualified by the notion of "as it were," as Philip Sidney puts it in the case of psalmic images of God's approach.

In literary fiction, personifications are continued metaphors that persist through a narrative. As a result, readers have often understood them as allegorical. If this is correct, then a further basic description of prosopopoetic agency is required. Allegorical signs do not necessarily behave as agents. The building called the Castle of Perseverance and the market called Vanity Fair signify something in relation to other signs in their allegory, and events may take place in them, but they do not perform actions. If personifications are likewise signs, perhaps it makes sense to group them more closely with signifying objects such as castles, spears, and forests, and less closely with characters who behave as literal agents.

In short, we need an account of the relation between personification's characterhood and its signhood. Critics have sometimes gestured at such an account under the rubrics of "concrete versus abstract" and "realistic versus allegorical." Yet the first binary does not make much sense of personifications of things such as rivers or cities, and the second commits us to a psychological mimeticism that is probably alien (as I will argue shortly) to the premodern experience of literary character. Instead, in this section and the next I propose to examine personification's allegorical dimension under the rubric of "example and sign." Doing so will allow us to specify the range of ways in which personified figures, as signs and characters, interact with the narrative that contains them.

The first thing to ask is whether literary personifications are indeed allegorical or not. There is no general agreement about this question. Some scholars claim that allegory emerges from a tradition of latent or hidden meaning (*allos, hypnoia, mysterium*), whereas personification offers patently obvious meaning.[50] Furthermore, allegories (unlike individual tropes) require narratives that develop in time in order to unfold their meaning.[51] These scholars also point out that medieval and Renaissance theorists of allegory never mention a relation to personification. Hence, that personification sometimes occurs in allegorical narratives is a mere coincidence. Other scholars have argued, to the contrary, that no device partakes more thoroughly of allegory than personification. The trope forces us to attend to ideas signified by the characters in the story, implying multiple levels of meaning. Personifications wear a mask or face (*prosopon*) linked to an idea or feeling, and so involve an inside/outside structure analogous to the surface/depth structure of allegorical narrative.[52]

My own view is rather ecumenical on this question. The object of study in this book is personification, not necessarily personification allegory. Personifications do not, in themselves, yield allegory, which I assume to involve a narrative that announces, with greater or lesser degrees of explicitness, its secondariness to an order of nonfictional ideas. *Secondary* here doesn't mean boring or useless;

instead, it means instrumental. In allegory, the story reveals itself, at least at times, as an instrument for pointing at these nonfictional ideas.

This definition remains deliberately silent about a number of hot-button issues surrounding allegory. It says nothing about whether allegory must involve abstract ideas or whether these ideas are hidden by or transparent within the narrative. The definition offers no rules for how allegorical narratives signal their secondariness. The rubric of "greater or lesser degrees of explicitness" is pitched broadly enough to all but ensure that borderline cases—is it allegorical or not?—will occur. My silence about these issues constitutes an attempt to avoid entanglement in long-standing debates about allegory that, although interesting, have little relevance to the manner in which personifications operate. It is the issue of secondariness, as we will see, that most impinges on prosopopoetic function.

Yet even in this regard I must make an important qualification. For the sake of convenience, the pages that follow will assume a ready distinction between allegorical and nonallegorical fiction, but that distinction was far cloudier in the Renaissance. According to some modern scholars, the early modern category of allegory is very wide indeed. Kenneth Borris's important study of allegorical epic, for example, at times seems to include any text "stressing moral significance and profundity of content."[53] Judith Anderson casts allegory in similarly broad terms, ranging from "realistic improbability and disjunction to conspicuous mythic characterization, sustained structural significance, radical puns and thematic words, insistent reiteration of meaning, allegorical projection, interiorized landscapes, persistent allusion to the forms, images, and words of earlier literary texts, and in short, to a concern with meaning that is not naively abstracted from earth but is radically discontinuous with it."[54] Allegory in these descriptions sounds almost coextensive with the possibility of meaning itself, and it is hard to imagine a nonallegorical work of fiction under these rubrics. Yet I confess that I can find no Renaissance definition of allegory that would exclude these conceptions. The lesson I take from Borris and Anderson is this: we should not expect to find a category of "nonallegorical fiction" explicitly informing the sensibilities of premodern readers and writers. In the terms I am using, *any* fiction can potentially be considered secondary to an order of nonfictional ideas. Nonetheless, not all fictions equally call attention to a secondariness that marks them as allegorical.

If allegorical narrative features this quality of secondariness, then to what degree does this formulation help us say whether a given character is allegorical or literal? The nature of literal character is immensely complicated, but I will suggest three conditions: (1) it openly represents a historical person; (2) it does not announce (via name or behavior) its secondariness to an order of nonfictional ideas—that is, it can be understood *primarily* in terms of its relation to other elements in the same narrative plane; (3) it displays emotions, dispositions, or intentions of sufficient range to make it difficult to identify the character with a single trait. Renaissance writers and readers would affirm (1) explicitly and (2) implicitly and would probably regard (3) as rather oblique. (For the modern sense of literal character, simply reverse this order of priority.) In any case, these criteria allow for plenty of ambiguity but are at least minimally relevant to the Renaissance recognition of literal character, allowing us, for example, to include Shakespeare's Lord Bardolph, who spreads rumors in *2 Henry IV*, but to exclude Shakespeare's Rumor. Shakespeare's contemporaries would probably see this distinction, even if they had no interest in theorizing or formalizing it.

Signs and Examples

The second condition of the above definition of literal character— that a character not announce its secondariness to an order of nonfictional ideas—promises to give the most insight into the relation that personifications have with the fiction that contains them. Within a fiction, what counts as announcing or not announcing one's secondariness? The distinction between sign and example offers a way to think about this question. In the play *The World and the Child* (1522), for instance, Folly urges Mankind to abandon virtue, and Conscience urges him to return to it. If we say that Folly and Conscience *signify* the operation of certain mental inclinations in the human soul, and therefore understand the characters as secondary to ideas about these mental inclinations, then we are close to allegory. But we don't have to say this: perhaps Folly and Conscience *exemplify* foolish and conscientious moral advisers, in which case there is no particular urgency to call the story allegorical. One can have examples without allegory. Goethe defined allegory as a mode "where the particular serves only as an example of the general," but this is probably not quite right.[55] Examples don't signify another order of meaning: an apple is an example of fruit, but it does not necessarily signify fruit. But an apple might signify, in an allegorical interpretation of Genesis 3, the sinful desire to transgress divine law. Allegory, in this respect, seems to treat its elements as signs more than as examples.

The difference between signs and examples very quickly raises problems, however. For one thing, all the words and characters and events in a fiction might be understood as signs—say, in a Peircean sense—but this doesn't help us distinguish allegorical from literal character or agent from nonagent. For another thing, examples appear to refer in ways that are different from signs, but what is the difference? Do examples have a natural or logical relation with their categories rather than a conventional relation? In a fiction, does the character named Youth exemplify or signify the concept of youth?

We can get some clarification on these matters from the work of the art philosopher Nelson Goodman, who postulates a distinction between *denotation* and *exemplification* that corresponds, roughly, to the distinction between sign and example obtaining in allegory. Goodman suggests that denotation involves the relationship of a label, such as the title of a painting, and the thing it labels, such as the painting. Denotation includes all sorts of labels, linguistic, gestural, and pictorial: a painting of the Eiffel Tower may function as a label of the Eiffel Tower. Importantly, the "realism" of such a painting, its resemblance to the actual Eiffel Tower, is merely incidental to its denotational function. After all, as Goodman points out, such a painting far more closely resembles other paintings of the Eiffel Tower than it does the actual building, yet we do not claim that the painting represents other paintings.[56] The relation between labels and the things they label is purely arbitrary and conventional, not natural or based on shared properties (34–39). In short, denotational labels do referential work, pointing us to things other than themselves.

By contrast, exemplification requires that the symbol under consideration possess the property that it exemplifies. Goodman offers the example of tailor swatches: a plaid swatch not only refers to plaidness but also possesses the quality of being plaid. In Goodman's formulation, "Exemplification is possession plus reference. To have without symbolizing is merely to possess, while to symbolize without having is to refer in some way other than by exemplifying" (53). In denotation, the arrow of reference travels only in one direction, from the word *plaid* to the property of plaidness, for instance. But exemplification involves a bidirectional relation between symbol and the thing symbolized. The word *plaid* denotes the tailor's swatch, but the swatch likewise refers to plaidness. The relation between example and the properties exemplified is not arbitrary as in the case of labels: the example must partake of the nature of the property it exemplifies.

It is worth emphasizing that Goodman's definition of example does not necessarily imply a Platonic notion of Forms. As Goodman notes, we can say equally that what is exemplified is a property (plaidness) and a predicate ("is plaid") (54–57). This leaves open the question—which I think ought to be left open—of whether to understand literary personification as philosophical realism or nominalism.[57] After all, we can find both views expressed within a single personification fiction. The speaker of Dante's *Vita nuova*, for example, assures us on the one hand that personifying Love "as if it were a human being" is, strictly speaking, "patently false, for Love does not exist in itself as a substance, but is an accident in a substance." On the other hand, he also speaks of this personification in terms that resemble the metaphysical realism of Socrates in the *Cratylus*: "The name of Love is so sweet to hear that it seems impossible to me that the effect itself should be in most things other than sweet, since, as has often been said, names are the consequences of the things they name."[58] As with Dante's figure of Love, we can think of literary personification either as giving a name to that which does not really exist as a substance or as embodying independently existing abstract properties.

In any case, Goodman's distinction between denotation (which I am calling a "sign") and exemplification offers a valuable means for thinking about the intersection between prosopopoeia's agentive and figurative dimensions.[59] In particular, it supplies a template for the range within which personifications act out their concepts. In some cases, personifications signify their concept by performing actions that share no characteristics with that concept. Take, for instance, the character of Chastity (Pudicitia) in Prudentius's *Psychomachia*, who defeats her opponent Lust by thrusting a sword into the vice's throat.[60] Now, if Lust had sexually propositioned Chastity, and Chastity had said no, then we might have an example of chastity. But that is not the case here. Even if the scene of combat plays on traditional language about fighting against temptation, slicing open your opponent's windpipe is not literally a chaste thing to do. The link between violence and chastity is merely conventional. Like a denotational label, Chastity signifies her allegorical meaning by pointing toward an idea to which she herself has no necessary relation. The idea of chastity does not point back to her.

Personifications like Prudentius's Chastity bear a considerable resemblance to allegorical signs such as the Castle of Perseverance or the Apple of Temptation. What they signify has little to do with what kind of thing they are or what actions they perform. We could just as readily have a Castle of Temptation and an Apple of Perseverance. The Wandering Woods might deny its victims a clear path, but it equally might offer them a clear path to the wrong destination. Of course, some limits exist: the Armor of Vulnerability would be a strange allegorical sign, and a Chastity that eagerly coupled with Lust might confuse us.[61] George Puttenham rightly observes that in allegory a figure cannot be "altogether contrary" to its meaning but has "much convenience with it."[62] But aside from cases of direct self-contradiction, anything goes. Allegory signifies so sup-plely because its signs are arbitrary and almost anything can stand for anything else. This quality of allegory sometimes inclined religious opponents during the Reformation to accuse each other of capricious biblical interpretation under the charge of "allegorical" reading.

Since Chastity's denotational function does not depend on the particular actions she performs—in the sense that she could signify chastity by means of an arbitrary range of actions—her allegorical significance has nothing to do with what kind of character she is. Certainly, she has a character in the fiction: a warrior princess who exalts over the fall of her enemy. But she could equally be a humble peasant who looks with pity at the victims of desire, or the master of a household who keeps his bedroom neat and uncluttered. None of these actions are literally chaste things to do, so such characters denote chastity by pointing away from themselves toward an order of nonfictional ideas outside the frame of the fiction. They do not signify as characters; rather, they signify and also happen to be characters.

Contrast Chastity, however, with Prudentius's figure of Patience, who stands "with staid countenance, unmoved amid the battle and its confused uproar."[63] Patience endures her opponent's attacks patiently. Wrath throws a spear, and Patience stands unmoving as the spear bounces off her breast armor. Wrath smites her in the head with her sword, but the sword breaks upon the virtue's bronze helm. Wrath finally becomes so frustrated that she kills herself.[64] Throughout the encounter the poet describes Patience as unmoved, calm, and waiting. In Goodman's terms, Patience the character exemplifies her concept in a way that Chastity the character does not. The things that Patience does are literally patient. Like Chastity, she points to a nonfictional idea, but unlike Chastity this idea also points back at Patience.

Notice that the difference between sign and example does not involve verisimilitude: Patience's impassivity as her opponent attacks her is surely less "realistic" than Chastity's victory over Lust.[65] Instead, the difference involves the nature of the relation between

an example and its meaning. Unlike Chastity, what Patience signifies depends on what she does and on what kind of character she is,
because she exemplifies what she signifies. Her character does not
perhaps have a *necessary* relation to her allegorical meaning (she
could perform patient actions different from the ones she does), but
this relation is not arbitrary. As Goodman observes, "Labeling seems
to be free in a way that sampling is not. I can let anything denote red
things, but I cannot let anything that is not red be a sample of red-
ness" (58–59). To the degree that Patience offers a sample—an
example—of patience, her range of action and character is limited.
She signifies her meaning by means of her character, not in spite
of it.

Over a long enough narrative, of course, a single personification
can alternate between signification and exemplification. This imposes a programmatic ambiguity on the question of whether personifications are literal or allegorical agents. The condition of literal
character that I posed a few pages ago—that a character not announce its secondariness to an order of nonfictional ideas—seems
to apply to Patience but not to Chastity. Chastity's actions and character serve as instruments for signifying an idea of chastity that
plays no role in the literal fiction. We need to go outside the literal
narrative plane if we wish to access the concept of chastity that this
character references. By contrast, Patience's character and actions
offer examples of patient behavior that interact with the literal narrative. This does not make Patience antiallegorical, to be sure, but
it does provide grounds for interpreting her as nonallegorical. As
I observed before, one can have examples without allegory: Mr.
Darcy's behavior toward Elizabeth Bennet's family exemplifies the
character flaw of pride, but we do not therefore conclude that he is
a sign in an allegorical narrative. Likewise, Folly and Conscience
offer foolish and conscientious advice in *The World and the Child*,
so we can understand the ideas they reference in terms of the literal
plot of the drama.

So sometimes personifications signify by exemplifying, and
sometimes they just signify. One can find plenty of cases like Pru-

dentius's Chastity, where the property referred to has no literal presence within the fictional character. Spenser's Error does not literally make any mistakes, and Bunyan's Flatterer does not literally offer any blandishments to Christian and Hopeful.[66] The nonexemplifying aspect of literary prosopopoeia, incidentally, sheds light on the oft-disputed relationship between personifications and "character types" such as we find in the drama of Ben Jonson and others. Lady Saviolina, Fastidious, Morose, and their ilk will never exactly coincide with literary personification because a character type that does not exemplify fails its essential duty, and this is not true of prosopopoeia. On the other hand, character types and personification will always have some overlap because more often than not personifications possess an exemplifying dimension: their actions and character are samples, within the literal narrative, of what they signify. Fear behaves fearfully, Pride behaves pridefully, and likewise for Hope, Ignorance, Strength, Charity, and so on. Even personifications of the natural landscape, such as cities and rivers, might be understood as examples, at least to the degree that we can specify what it means to behave in a city-like or river-like fashion.

This means that, as examples, personifications do not have access to an arbitrary set of actions by which to reference their concepts. They signify with their actions and dispositions, which is to say that they signify as characters, not only as signs. Like most characters, they engage the narrative and therefore find themselves limited and manipulated by that narrative. Indeed, in narrative (and perhaps in real life, though that is not the question here), circumstantial constraint is one of the conditions of agency: the fact that the features of a landscape resist a character indicates that the character is trying to push these features around in the first place. In rare cases, the narrative manipulates personifications in such a way that they appear to behave contrary to their concept. Guillaume de Lorris's Resistance promises to stop resisting; the Seven Deadly Sins in Langland "confess" their sinfulness and promise to reform; in the interlude *Hick Scorner*, a repentant Free Will gives his companion Imagination the new name of "Good Remembrance."[67] Narrative circumstances appear temporarily to cause these personifications to lose focus and to drift or fall into behavior that contradicts their putative allegorical significance.

Personifications, then, have at least two ways of interacting with a fictional narrative. They can float above it, as signs, violating or reorganizing or ignoring its typical causal rules, or they can engage its causal landscape, as examples, manipulating and being manipulated by its literal features. And they can do both at the same time. Spenser's Furor, as a sign of rage, is partly exempted from the rules of combat operating elsewhere in the poem, but he is also an angry man, exemplifying rage and transmitting it to others. When personifications are more sign than example, we are inclined to think of them as metaphors; when they are more example than sign, we sometimes describe them as extreme character types.

Personifications are thus agents who have one foot in character and one foot in signhood. They resemble allegorical signs, signifying their concept through action that sometimes has only an arbitrary and conventional relation to this concept. Yet as examples they also differ from allegorical signs in that their relation to their concept is not arbitrary; they need a certain kind of character to achieve their signifying work. Whether as daemonic characters or as signs free from narrative causality, personifications extend passion into activity and concept into volition.

Personifications animate things; they draw action out of otherwise inactive objects or states. This is what I meant by my opening claim that personification produces a transition from the order of being to the order of doing. I also admitted in that opening that the reverse movement can occur: narrative action may seem to lapse into abstract states of being. In some fictions, when personifications multiply and enter into regularized, repetitious interaction (pageants, ritualized battles, genealogies, etc.), they do not appear to daemonically interrupt the rules of a narrative but instead seem to translate these rules into signs. It is probably fair to say that the paired combats in Prudentius's *Psychomachia*, exciting though they are, become less exciting as the narrative continues. And when in *Piers Plowman* Anima (as she is named in the B-text) tells Will at some length that in her other modes of being she is called Animus, Mens, Memoria, Racio, Sensus, Conscience, Amor, and Spiritus, we may conclude that Langland does not here ramp up the action but rather temporarily suspends it to demonstrate a set of psychological affiliations.[68]

This enervating effect, although certainly present in literary personification, remains secondary to the main daemonic force of prosopopoeia as it operates in premodern literary texts. A few critics, such as Theresa Krier, see personification as essentially energetic. Yet the contrary conclusion that personification first and foremost depletes the fiction—and that personification is a kind of frozen or hollow version of literal characters—has become an unstated scholarly consensus. It is time to explore this consensus.

VOLITION OR COMPULSION? MODERN VIEWS OF PERSONIFICATION

Nearly everyone recognizes that personification is linked to agency in some way. One commentator has even referred to it, in passing, as "the pre-eminent rhetorical figure of agency."[69] Yet most critics have come to understand the link as an ironic or negative one. Personification implies agency by foreclosing or objectifying it.

The most familiar and naive version of this view involves the claim that personifications are missing something as characters: they have only two dimensions rather than three, they are flat rather than round, they sound only one note rather than a complete melody, and so on. Now, once one has the modern novel, these kinds of claims begin to make sense. Steven Knapp may be right that eighteenth- and early nineteenth century writers associated personification with a troubling confusion between people and things, thereby using personification as both an embodiment of and a contrast to a notion of sublime agency.[70] And it may be true, as William Jewett has suggested, that Coleridge and Southey's *The Fall of Robespierre* (1794) ironizes an ideal of political agency by making its lead characters "congeal into abstract personifications of their leading traits."[71]

As long as we limit these kinds of claims to the modern era, they offer plausible insights about the perceived difference between real people and flat personifications. But such claims are not valid—or, at least, not generally valid—for the premodern period, whose readers and writers didn't have the modern novel and would have found such ideas puzzling. The standard template of literary character for these readers was not Emma Bovary, compared to whom the character Ennui appears flat, undeveloped, or obsessed.[72] Medieval and Renaissance readers would probably understand Ennui, if this character appeared in Flaubert's story, as a piece of Emma, but a piece that illustrated how Emma worked and that showed Emma taking action in the world. They would not assume that Ennui risked congealing flesh-and-blood Emma into a cold abstraction.

This does not mean that premodern readers thought that all literary characters were simplistic. As Elizabeth Fowler has shown us, one may have a highly complex experience of a literary character without bothering with modern notions of psychological depth.[73] Nor would I deny that premodern literature sometimes features characterological effects that resemble modern fiction.[74] But the dichotomy between real person and artificial trope did not dominate the sensibilities of premodern readers.

Many critics would readily grant what I've been arguing here, and most would eschew the naive version of the complaint that personifications are flat and lifeless. Nonetheless, some of the most sophisticated scholarly accounts of personification betray a whiff of this complaint, albeit at a highly amplified conceptual level. One form this line of thinking has taken involves associating prosopopoeia with death and with the inhuman. Paul de Man, for example, as we have already briefly discussed in the Introduction, influentially argued that prosopopoeia invites a commerce between life and death, so that as the trope imbues nonliving things with animation it simultaneously inflicts speechlessness and death upon the living who behold it.[75] J. Hillis Miller and Margery Garber have extended these ideas in discussions about the petrifying and epitaphic effects of personification on readers and writers.[76]

To be sure, these accounts of personification turn on a special theory about the relation between language and human experience, namely, the idea of the priority of the former over the latter. De Man offers a version of this argument in rich, if somewhat elliptical, terms: "If there is to be consciousness (or experience, mind, subject, discourse, or face), it has to be susceptible to phenomenalization. But since the phenomenality of experience cannot be established *a priori*, it can only occur by a process of signification. . . . Once the phenomenal intuition has been put in motion, all other substitutions follow as in a chain. But the starting, catachretic decree of signification is arbitrary."[77] That catachretic decree, that abusive juxtaposition of the person and nonperson, is prosopopoeia, which gives a human face to things that properly have none. For de Man, personification is the ur-figure reminding us that concepts such as time or mind require sensuous, phenomenal correlatives and, further, that such correlatives become intelligible through language. Time enters the human order, for example, through the "face" of the clock. Yet, in de Man's reading, this kind of prosopopoetic reminder troubles human experience—"Prosopopeia is hallucinatory. To make the invisible visible is uncanny"—and personification imposes a programmatic uncertainty about the mediated nature of our consciousness: "It is impossible to say whether prosopopoeia is plausible because of the empirical existence of dreams and hallucinations or whether one believes such a thing as dreams and hallucinations exists because language permits the existence of prosopopoeia."[78]

This is not the place to query the understanding of language that underwrites de Man's account of prosopopoeia. Instead, let us ask about the extent to which this account might pertain to literary personifications that behave as characters in narrative. De Man is silent on this issue, confining his examples to brief, prosopopoetic moments occurring in lyric. In this respect, Michael Riffaterre has complained that de Man does not sufficiently distinguish between full-scale personification, which requires some degree of "descriptive realism," and prosopopoeia, a simple figure of speech that involves "no mimesis, no restriction justified by referentiality."[79] Riffaterre thinks that prosopopoeia is a function of linguistic or poetic convention, not a protraction of language into the sphere of sensuous experience or real life: "Figural meaning does not depend on sensory perception, referentiality or a descriptive grammar" (113). The implication here, *contra* de Man, is that prosopopoeia is not the trope that enacts an uncanny or petrifying double of the person.

But if prosopopoeia as trope does not produce this uncanny effect, what about personification as character? Unfortunately, Riffaterre does not pursue this question, merely noting that the conspicuous artifice of prosopopoeia can be only comic in narrative "because the basic rule of fiction is verisimilitude."[80] (It would be interesting to know how this dictum might account for personification fictions such as *The Romance of the Rose*, *The Faerie Queene*, or *Pilgrim's Progress*.) In any case, it is hard to deny that at the level of narrative personification does indeed mix trope with personhood. From this perspective, James J. Paxson is probably right to say that "personification involves a kind of epistemological error— a sort of forgetting of the textual status belonging to animate metaphors."[81] Personifications are words strutting around as if they were people.

But to conclude from this that in literary narrative personification functions to deaden or paralyze imposes a curious burden upon personification as a figure among figures. Why not conclude that prosopopoeia enlivens rather than enervates? The assumption in operation here, I suspect, is that personification attempts to approximate the person and that therefore its conspicuous failure to do so leaves the person distorted, uncanny, or troublingly mediated. But, as this book has been arguing, this is not how premodern rhetoricians talk about the trope. When Henry Peacham notes that via prosopopoeia the poet "raiseth again as it were the dead to life, and bringeth them forth complaining or witnessing what they knew," the emphasis of direction here is from lifelessness to animation, not the other way around.[82] In any case, if we associate language with death or the inhuman, then all tropes are liable to pull the living into the nonliving. Personification does not deserve a special distinction in this regard.

Other critics have understood the textual and iconographic status of personification to link it to constraint and immobility. One of the finest accounts of this kind comes from Susanne Wofford's *The Choice of Achilles*, which devotes several chapters to Spenser's *The Faerie Queene*. In her reading, the poem imagines "an apparently inevitable link between prosopopoeia and imprisonment, bondage, enclosure, or death."[83] Personification does indeed rely on "daemonic possession," yet for Wofford this possession never yields inspiration, only dispossession: "Sin itself comes to be defined as the moment when a human being allows a daemon to overtake him or her, becoming as it were completely 'obsessed' by the one devouring trait" (303). Agency resides in *resisting* personification allegory: Britomart is a "non-allegorical heroine" (310) in her victory over Busirane, and in general we should read the success of virtuous characters in the poem "not as an allegory, but as a fiction of release" (320).

In a somewhat similar vein, Jeff Dolven has offered an elegant description of personification allegory as a form of poetic justice, one that emblematically includes the consequences of crime with the crime itself. Via a consideration of the activities of Arthegall in book 5 of *The Faerie Queene*, he suggests "how close to the conceptual root of personification allegory the idea of punishment lies."[84] Rather like Wofford, Dolven equates moments of relief from the poem's punitive zeal with moments of release from allegorical meaning. As the wicked Munera suffers destruction at the hands of Talus, the poet mentions that she has "a sclendar wast," preventing us from fully relishing her deserved punishment: "Now we know that she has this *unallegorical* middle, a surprising and touching detail, almost felt in the crook of an arm before she is gone from the poem for good."[85]

Both these readings provide rich insight into how a poem like *The Faerie Queene* manages its allegory. Yet they are, after all, interpretations of particularly sadistic-seeming moments in the poem: Busirane's torture of Amoret and Talus's execution of violence on a defeated opponent. My concern is that if we extrapolate from scenes such as these to personification generally, we will get a skewed view of how readers before the novel experienced it. That is, we might find ourselves pursuing interpretations that seek out moments when the characters *escape* from the tyranny of personification and allegory and then taking these moments as the genuine nodes of interest and energy within the fiction. Personifications, in this view, will not be the trajectories of volitional energy I described earlier but rather the sinkholes the narrative must negotiate if it wishes to remain alive.

This kind of interpretation, at any rate, appears to inform even some of the best recent discussions of personification allegory. Masha Raskolnikov, for example, has written a wonderful survey of medieval literary texts that use personification to ruminate about the relationship between body and soul. She argues persuasively that personification allegory produces an "immanent psychological theory," one that involves "the division of the parts of the self into forces capable of action."[86] Yet in a number of her actual readings, personification becomes most notable insofar it appears to resist being personification, as when in the *Psychomachia* Chastity contradicts her meek nature by exercising extreme violence, or when Boethius's Lady Philosophy argues for a freedom of the will that she, as a personification, can never enjoy.[87] Another paradigmatic example for Raskolnikov is Guillaume de Lorris's Resistance (*Dangier*), who, by allowing Openness and Pity to soften his aversion to the lover, "offers an example of an allegorical character who stretches the limits of his named nature until *forced to snap back into its confines*: Insofar as he is a person, and subject to persuasion and charm, he can be nice to the Lover, but insofar as he is an allegorical figure for the Rose's reluctance to yield to the lover, he must not. Dangier's will is not entirely free because he is an allegorical character."[88]

I admire the ingenuity of Raskolnikov's arguments here, but I worry, as I did above, that they channel a modern notion of literary character that premodern readers would not have brought to the table. Resistance does indeed obsessively resist the Lover's courtship of the rose, and to do otherwise compromises his nature. But he isn't "forced" to resist the lover; instead, he is doing what he wants. And it is unlikely that Guillaume's readers imagined that

Resistance possesses volition "insofar as he is a person": it is not Resistance's job to be like or unlike a person, but rather to put into action the beloved's aversion to the Lover. His will does not become free as he begins to succumb to the persuasions of Openness and Pity. Rather, he suffers a loss of energy: the inertia of narrative obstacles slows down his momentum, and he loses his volitional focus. (Let us recall that the first thing Resistance does upon relenting is fall asleep.) We will do better if we call Resistance's violation of his nature at this point something like "semantic drift" instead of "free will." Even personifications, as they interact with other characters and events, sometimes find their energy diffused by the entropy of the narrative. But such diffusion does not represent an entrée to personhood or freedom.

Two Touchstone Studies

The implicit critical consensus about personification that I am trying to contest here perhaps finds its most important articulations in two highly influential studies, Angus Fletcher's *Allegory: Theory of a Symbolic Mode* (1964) and Gordon Teskey's *Allegory and Violence* (1996). Although the official topic of both books is allegory, they assume, to a degree other critics do not, that personification is the paradigmatic figure of the allegorical mode. These two books have offered crucial resources for my work on personification, although I have important disagreements with some of their arguments. Engaging those arguments, even if briefly, will help clarify my own view of personification as an expression of will.

More than any other modern critic, Angus Fletcher anticipates my claim that personification indicates a kind of energy. For Fletcher, allegory is concerned above all with quantities of power: "His [the allegorical hero's] essentially energetic character will delight the reader with an appearance of unadulterated power. Like a Machiavellian prince, the allegorical hero can act free of the usual moral restraints, even when he is acting morally, since he is moral only in the interests of his power over other men."[89] Fletcher's account is perhaps best known for the way it describes this energy as resulting in an obsessed, fixated persona: "If we were to meet an allegorical character in real life, we would say of him that he was obsessed with only one idea, or that he had an absolutely one-track mind" (40). In a fascinating intuition, Fletcher associates this obsessed persona with psychological compulsion (279–303). What we now describe as a clinical condition that compels repetitive action, the premoderns described with the literary figure of personification.

This is a justly celebrated interpretation of personification allegory. Yet critics who rely on Fletcher's account have tended not to inquire into the literary basis on which he makes this interpretation. That is, compared to what notion of character are we to understand personifications as compulsive? Fletcher bases his account on what we might call the felt distance between a personification and a psychologically mimetic character. For example, as Spenser's Malbecco begins to transform into the personification Gelosy, the character moves "away from realism and mimesis" toward allegory, which denies Malbecco his previous role as a jealous husband, a role that Fletcher calls "eminently real and natural and comic" (49). Likewise, in splitting Arthegall into prosopopoetic parts, such as Talus, the poet "denies true human character to that hero" (38).

For Fletcher, allegory in general lacks "the feeling one gets of common humanity binding together the characters of a mimetic drama" (30). This is because, in part, personifications cannot grow organically in the way literal characters do, in the sense of "maturation" (66). And personifications cannot achieve maturation because, significantly, they lack free will: "Realism of character is related to freedom of choice in action. The truly 'real' character, the Pierre of *War and Peace*, does not necessarily change radically, but he does have the power to change radically, if need be, and we are made to feel this potentiality. He can act according to probability, not solely according to fixed necessity, nor is he a victim of random chance" (66–67). A personification, by contrast, is best described as a "caricature" (34) or "a robot, a Talus," or the monster in *Frankenstein*, or a cyborg in modern science fiction (55).

I have no interest in faulting Fletcher for appealing to notions of "natural" literary character, "true human character," or "common humanity." He is talking about the experience of character that we often find in novels. We don't have to deny that all literary characters are tropes in order to acknowledge that novelistic characters affect us differently than do caricatures. Pierre Bezukhov and Emma Bovary and Charles Swann appear designed to encourage us to identify with them; an appeal to common humanity is partly how they work.[90] Compared to them, personifications like Folly or Furor do perhaps appear like robots or reanimated corpses.

My concern, rather, is that comparing Folly and Furor to such characters puts us on the wrong track. There is no evidence in the vast archive of premodern literary characters, or in premodern literary theory, that readers and writers *typically* had an expectation of psychological depth or mimetic realism. The contrast between Pierre and Folly that seems so obvious to us would probably not have seemed obvious to them, or at least not obvious in the same terms. Yet I believe that the perceived affinity between mimetic, novelistic characters and real human beings continues to underwrite the critical inclination to describe personifications as constrained or enervated. What Fletcher does openly we still do implicitly: we *start* with the notion of psychologically deep, mimetically probable literary character and then peel away its complexity and nuance until all that remains is a single, simplistic kernel.[91] This is the modern view of personification. But to apply this modern view as the default template for prosopopoeia would seem to require that we produce a premodern model of novelistic character *avant la lettre*.

Does Fletcher produce such a model to contrast to personification? He implies that he finds it in mimetic drama, especially as described by Aristotle. The *Poetics* repeatedly recommends that tragic drama maintain a probability of plot because the effect of wonder (*thaumasia*) is most intense when events occur unexpectedly but in a recognizable causal sequence.[92] It seems fair to say that Aristotle would find the narrative improbability of a personification to make it unsuitable as the protagonist of a tragedy. But Fletcher pushes this idea to a broader range of application, concluding that "mimetic drama . . . questions whatever will prevent human character from gradually modifying itself. . . . Above all, natural growth and natural decay seem to be the prime concern of the mimetic artist" (150).

This smacks of bootstrapping. Aristotle has no interest in the natural growth of human character in tragedy: he cares about character only insofar as it helps to produces certain plot effects.[93] For him, what matters is choosing the right *type* of character—elevated or base, virtuous, wicked, or in between—that fits the kind of fiction the dramatist or poet is creating.[94] Character leads to certain *kinds* of action rather than enabling the free selection of multiple possibilities.[95] So although Fletcher suggests that Aristotle would prefer to see a "free agent" on the stage rather than an obsessed one (67), and refers to the "Aristotelian notion that art must deal with the variable and with matters of 'choice'" (306n4), we will search in vain for such ideas in the *Poetics* itself.

Fletcher, I suggest, can find the stark contrast to personification that he seeks in modern novels but not in Aristotle. Nor would he find it in ancient drama if he looked. Athenian tragedy features, not the natural growth of its characters, but rather the shocking effects of the morning after: Herakles waking up after killing his family while possessed by madness; Ajax realizing to his horror that he has slaughtered cows, not warriors; Oedipus learning that he is the cause of Thebes's plague. The actions of these characters result from a combination of their mostly fixed nature and external daemonic forces.

I don't intend these comments as a wholesale rejection of the account of personification in Fletcher's *Allegory*. My view in many ways is Fletcherian: personifications are trajectories of energy driven by daemonic force. Such figures do indeed appear fixated on a single objective and mode of behavior. But fixation is only part of the story: daemonic possession also inspires and enables personifications to do what they are in an untrammeled manner.

Along with Fletcher, the other account of personification I must address is Gordon Teskey's undeniably brilliant *Allegory and Violence*. Teskey rejects Fletcher's view that personifications express compulsive, daemonic energy, and he has no interest in contrasting them with mimetic literary characters. Instead, he argues that personification offers the definitive instance of allegorical violence. In his view, allegory expresses, and seeks to accomplish, the desire of the realm of ideas to impose itself on the realm of material things. Allegory aggressively foists meaning onto the world. Teskey associates this imposition both with the notion of "participation" in Platonic metaphysics, whereby an object has a quality only by merit of its connection to an Idea of that quality, and with Aristotelian hylomorphism, in which form actively imposes itself on passive material.[96] In Teskey's account, the medieval Scholastic doctrine that feminine Matter secretly desires masculine Form to ravish it aptly signals the gender dimension of the struggle between ideas and things (20). The violence of allegory is above all a sexual violence.

Teskey's view of allegorical violence crucially influences his description of personification, which, he suggests, ought to be understood as only one side of a coin. On the other side is "capture": "What the act of capture exhibits is the truth over which allegory is always drawing its veil: the fundamental disorder out of which the illusion of order is raised" (19). The material world resists the effort of Ideas to organize or process it. This resistance occasionally erupts in an allegory as disturbances or discontinuities on the otherwise smooth conceptual surface. In the case of personification, the poet sometimes allows us to glimpse matter resisting the violent procedure by which Ideas translate the world into signification. For Teskey, paradigmatic examples of capture include Dante's Francesca da Rimini—trapped for eternity in hell—who refuses to behave as a simple personification of lust, and Spenser's Amoret—bound, heart ripped from her chest—who refuses to transform into an obliging object of male desire (19, 25–29). Capture is the aggressive process leading up to a finished product, personification, but the product then conceals this process.

Teskey's account offers a profound sense of the metaphysics in operation in allegory generally and in personification specifically. Yet an implication of this account, as in several of the critical views I have discussed, is that personification becomes most interesting when it stops behaving like ordinary personification. The *prosōpon* of personification is a deceptive one: Charissa nursing her babes in the House of Holiness may seem sweet, but just below the surface is a bloody Amoret struggling to escape from bondage. Indeed, for Teskey it is primarily insofar as we can still perceive repressed matter resisting its prosopopoetic mask that personification attracts our interest.[97] When personification effectively erases the process of capture, it threatens to drain vital energy from literary narrative. As Teskey puts it in an essay about the idea of death in allegory, "The very liveliness of the allegorical figures, their frenetic, jerky, galvanic life, makes us think of dead bodies through which an electric current is passed."[98]

Teskey's account of personification as an undead figure, one that seems energetic only when the remnant of suppressed materiality twitches within it, relies in no small part on his strict separation between the Greco-Roman daemon and Christian personification. In this he follows Coleridge's distinction between ancient mythic figures such as Love and Psyche, on the one hand, and Christian allegory, on the other, which features the "known unreality," as Coleridge put it, of personified characters.[99] Along these lines, Teskey argues that in ancient literature the landscape is numinous and local: gods, daemons, and spirits coexist with the natural order of things. Christian thought, by contrast, reconceives of this local numinousness as God or the One or absolute meaning and situates it outside the natural order, leaving in its place a system of signs that point back to it.[100]

According to Teskey, this means we cannot understand ancient literary figures such as Hesiod's Eros or Homer's Eris or Euripides's Philotimia as personifications, but only as supernatural beings whose agency is real, not merely a sign of an abstract idea (40–41). Prudentius's Ira, by contrast, is an abstraction to which the poet has retroactively given agency: Ira's power to act does not belong to her but comes from her relation to a system of signs. This system animates her otherwise empty shell, an electric current, as it were, passing through a dead body.

I am dubious that the distinction between daemon and personification can be made as sharply as Teskey would have it. Most scholars agree that the two figures differ from one another, but most also concede that it is often hard to be sure of the difference.[101] Classicists such as Emma Stafford have suggested that the ancient Greek world implicitly made use of a sliding scale, at one end of which stood the fully individualized deity, while on the other stood a figure of speech with no personality: in between were more and less figurative versions of personification.[102] Likewise, medievalists such as Barbara Newman have demonstrated the persistence of numinous deity in Christian literary figures such as Natura, Amor, and Sapientia.[103]

Premodern Christians did not build altars of worship to Chastity and Health, it is true, but many of them did believe that the world was inhabited by invisible spirits and energies, good, bad, helpful, and mischievous.[104] For example, in Lewis Wager's moral interlude, *The Life and Repentance of Mary Magdalene* (1566), Christ brings Mary to repentance by banishing her longtime companion Infidelity from her presence, along with "the seven devils which have her possessed."[105] It is nearly impossible to understand Infidelity here as purely a figurative sign of an abstract vice. After all, Christ is *literally* performing exorcisms when he speaks of the seven wicked spirits in scripture (Luke 11:26), which Wager references in the above line. Infidelity is a walking metaphor personifying faithlessness, but he also operates as the daemonic agent that has led Mary along the primrose path to sin.

And a regard for daemonic agents was not limited to popular belief. A Renaissance intellectual like Leone Hebreo is happy to nod to both numinous presence and Platonic metaphysics:

[The ancients] called human virtues, vices, and passions "gods or goddesses," principally because, apart from the fact that *the nobility of the first and the might of the others has in it some godlike element,* each of the virtues, vices, and passions of men in general has its own Idea, and manifests itself in them with more or less intensity in proportion as it partakes of the Idea.

> Therefore it is that among the gods are numbered Fame, Love,
> Grace, Cupidity, Pleasure, Discord, Labour, Envy, Deceit, Per-
> severance, Sorrow and many other of the same kind, forasmuch
> as each has its own Idea or incorporeal principle, (as I told you),
> on account of which it is declared a god or goddess.[106]

Human passions, virtues, and vices in themselves possess daemonic
intensity. Leone's personified figures participate in the primacy of
the Forms without quite sliding completely from deity to sign.

Part of the difficulty here involves Coleridge's distinction between real and unreal characters. In an anthropological sense it is
perfectly clear what this means: Ovid's Envy links an abstraction to
the name of a personality believed to be real (a daemon), whereas
Langland's or Spenser's Envy links an abstraction to the name of an
openly fictional personality (a personification). But in a narrative
sense it is less clear what this difference means. All three of these
figures take action in narratives, imposing themselves on other characters, seeking to achieve their envious projects. For Ovid, Langland, and Spenser alike, I suggest, envy is in us and also out there in
the world. We express envy through acts of will, and Envy pricks us
into feeling envious.[107]

In arguing for the daemonic basis of personification, I suppose
I am claiming, as in the case of Fletcher, that Teskey gives us only
part of the story. The part he provides is fascinating: personification foists an idea onto a human figure in a kind of aggressive hylomorphism, whereby form tries to ravish and impregnate matter. As
a consequence, a personification has an agency that does not quite
belong to it. This accounts for its curious heterogeneity to the narrative in which it acts. But at the same time personifications channel daemonic agency. They represent the energies passing back and
forth between us and the landscape. Chastity and Envy figure the
nobility and might, as Leone puts it, of our will to virtue or to vice.

Thus far I have argued for a continuity between daemonic and
prosopopoetic representations of agency. What Envy did for Ovid,
she does similarly for Langland and Spenser. Nonetheless, there is
no denying that characters with names such as Envy occur in me-

dieval and Renaissance literature far more than they do in classical literature. Premodern Christianity sponsored the great age of literary personification. Why was this so? Scholars have long identified an answer: monotheism requires that the gods transform into metaphors. "The twilight of the gods is the mid-morning of the personifications," as C. S. Lewis once put it.[108] Yet as rich and important as this explanation is, medieval readers and writers understood personifications as more than pagan deities translated into figures. The next chapter thus explores a different kind of explanation for the rise of literary personifications in the early Middle Ages and after, one that involves examining several developments in the concept of the will in this period. In doing so, I will suggest that ancient daemons and Christian personifications, despite their broad overlap, also imply disparate notions of agency.

"Free Will." Detail from Caesar Ripa, *Iconologia, or Moral Emblems* (1603; repr., London, 1709), 49. Reproduced with permission of the Folger Shakespeare Library.

THE PROSOPOPOETIC WILL

Ours, though Not We

The history of the will has become an academic favorite, and the field has grown rather crowded. Anyone hoping to offer a complete view of the concept must master dozens and dozens of subthemes. My more modest purpose in this chapter is to offer a series of snapshots of Western views about the will. I make no claims to comprehensiveness. I am not telling *the* story of the will, but I am telling *a* story of the will, one that considers the relation between volition's freedom and its causation. In doing so, I try to isolate what aspects of medieval and Renaissance conceptions of the will made this faculty especially susceptible to prosopopoetic representation.

The short answer is this. Antiquity, insofar as it had a concept of will, affirmed the will's agency by emphasizing its *dependence on and continuity with* the various capacities of human beings, such as reason and moral character. Modernity, by contrast, affirms the will's agency by emphasizing its *independence from and discontinuity with* these various capacities, instead identifying the will closely with the orientation of the ego or deep self. Medieval and Renaissance Christian writers, unlike ancient writers, often held that the will enjoyed independence from reason and moral character; yet, in contrast to modern commentators, these writers did not possess a notion of autonomous ego or deep self to posit as the source of the will. Hence, the postclassical will was free (the other faculties of human psychology did not determine it) but was potentially hard to account for (*what* exactly did determine it?). Our acts of will belonged to us, of course, but were partially independent from any particular part of us. As John Donne says of lovers' bodies, "They're ours, though they're not we."

ANCIENT VERSUS MODERN

Histories of the will often start with Aristotle, probably because his philosophy of action illustrates so well the ancient habit of thought that subordinated volition to other human components. A basic notion of causation governs Aristotle's account of human activity. For example, in the *Physics* Aristotle describes the string of causes by which a stick moves a stone, a hand moves the stick, and a man moves the hand. The man occupies a special place in this series, because, unlike the hand and the stick, his role as mover "is not so in virtue of being moved by something else."[1] How are we to understand Aristotle's statement here: is he saying that human actions are uncaused causes? Almost surely not, since a few pages earlier in the *Physics* he pointedly rejects the suggestion that animate things like animals can spontaneously transition from motionlessness to motion. Instead, factors in the environment prompt already-animate elements within the animal, such as intellect or appetite, and these respond in turn by setting the animal in motion.[2]

Anything that moves is moved. Aristotle distinguishes the man from the hand and the stick, then, not in terms of a freedom from causation, but rather in terms of the manner in which the man occupies a place on the causal chain. In order to say that the man moves the stone, we can do without the stick, and maybe even without the hand, but not without the man. But the man himself is made up of parts that respond to a variety of prior causes. This constitutes the man's nature. Aristotle appears uninterested in the kinds of questions that often occupy modern thinkers, such as how we might distinguish a human agent from an automaton or complex machine, or how we might distinguish the parts of the self from the self itself, or how we might distinguish persons from nonpersons.

Aristotle's account of human action includes plenty of features that seem familiar to modern readers. According to the *Nicomachean Ethics*, we wish for what we take to be the good, we deliberate about the right means to achieve this good, and, on the basis of that deliberation, we choose a course of action.[3] But what is missing, if that is the right word, is a notion of will as a moment of executive decision, the selecting of option X out of a range of options. This absence has implications that do indeed seem strange to us. For example, Aristotle doesn't think that when we choose (*prohairesis*), we choose between two options, such as good and evil. Instead, to choose is to follow rational desire to the action leading to the good. This means that if you act irrationally, you haven't chosen; rather, you have voluntarily acted against your choice.[4] You can choose to follow reason, but you cannot choose to follow irrational appetite.

If Aristotle has a concept of will, it involves the entire process of wishing, deliberating, and choosing.[5] Without denying the important differences between Aristotle and other philosophical schools such as Platonism, Stoicism, and Epicureanism, we can say that this notion of choice as a capacity to follow reason into action broadly pervades ancient thought. The fact that we can act against our rational choices does not, as in modern thought, underwrite our agency but rather reveals the limits of our powers and the inconsistency of our character.[6] When the will is functioning properly, it has a deep continuity with the psychological causal process of desiring, deliberating, and deciding, insofar as ancient writers bother to distinguish the will from these things.

This is not to say, however, that the Christian era received the concept of the will in exactly Aristotle's terms. Stoicism added influential features to the philosophy of action. According to Chrysippus, for example, even our irrational impulses require that our reason assent to them.[7] This means that, contrary to Aristotle, all our effective desires, even irrational ones, are "willings": we assent to both the good and bad. Also, the idea of assent renders decision making more explicitly internal, so the will functions as a mental capacity over against obstacles in the external world. This is the tenor of Epictetus's famous phrase, "You may chain my leg, but not even God can conquer my will."[8] Furthermore, Roman philosophers in the period just prior to Epictetus adopt the term *voluntas*, which has resonances much closer to the idea of volition than does Aristotle's *prohairesis*.

However, Greek Stoics and Roman philosophers alike continue to conceive of the will as deeply embedded in a psychological causal process, which itself interacts with external causes. In Latin texts, *voluntas* usually refers to a single act of will, not a freestanding capacity to will. Seneca, for example, distinguishes between flashes of anger, for which we bear no culpability, and the passion of anger, for which we do. He argues that we experience the former involuntarily (*non voluntarius*), but that in the case of the latter we make a voluntary affirmation (*cum voluntate*) that it is reasonable to seek revenge against the one who injured us.[9] The threshold for culpability here does involve a distinction between willed and unwilled, but it remains hard to say exactly what *voluntas* contributes. Reasoning that the injury merits revenge sounds like an error of judgment (at least from a Stoic point of view) as much as it sounds like an act of volition. Seneca keeps the will very close to intellect.

Although he speaks from a philosophical perspective almost the antithesis of Seneca's, Lucretius likewise describes the will as a function of intellect when he offers an Epicurean account of bodily movement. He explains that when images of motion (thin films of atoms) strike the mind they prompt the will into action: "After this comes will [*voluntas*]; for no one ever begins anything until the intelligence [*mens*] has first foreseen what it wills [*velit*] to do."[10] Again, the will marks a transition from passive perceiving to active doing, but its work seems confined to carrying out what the intelligence has already determined. The intelligence expresses its activity in an act of *voluntas*, but *voluntas* is not a distinct faculty in itself.

Lucretius is probably best known, however, for his remarkable image of free will (*voluntas libera*) as produced by a "swerve," the atom's random shift from its existing trajectory.[11] The idea of the swerve, suggested by Epicurus, probably sounded even stranger to antiquity than quantum mechanics sounds to us, and it prompted many expressions of ridicule. Epicurus probably suggested it not to argue for free will but rather to deny the impression that the surface phenomenon of physical orderliness in the universe implies intelligent design.[12] Nonetheless, Lucretius's metaphor of free will is arresting: racehorses, crouched in their cells, waiting for the gate to be thrown open. So eager are they that their desire to burst out exceeds their bodily ability to do so.[13] In this image, at least, we have a sense of sudden, sheer volition that would capture the imagination of later writers.

Yet overwhelmingly for ancient writers, the idea that a motion would lack a cause reeked of nonsense. Cicero's *De fato* insists that Epicurus's doctrine would mean that "something comes out of nothing," a proposition that flies in the face of known natural philosophy.[14] Cicero thinks it suffices to distinguish between intrinsic causes that constitute the nature of an object and extrinsic causes that affect it from the outside. His principal analogy is instructive. Just as an atom is not externally determined but follows gravity because of its intrinsic nature, so the will needs no extrinsic prompting but "possesses the intrinsic property of being under our control [*in nostra potestate*]."[15] This analogy dispenses with random motion, to be sure, but offers little sense of how to distinguish between the movement of a particle hurtling through space and the volition of a human being. Like Aristotle, Cicero does not appear alarmed by this.

Nothing in the model of will that I have just sketched would have prevented ancient literature from developing a full-scale tradition of personification. Antiquity very much thought of human agency in terms of parts; personification deals with parts. And the ancient daemon, as some commentators suggest, sometimes slides very close to personification. Nor do I wish to imply that ancient literary personification was a monolithic phenomenon that remained the same over the centuries.[16] But if we think of personification as a "piece" of the agency of the human psyche or of the natural landscape, a piece that bursts out in a partially independent expression of volition, then we might have an insight into the *relative* scarcity of literary personification in ancient writing, compared to the centuries following. Ancient writers, as we have seen, did not conceive of the will as particularly distinct or independent from the rest of the self. Human agency, although in constant daemonic interaction with the external world, did not express itself in a volition whose force was separate from other human faculties. Yet medieval and Renaissance personification seems to intimate precisely this sense of separateness and independence.

If, as I'm suggesting, the ancient notion of will did not encourage a tradition of literary personification, the modern notion of will downright eschews it. But this eschewal stems from different reasons, because the modern view ascribes a great deal of independence to the will. We moderns don't approve of the idea that something comes of nothing any more than does Cicero, but we also find it odd to say that our will is "caused." We tend to conceive of volition as highly distinct from other cognitive activities: our will represents our executive decision *after* assessment, deliberation, and emotion have had their say. We usually assume a gap between the question *What should I do?* and the question *What shall I do?* It doesn't surprise us that our answer to the second question (our will) sometimes differs from our answer to the first question (our judgment). That we can choose against our practical judgments demonstrates our will's freedom, its partial independence from the machinery of cognitive activity. Modern volition emphatically differs from a particle following a gravitational trajectory.

This is not the whole story, however, because many of us also sense a tension involved in the modern idea of a will free from causal determinism. If, for example, someone asks us *why* we willed against our better judgment, we might say that we had a good reason for doing so. But then it is hard to explain why this reason does not count as the cause of our will. And if we respond that we willed for no reason in particular, then volition risks taking on the random quality that inclined antiquity to ridicule the Epicurean swerve. Modernity softens this impression of randomness by identifying the will with the ego, or the self, or the "real me." In this respect, the modern notion of an ego isolatable from intellect and emotions serves the modern will aptly. My feelings, moods, and even judgments may sometimes happen to me, but my will expresses *me*. Insofar as the world frustrates my will in its projects, it also frustrates my selfhood. My will's autonomy is all but synonymous with my autonomy. What caused my will to choose against my best judgment? *I* did. Our wills are not only ours; they are also we.

These comments describe what I take to be a common modern intuition about the will, but we can find this view expressed formally in modern philosophy. Immanuel Kant, to select an influential example, acknowledges the oddness (from an empirical point of view) of claiming that the rational will enjoys freedom by initiating a series of causes without itself having a prior cause.[17] But he insists that when we exercise our moral will we become the authors of the very moral obligation requiring our obedience. We give the law to ourselves, as Kant puts it, and achieve autonomy. Thus, although a moral agent feels himself subject to causality in terms of appearances and inner sensations, "he must necessarily assume something else lying at their basis, namely his ego as it may be constituted in itself."[18] Moral autonomy frees itself from ordinary causality through a transcendental accord between will and self: "So it is that the human being claims for himself a will which lets nothing be put to his account that belongs merely to his desires and inclinations.... It is there [in the noumenal sphere], as intelligence only, that he is his proper self."[19]

Much philosophy of will following Kant does not play for the same transcendental stakes, but it nonetheless assumes that acts of will coordinate deeply with our sense of self. John Stuart Mill is a psychological determinist, but he still suggests that we adjudicate our conflicting desires according to who we think we really are: "What causes Me, or, if you please, my Will, to be identified with one side rather than with the other, is that one of the Me's represents a more permanent state of my feelings than the other does. After the temptation has been yielded to, the desiring 'I' will come to an end, but the conscience-stricken 'I' may endure to the end of life."[20] And

Henri Bergson, no psychological determinist, argues that we exercise our freedom when our actions spring from our "fundamental self" rather than our "parasitic self": "But then, at the very minute when the act is going to be performed, something may revolt against it. It is the deep-seated self rushing up to the surface. . . . We choose in defiance of what is conventionally called a motive, and this absence of any tangible reason is the more striking the deeper our freedom goes."[21] Motives exert causation, but the self is free.

This association between will and deep selfhood continues into twentieth-century philosophy. Jean-Paul Sartre claims that when we choose, we choose ourselves.[22] Hannah Arendt suggests that our freedom to will is rooted in our *natality*, in the fact that we were each born as a unique and individual self, prompting the introduction of novelty in the world.[23] Roderick Chisholm, arguing for the will's freedom from determinism, takes Aristotle's example of a hand moving a stick to move a stone and arrives at a rather un-Aristotelian conclusion: "We may say . . . that the motion of the hand was caused by the motion of certain muscles; and we may say that the motion of the muscles was caused by certain events that took place in the brain. But some event, and presumably one that took place in the brain, was caused by the agent and not by other events."[24] In Chisholm's description, the source of the will is the self, and this self is strictly distinguished from its parts.

I am, needless to say, stacking the deck by selecting the above examples. Modernity features intense skepticism about the will at the same time that it celebrates its intimacy with the human ego. People who teach in academic philosophy departments have plenty of reservations about a libertarian agent-causation position like Chisholm's. Modern perspectives doubting our conscious control of our will, such as psychoanalysis or neuroscience, have deeply affected the popular and intellectual imagination. Friedrich Nietzsche carries out an interpretation of biological existence under the rubric of "will to power," but he does not appear to believe in a faculty of human will.[25] Nonetheless, such skepticism operates over against the dominant modern intuition of a deep connection between free will and ego. We do not, for the most part, understand our volition in terms of causes flowing into and out from the self. On the contrary, the modern will helps to maintain the boundary between self and not-self.

Since literary personification thrives on the ambiguity between self and not-self, it represents modern volition ineptly and awkwardly. Characters with names like Justice or Lust or Fear seem to objectify the subjectivity of the agent. On the one hand, such characters externalize the will, severing its link with the ego. On the other hand, they freeze the will in a series of causes, through allegorical genealogy or through mechanical interaction with each other. Little wonder that we now tend to think of them as lifeless, compulsive, or freakish. Yet premodern readers and writers did not think of them in this way, and part of the reason is that their notion of will differed from our own.

THE MEDIEVAL WILL: PUZZLES OF CAUSATION

There is little agreement about when in late antiquity a notion of the will as an independent faculty arises.[26] Scholars used to routinely point to Augustine: Hannah Arendt once called this theologian "the first philosopher of the will," and plenty of commentators have concurred.[27] Recent scholars, however, have argued that Augustine's view of the will in fact resembles the Stoic model that he thinks he is critiquing.[28] Nonetheless, Augustine holds a special place in this history of the will because he explicitly questions the will's causality. In this respect, he breaks substantially from earlier Greek and Roman accounts of volition.

We should note up front that our interest does not lie in precisely what sense or to what degree Augustine believes the will to be *free*. It is easy to come to grief with such a question when one is studying this early Christian theologian. Throughout most of his writings he makes it clear that human beings, because of their postlapsarian nature, cannot simply will themselves to do the good; a will to virtue requires the gift of God's grace. Yet even though sinners cannot will the good on their own, they commit their sins voluntarily: "Nothing else makes the mind the ally of evil desire except its own will and free choice."[29] Since sinners are doing what they want, they are, in a limited sense, free. What remains debatable in Augustine's writings, however, is whether sinners can, *on their own*, ask God for the grace to start willing the good (which would imply a deep freedom), or if even that act of asking requires the prior presence of grace, over which sinners have no control (which would again imply only limited freedom).[30] And it may be that Augustine deliberately leaves ambiguous the precise interaction between divine and human agency, perhaps an effect of his commitment to the mediations of Christology and the institutions of the church, as David Aers has recently suggested.[31]

In any case, leaving aside the thorny issue of ultimate human freedom in Augustine, our concern centers on the psychological causal structure informing the will. His treatise *On the Free Choice of the Will* (*De libero arbitrio*) is a good place to start, since early in this text he makes many assertions implying that our will can equally and freely choose good or evil.[32] Indeed, in this earlier part Augustine appears to think that the human will to evil presents a puzzle and requires explanation. He claims—as he will later claim in the *City of God*—that an evil will comes from an absence rather than a presence: the will's movement to sin is a *defectivus motus*.[33] This explanation does not satisfy Augustine's interlocutor, Evodius, who—granting that evil is an absence—still wants to know what *causes* an evil movement of the will (3.1–2). Augustine responds that the will by definition is freely in our power and therefore is never controlled by external determinism.[34] But Evodius does not stop pushing: If all men have free will, then what causes *some* of them to will the good while *others* will the bad? He insists, "I will not accept the answer 'the will,' because I am asking for the cause of the will itself" (3.163).

The treatise thus presents us with a thrilling conflict between causation and freedom. It is at this point that Augustine becomes most interesting for the story I'm telling. He responds to Evodius, with apparent irritation, that he cannot answer his companion's question: if he offered an explanatory cause, Evodius would simply ask the cause of that cause, and then the cause of that cause, on to an infinite regress (3.164). "After all," reasons Augustine, "what cause of the will could there be, except the will itself? It is either the will itself, and it is not possible to go back to the root of the will; or else it is not the will, and there is no sin" (3.168). This is remarkable: it suggests, for one of the first times in Western writing, that the language of causality is inappropriate for talking about the will.

Aristotle, the ancient philosopher, follows the causal chain of action back to a human agent, who is himself a special link in a chain of prior causes. Chisholm, the modern philosopher, follows the causal chain of action back to the self as agent, where the chain stops. For Augustine also the causal chain stops, but not at the self: it stops at the will. But what causes the will? Augustine rejects, at least at this moment in the treatise, an Aristotelian sense of prior causes leading up to and determining the will, but he also indicates no sense of a freestanding ego that spontaneously expresses itself in will. Instead, the Augustinian will is freestanding and self-causing, which makes its relation to other psychological capacities somewhat perplexing.

Augustine's notion of human freedom changed throughout his career, and I am singling out only one aspect of it. But it is an important aspect, and it comes up elsewhere in his writing. For example, near the end of *On the Free Choice of the Will*, he tries to compare Adam's state of indifferent freedom—balanced between wisdom and folly—to the experience of waking from sleep prior to full wakefulness. But he cautions that the analogy is imperfect: waking is involuntary and caused, whereas Adam's act was voluntary and free (3.254). Augustine can find no way, finally, to describe the indifferent will through comparison to natural phenomena: "This intermediate state cannot be understood in this life by men, except through contraries" (3.252).

Likewise, in the *Confessions* he speaks of a doubled will—part carnal, part spiritual—that has the freedom of self-command precisely because it always has two ways of expressing itself. Yet Augustine acknowledges the curiousness of this free will as he strives to will himself to convert: "But when the mind commands the mind to make an act of will, these two are one and the same and yet the order is not obeyed. Why does this happen? What is the cause of it? The mind orders itself to make an act of will, and it would not give this order unless it willed to do so; yet it does not carry out its own command."[35] Augustine finds himself perplexed by the elusive play of cause and effect, which we may spell out sequentially: (1) the mind fails to will; (2) this failure to will was preceded by a command to will; (3) this command to will was caused (Augustine reasons) by an even earlier will to command. Although Augustine does not go further, he implies that (4) this will to command was caused by an earlier will to will this command, and so on. We have here, *in ovo*, the infinite regress threatened by Evodius's persistent questioning about the cause of the will.

It is important not to overstate the independence of this causeless will. Elsewhere, Augustine finds volition's causation perfectly obvious: our sinful character (for wicked choices) and divine grace (for good choices). Later medieval commentators, such as Peter Lombard, likewise seek to balance the will's freedom from necessity with its enslavement to sin.[36] Nor is the specifically causal relation between reason and will the only way medieval thinkers wrote about these two faculties. Sometimes they described them as passages of reception by which human beings could be influenced. James Simpson has discussed the medieval tradition of moral address that distinguishes between reason and the will: "Modes designed to move emotionally . . . appeal to the will, whereas analytical procedures . . . appeal to the reason."[37] Configurations of faculty psychology such as this do not emphasize the question of whether reason determines the will but rather focus on the distinctive receptivity of each separate faculty. In other medieval descriptions, reason signals a tendency toward godly understanding, whereas will signals a tendency toward concupiscence.[38]

In this respect, we should hesitate in asserting that these early theologians are necessarily taking about "free will." Although they occasionally use the phrase *voluntas libera*, the far more common expression is *liberum arbitrium voluntatis*, the free decision of the will. As a number of recent commentators have suggested, this expression does not really make any claim about the will's freedom per se.[39] Instead, it claims that the choice or action rendered by the will is uncompelled, insofar as the will is acting as it wants. But this leaves unanswered—and even unasked—the question of whether the will is free to want different kinds of things.

This is why a theologian like Thomas Aquinas can posit a robust sense of the will as an isolatable faculty but nonetheless describe human action in terms of Aristotelian eudaimonism. For Aquinas, the universal human drive to happiness means that, in a general sense, our decisions are foregone conclusions. When it acts, our will selects whatever object our reason judges as good.[40] Evil acts of will involve some degree of error on the part of reason. This still amounts to *liberum arbitrium*, because reason doesn't compel the will to act: Aquinas says that our will can opt to do nothing at all (2[1].10.2). But if it does act, it acts in harmony with reason. Aquinas does not set out to prove the freedom of the will; instead, he proves the freedom of human action. Indeed, for him, reason and will have a distinct cause-and-effect relationship, and he has little sense of Augustine's puzzlement over the causeless nature of the will.[41]

This priority of reason over will suffered a major reversal in the Paris Conference of 1277, which condemned a number of theological positions deemed heretical by the church. Among the condemned items were Aquinas's statements about the will's subordination to the intellect. This represents a crucial turning point in the series of snapshots offered in this chapter. Earlier theologians had discussed the will under the rubric of *liberum arbitrium*, but after the Paris Conference a new rubric emerged: *libertas voluntatis*, the freedom of the will.[42] This rubric makes central the question of what freedom accrues to the will itself, rather than merely to its decisions. In this respect, it may be significant that the major work of literary personification in fourteenth-century England, *Piers Plowman*, names its main character "Will."[43] Yet for my purposes the

Paris Conference debate highlights a problem generally inherent in the Christian notion of the will since Augustine. Because Aquinas's critics insisted that the will preceded and dominated the intellect, Augustine's problem of volition as its own cause returned with renewed vehemence.

How did the post-Conference theologians of the late thirteenth and fourteenth centuries argue for both the will's freedom and its intelligibility? Sometimes they offered highly subtle explanations of what counts as a "cause." Henry of Ghent, for example, argues that the distance between cause and effect differs from case to case. There is maximum distance in the case of an agent moving an object, a complete dichotomy between active (the agent) and passive (the object). On the other end of the spectrum, there is minimum distance in the case of God moving himself, an almost perfect identity between activity and passivity. Henry claims that the movements of the human will more closely resemble divine self-movement than they do the agent/object dichotomy.[44] This means that although the will needs reason to identify its objects, it is in no sense passive in this transaction. On the contrary, the will commands reason to begin deliberating in the first place.[45]

John Duns Scotus, to select another post-Conference example, is more willing than Henry to concede a causative dimension in the intellect's presentations to the will, but, like Henry, he insists that the will suffers no passivity in this regard.[46] The will operates according to a deep contingency, even at the moment of willing, such that it always retains the potential to will the opposite of what it wills.[47] Scotus sometimes calls this quality of the will a "superabundant sufficiency" (152, 194). When it follows the judgments of reason, then, the will's action is nonetheless self-elicited (157). But what causes the will to self-elicit in one direction rather than another? Scotus's answer resembles Augustine's: "If there is some reason or cause, such as 'The will wills A because of B,' then one inquires further. Somewhere, however, you must stop. Where? Why does the will will this last? There is no other cause to be found except that the will is will" (153).

A final example of the late medieval notion of the will can be found in the philosophy of William of Ockham, who insists on the autonomy of the created will to a degree even greater than that claimed by Henry or Scotus. Ockham redescribes Scotus's notion of the will's contingency in terms of a "liberty of indifference": not only is the will free to act against reason's judgments, but it also enjoys liberty from any natural inclinations.[48] Scotus had conceded that the natural human tendency to seek happiness meant that the will could not actively will misery, although it was free to not will happiness (i.e., to remain inactive) (193). Ockham, by contrast, releases the will even from that constraint: the will can will misery and can will evil *qua* evil.[49] He sharply distinguishes objects of nature, which operate according to efficient causality, from the free agency of the will, which operates according to reasons, that is to say, according to ends rather than efficient causes: "It can be proved evidently through experience . . . that a free agent acts because of an end."[50] If reasons are not causes in any sense—if they do not incline the will one way or another in the slightest—then it might seem that the will functions arbitrarily rather than intelligibly. As one commentator has suggested, Ockham's account of human agency "cuts the will off from nature."[51]

These post-Conference accounts assume that, insofar as the will is caused at all, it is a special kind of causation very different from natural determinism. Yet this assumption also makes it difficult for them to explain the will's relation to other human faculties. Henry compares the intellect's "modification" of the will to the manner in which differing temperatures can modify our appetites and sensations, but he quickly corrects himself: the appetites passively respond to external stimuli, whereas the will is self-moving.[52] We saw this gesture of self-correction earlier, when Augustine tried to compare Adam's freedom of indifference to the state between waking up and full wakefulness. Similarly, Scotus compares the will's contingency to the potential of certain objects to produce either heat or cold, but he notes that this example is "deficient": "In short, there simply is no appropriate example whatsoever that could be given,

because the will is an active principle distinct from the whole class
of active principles which are not will, by reason of the opposite
way in which it acts. It seems stupid, then, to apply general propo-
sitions about active principles to the will, since there are no instances of the way it behaves in anything other than will. For the
will alone is not this other sort of thing" (159). The will is not like
other natural objects and faculties. But then what is it like? Answer:
the will is like the will.

The point here is not that after the fourteenth century everyone
agrees that the will enjoys freedom from reason. Aquinas's intellectualist position has plenty of defenders all the way through the Renaissance period. The point, rather, is that the late medieval attacks
on this position make the question of the will's vexed relation to the
other components of human psychology explicit and almost ines-
capable. As we will see shortly, even later intellectualists, who assume that the will acts according to reason's judgments, tend to
ascribe wayward volitions not to a failure of reason but to the will's
perverse deviance from sound judgment. The will's causality, always
a puzzle, becomes even more so in the late Middle Ages. Augustine,
Henry, and Scotus believe, of course, that human volition has a relation to the other capacities of the soul. But the precise nature of
that relation is difficult to articulate, since it cannot be one of ordinary causation.

This account of the history of the will thus assumes a significant
continuity between early Christian writers such as Augustine and
later ones such as Scotus and Ockham. They all share a commitment
to the idea of the will as at least partly independent of the cognitive
machinery of the self; the difference between these thinkers on this
issue is a matter of degree, not sharp difference. I therefore need to
address, at least briefly, recent intellectual histories that see Ockham
and his fellow nominalists as more starkly breaking with medieval
tradition, even to the point of initiating a "modern" conception of
the will and the human self. Michael Allen Gillespie, for instance,
has argued that by divorcing God's goodness from his omnipotence
and human volition from human reason, Ockham "undermined
the metaphysical/theological foundation of the medieval world."[53]

Likewise, Thomas Pfau has charged the nominalists with producing a cosmos "stripped of any intrinsic telos or dynamism," one in which nature consists of a collection of disconnected entities, including singular instances of human consciousness, a theology that "was to prove vital to the construction of modern subjectivity over subsequent centuries."[54] By making the human will radically free, unconstrained by either reason or nature, Ockham ends a medieval dispensation and begins a modern one: "Here are the origins for the long process of 'theoretical self-determination' (*theoretische Selbstbehauptung*) that Hans Blumenberg and others view as defining the modern era."[55] In Gillespie's and Pfau's version of the story, the late medieval theorists of the will have little in common with earlier Augustinian and Thomist accounts.

No doubt, one can coherently and productively tell the story in this way. The nominalist position was considered radical in its own time. David Aers has recently observed that Ockham's theory of human volition "abstracts freedom from the intrinsic bonds connecting reason, will, and *liberum arbitrium* with their divinely given teleology (the true, the good, beatitude participating in the divine life), intrinsic bonds characteristic of Augustinian and Thomistic Christianity."[56] Although I suspect that the bond between reason and will is less secure in Augustine than it is in Aquinas, this statement offers a just assessment of the nominalists' break with important strands of medieval theological tradition. Ockham in particular replaced a long-standing teleological notion of nature with one governed solely by efficient causality, creating a sharp gap between the natural world and the human psyche.

Yet, regarding the causation of the will, accounts such as Gillespie's and Pfau's underestimate the extent to which the post-Conference philosophers are closer to Augustine than they are to Kant or Schopenhauer. Henry, Scotus, and Ockham liberate the will from reason and habit and in the process leave its causal motivation underdetermined. Yet this is not a brand-new move: we have already seen how Augustine, despite his account of the influences of original sin and divine grace, has a difficult time explaining exactly *why* the free will does what it does. The same is true of many other early Christian theologians. In the eleventh century, for example, Anselm of Canterbury tried to explain the freedom of the will according to a "two-will theory": we have within us a will to advantage and a will to justice, and on any given occasion we are free to select which of these two wills leads to action.[57] This two-will structure allows Anselm to explain how it is *possible* for even an unfallen agent like Lucifer in heaven freely to will rebellion. What remains unexplained, however, is *why* an agent wills the will to advantage over the will to justice in a given case. As one commentator has aptly put it, "We so act, as Anselm insists, because the will is the will."[58] Anselm thus struggles with essentially the same issues of causal regress that Augustine did before him and Scotus does after. This suggests, *contra* the implication in Gillespie and Pfau, that the late medieval nominalists did not invent the problem of the undetermined or libertarian will; instead, they intensify a problem endemic to any psychological model in which volition enjoys partial independence from the other components of the self. Such a model entails a sliding scale of *degrees* of emphasis, either on judgment's influence on the will (which risks scanting freedom) or on the will's independence from judgment (which risks scanting intelligibility).

We likewise have reason to qualify the alleged continuity between the nominalists' position and the modern conception of will. For Henry, Scotus, and Ockham, like the theologians that precede them, the will is not an essential expression of the ego or real self. Significantly, when these writers use the term *agent* (*agens*), as often as not they refer, not to a person, but to a faculty within the person or to an object in the natural world.[59] This does not mean that they had no notion of the whole human being; certainly they did. But it means that they thought of human agency in terms of parts, and one of these parts was the will, the executive source of action that remained awkwardly nonadjacent to the other components of agency.

By contrast, modern philosophers, as we have discussed, usually talk about the will in a quite different way, grounding its freedom in the self or core personality. Even skeptics about the will (and there are plenty in modernity) usually make this assumption. For example, R. E. Hobart, in one of the most influential twentieth-century critiques of undetermined free will, insisted that the heart of the error involved an idealist conception of an "inmost self" that might in some curious way "rise up in its autonomy and moral dignity, independent of motive, and register its sovereign decree."[60] The relevant point at issue is not whether Hobart was right or wrong to find this conception incoherent. Rather, the point is his assumption that to critique free will amounts to critiquing the "inmost self." The modern will is not a faculty or instrument of the human agent; rather, the will is the agentive expression of the true "I." Henry, Scotus, and Ockham, like their medieval predecessors, remain distant from any such conception of volition.

The premodern will is part of the self but also independent from the other parts of the self. The implication this dynamic has for literary personification is probably growing a bit obvious. Personifications represent the parts of a human being (Fear, Joy, Rage) or a landscape (Rome, Thames, Peace), but they also assert an independence from the thing they are part of by behaving as separate agents in the narrative. Personification, I suggest, is the literary equivalent of a model of will in which volitional acts enjoy a partial freedom (or suffer a partial deviation) from the causation of other psychological activity. It is perhaps opportunistic to make too much of the fact that three of the most important early Christian theorists of the moral will—Augustine, Prudentius, and Boethius—all feature personification in some crucial way in their writing. Augustine converses with Reason in the *Soliloquies* and encounters Continence in the throes of his spiritual trials in the *Confessions*.[61] Prudentius, author of the free-will theodicy *Hamartigenia*, also writes the *Psychomachia*, and Boethius learns about the moral will from Lady Philosophy. Yet if we should refrain from charging these coincidences with too much significance, it would be as great an error to ignore them entirely. The personification of Continence signifies the yearning in Augustine's soul to turn to God—"as I wrangled with myself, in my own heart, about my own self"[62]—but her externality indicates that this act of will is not entirely within Augustine's control. Augustine's will is his but is also partly free from the cognitive machinery of the self.

Crucially, as we discussed in chapter 1, medieval and Renaissance thinkers did not place this freedom under the aegis of an ego or deep self. The will floated in and out of the self, connected to the other faculties but not entirely determined by any of them. To have your anger personified by a character named Rage, then, did not alienate your agency from your ego but depicted a part of you sliding into agency. There was no freestanding ego, no "true self," to be alienated. Yet the prosopopoetic figure of Rage also signaled the degree to which your will was not absolutely in your control because, although it was certainly yours, you could claim only an incomplete identity with it.

The postclassical, premodern notion of will, semi-independent of other psychological faculties but not embedded in an autonomous ego, provided a congenial landscape for literary personification. It is roughly this late medieval notion of will as special faculty that informs Renaissance conceptions of volition. With respect to its freedom from ordinary causation, at least, the early modern will was forged in the debates of late medieval theologians rather than in the imagination of fifteenth- and sixteenth-century humanists. This continuity is important to my argument in that it helps to explain why literary personification remained as natural to the Renaissance as it was to the medieval period. Of course, Reformation thought and seventeenth-century philosophy posed major challenges to this model of will. The next section will consider these challenges but will argue that the late medieval conception of volition remains largely intact through most of the seventeenth century.

The Renaissance Will: Alterations and Continuations

When I claim that Renaissance Europe inherited its model of will, broadly construed, from the late Middle Ages and not, say, from Italian humanism, I am not weighing in on the vexed debate about whether a new notion of self as individual emerged in the Renaissance, as Jacob Burckhardt, Ernst Cassirer, and others have argued.[63] There is no need to do so: the early modern will had a constitutive relation to action but not to the self (although it had *a* relation to the self, like all psychological faculties).[64] For my purposes, it is enough to claim that no notion of freestanding ego arose as the typical template for thinking about selfhood. Thus, when Marsilio Ficino praises the will as the power of our soul to engage the outside world, and when Nicholas Sander sees in the human will an analogy with the divine governance of the cosmos, and when John Bramhall argues for the will's power to determine itself apart from the causation of reason, these writers channel the late medieval primacy of the will.[65] None of them implies that volition represents the self-expression of a deep self. All of them assume that the will allows for a transaction—literally, analogically, or both—between human beings and their environment.

This is not to deny that European humanism revised the picture of human psychology in important ways. The fifteenth and sixteenth centuries saw the rediscovery of classical texts by Stoics, Epicureans, and Platonists that provided, in some cases, a new vocabulary for talking about freedom and action. For example, Lorenzo Valla's *De libero arbitrio* (1483) attacks Boethius's account of free will with a notion of the determinism of character derived from Stoic philosophy. His work had tremendous influence, cited approvingly by Luther, Erasmus, Calvin, and Leibnitz, yet it offers no theory of will that departs from medieval accounts. Indeed, Valla finds it natural to describe God's agency by *personifying* it, with Jupiter representing divine will and Apollo divine foreknowledge.[66] God is One, of course, but to describe how he works it is necessary to take him in parts. Likewise, if one consults Valla's rather different account of will in the *Dialectical Disputations*, where free volition enjoys a fierce independence from reason, one is struck by his readiness to engage not just Aristotle and Aquinas but also Stoicism, Epicureanism, and Platonism. But again, his basic notion of will as an autonomous faculty closely resembles that of Henry of Ghent and Duns Scotus.[67]

Likewise, Pietro Pomponazzi's exhaustively erudite *De fato* (1520) uses the Stoic theory of fate to dispute the findings of Aristotle, Alexander of Aphrodisias, Aquinas, and fourteenth-century voluntarists, among others. In this treatise he makes claims that are indeed hard to find in medieval authors—for example, that divine providence is the author of sin and that Stoic philosophy offers a better account of human action than does Christian theology.[68] Yet when Pomponazzi reaches his discussion about the specific operation of the human will, in book 3, the question at issue ends up sounding rather familiar: Does the intellect command the will, or does the will command its own action? Pomponazzi's answer involves a notion of multiphase causation in which the will first passively receives the judgment of reason but then actively moves itself into action.[69] He further grants the will the freedom to refrain from action at all, thereby eluding the determinism of the intellect (3.8.10).[70] Yet this essentially conforms to Aquinas's account of the will's freedom. The vocabulary and references are different, but Pomponazzi follows the medieval concern about the will's peculiar causality.

Again, these humanist formulations represent versions of the late medieval model of will, *broadly* construed. Beyond the fact of the will's independence (or deviation) from the intellect and other cognitive functions, no single conception of will dominated Renaissance thought. Early modern writers understand the will variously to point outward, as the means by which people aggressively assert themselves on others (as Gordon Braden has suggested), and also inward, as the means by which people regulate what goes into and out of their bodies (as Michael Schoenfeldt has described).[71] The Renaissance will plays multiple roles: it guarantees our moral responsibility, it governs the passions of our soul, and it perversely disobeys the judgments of reason. Nonetheless, these differing formulations share the conviction that the will is a *faculty*, part of me but not identical to a "real me." My will is mine but does not always coincide with me.

This conviction helps to clarify the difference between the early modern and the modern will. Medieval and Renaissance people used their will to control their appetites and passions, but they also had to control their will. What sounds like an odd turn of phrase to modern readers seemed much more natural to premodern ones. The French Catholic theologian Pierre Charron insists that the will's role in managing our soul requires that we manage it in turn: "The will is a great part of the reasonable soul, of very great importance, and it standeth us upon above all things to study how to rule it, because upon it dependeth almost our whole estate and good."[72] The will, ruler of our soul, becomes unruly without proper guidance from us. The premodern faculty thus remains distant from the modern notion of autonomy. Spenser's Redcross Knight is suffering a *loss* of self-control when the poet tells us that "will was his guide," and Sir Guyon exercises self-discipline by restricting, rather than exercising, his volition, "bridling his will and mastering his might."[73] The distance between willing and willfulness was much shorter for premodern people than it is for us. What is Guyon using to bridle his willfulness? Presumably, his will.[74] The peculiar causation implied by such a formulation was not lost on dramatic writers. When Shakespeare has Julius Caesar assert that "the cause is in my will; I will not come. / That is enough to satisfy the Senate," the playwright asks us to see the nonsense of the declaration—a decision with no reason determining it is more whim than choice—but also to appreciate the thrill of volition, the power of will to kick itself free of external causation.[75]

This dual quality of volition—the instrument of our self-control, but an instrument we must keep in our control—meant that the will's independence imposed liabilities as much as benefits. This impression comes through even in early modern writers who do not share the late medieval priority of will over reason. Thomas Wright, for example, although working from a Thomist assumption that volition follows the judgments of intellect, insists that the will is "the governess of the soul," charged with maintaining harmony among the passions. Yet he warns that the will exercises governance unreliably, often ready to make imprudent compromises with the appetites for the sake of the temporary avoidance of conflict over lasting harmony among the faculties.[76]

Likewise, Richard Hooker, channeling a distinctly Aristotelian eudaimonism, nonetheless affirms the will's fundamental freedom "to take or refuse any particular object whatsoever being presented unto it."[77] Yet this freedom also leads to perversity, and we act wrongly because of "the hastiness of our Wills, preventing the more considerate advice of sound Reason. . . . The search of knowledge is a thing painful; and the painfulness of knowledge is that which maketh the Will so hardly inclinable thereunto."[78] Both of these examples, echoing Philip Sidney's lament about the disparity between our "erected wit" and our "infected will," ascribe the perversity of our wicked actions not to a failure of reason but to our will's inclination to go its own way.[79] Our will gives us agency, but it remains unpredictable, inconsistently linked to our other faculties, regularly in need of discipline.

In short, there was a substantial continuity between the medieval and early modern conceptions of will. Yet even when viewed from on high, as I am viewing it, the Renaissance intellectual landscape reveals important changes. A major challenge to the medieval model of the will comes from Reformation theology and its intellectual architects, Martin Luther and Jean Calvin. This challenge involves two major aspects, divine providence and the bondage of human will to sin. For the first, Luther and Calvin's notion of providence posits a God who micromanages earthly affairs at a level of detail rarely conceived by earlier theologians. This providence leaves no room for contingency upon which human action might operate freely. Indeed, for Luther and Calvin the opposite of necessity is not freedom but accident.[80]

To say that they espouse a doctrine of determinism probably does not go far enough. If God let simple causal determinism do the work, the world would be like a machine that ran its course while its Maker observed it from a watchtower—both images that Calvin excoriates in the *Institutes* (e.g., 1.16.4, 1.28.1, 3.22.7). The world does not work that way: a leaf fated to fall on the west side of a tree will fall on the west side, even if hurricane-strength winds are blowing to the east as it falls.[81] Although Luther and Calvin object to the term *fatalism*, in part because of its associations with Stoicism, the label nonetheless captures a crucial aspect of their theology. Divine providence ordains all the events that happen with absolute necessity. In such a universe, what does the human will have to do?

In fact, it has plenty to do. Luther and Calvin distinguish between what we might call the sphere of *event causation*, which operates according to divine providence, and the sphere of *agent causation*, which operates according to the human will. In the terms of agency, the human will is the origin of our actions, which we can control in a way that inanimate objects cannot control their movements. Calvin finds it outrageous that some people think divine fatalism means that God designed his moral law for "blocks and stones" (2.5.7): "A wicked man . . . bent on following his own lust, can we compare to a stone, which, driven by an external impulse, is borne along without motion, or sense, or will *of its own?*" (2.5.14, my emphasis). Sin *qua* sin always occurs as an action, under the aspect of will. God isn't forcing us to sin against our will; we *want* to sin, due to our corrupt postlapsarian moral character.[82] When God extends his power to move our affections (without which we could will nothing), he simply activates into will the wicked inclinations already there. Luther offers the analogy of a man riding a lame horse: only with the man's prompting does the horse go forward, but its lameness determines that it goes badly, and this lameness belongs to the horse, not to the rider.[83] Our wills resemble injured creatures or damaged machines: they do what they do because of their impaired natures, but no external force coerces them to do what they do.

In Reformed theology, then, agent causation is to be distinguished from event causation not on the metaphysical terms of a free-will argument, as Scotus and Ockham maintained, or on the eudaemonist terms of rational judgment, as Aquinas maintained, but on what we might call "aspectual" terms, where the nature of the phenomenon depends on which register you use to consider it. That is, Luther and Calvin will grant that in one sense God caused an event, but they insist that in another sense the sinner performed the action. Consider, for example, Luther's response to Erasmus's claim that Judas freely chose to betray Christ: "We know . . . that

Judas betrayed Christ through an act of will, but . . . we are not discussing whether Judas became a traitor involuntarily or voluntarily, but whether at a time preordained by God it was bound infallibly to happen that Judas by an act of his will should betray Christ" (246). Judas performed an action and God preordained an event: the difference for Luther seems to inhere in which aspect of the phenomenon he is "discussing." It is similar for Calvin's suggestion that the prelapsarian Adam enjoyed the freedom to obey the Law or not. If Adam was free, does that mean that in this case God suspended his providence? "It were here unseasonable," writes Calvin, "to introduce the question concerning the secret predestination of God, because we are not considering what might or might not happen, but what the nature of man truly was" (1.15.8). Adam's transgression was an action, rather than an event caused by providence, because Calvin is at present "considering" it as a function of Adam's will.

Yet Luther and Calvin's account of agent causation, which allows for a description of human action beyond the strictures of divine fatality, itself implies the second challenge their theology poses to late medieval notions of volition, namely, the bondage of the will to sin and to Satan. Both Luther and Calvin concede that an ability to do what you want does not amount to free will. Human depravity means that, absent grace, agents can want only one kind of thing: sin.[84] For Luther, the human will resembles a beast of burden: either God rides it or Satan does, and the will cannot choose between them (140). For Calvin, likewise, the sinful will resembles a prisoner in a cell, bound in chains, whose only relief—a slit of sunlight—remains outside of his control (3.2.19). These metaphors of bondage imply that the human will is indeed abrogated, at least in some sense. Beasts bear onerous burdens, and prisoners remain in prison, against their will.

Reformed theology leaves many aspects of the medieval model of volition intact. Luther and Calvin, for example, everywhere insist on the sharp distinction between compulsion, which negates the will, and necessity, whereby the will acts according to its nature. Human sin, in other words, is fully voluntary.[85] Furthermore, Reformed theology retains the faculty psychology model, with reason, will, appetite, and imagination all playing a role.[86] Yet the relationship among these faculties has rather significantly changed, since the Reformers' psychology of action ends up eschewing both the intellectualist and voluntarist positions. The intellectualists, we will recall, held that reason determines the will, yet acknowledged that the faculty of volition has the potential for perverse and unexpected deviations from right judgment. Yet for the Reformers such deviations are no longer a surprise but rather the norm, since the will does not deviate from the judgments of reason so much as it carries out the imperatives of a darkened reason, as Lisa Freinkel has noted.[87] The Reformers' psychology of action likewise rejects the voluntarist notion that the will is "self-elicited," enjoying the potential for multiple options because of its independence from the faculty of reason. The depraved will of Luther and Calvin, as we have seen, enjoys no such independence, but rather follows almost automatically from the depraved character of the sinner.

The Reformers, then, preserve the medieval notion of the will as the power of asserting one's volition and as the source of human action. They deny, however, the traditional capacity of sinners to use the will to effect moral change in themselves. The wicked orientation of our will means that we naturally want to sin, and this orientation changes only if God gives us the grace to repent, at which point we *want* to eschew sin. Both before and after the arrival of grace, then, our will has a kind of automatic setting of bad or good. What remains often obscure in the Reformed psychology of action, however, is the role that the will plays in the transition from one state to the other. This obscurity, as we will see, inclines some literary writers to adjust the way in which they use personifications to represent the moral passions of the soul. Even here, though, the Reformed account retains continuity with medieval descriptions. For Augustine and Scotus, the cause of the will's activity is the will; for Calvin and Luther, the cause of the will's activity is its willfulness, its set orientation toward sin. In terms of the premodern conception of will, this amounts not to a contradiction but to a shift in emphasis.

The other major challenge to the medieval model of will comes from seventeenth-century philosophy, which made substantial alterations to the late medieval and humanist model of cognition. Perhaps most distinctively, this philosophy sought to replace the traditional compartmentalized account of the soul with a unitary one, which potentially alters the will's relation to other cognitive activity.[88] For example, René Descartes limits the soul to thinking beings, dispensing with its traditional separation into irrational and rational parts. He complains in *The Passions of the Soul* that previous commentators have erred in "identifying the different functions of the soul with persons who play different, usually mutually opposed roles. . . . There is within us but one soul, and this soul has within it no diversity of parts."[89] To associate internal human functions with agents that one might metaphorize as "persons" with independent agendas strikes Descartes as wrongheaded. This means, as he avers in the Sixth Meditation, that the unitary mind is the single source for all cognitive activity:

> For when I consider the mind, or myself in so far as I am merely a thinking thing, I am unable to distinguish any parts within myself; I understand myself to be something quite single and complete. Although the whole mind seems to be united to the whole body, I recognize that if a foot or arm or any other part of the body is cut off, nothing has thereby been taken away from the mind. As for the faculties of willing, of understanding, of sensory perception and so on, these cannot be termed parts of the mind, since it is one and the same mind that wills, and understands, and has sensory perceptions.[90]

This formulation undeniably revises the traditional premodern notion of self: the Cartesian self is single rather than compartmental, exclusive rather than inclusive. Descartes implies a sharp divide between me and not-me that would have seemed alien to Aristotle, Augustine, Scotus, and Valla. It is hard to imagine what a Cartesian personification allegory would look like.

Likewise, Thomas Hobbes, although writing from a materialist rather than dualist perspective, denies the faculty model of human psychology. Hobbes shockingly reverses the traditional hierarchy of reason over the passions, describing the soul as a bodily play of conflicting impulses in which there remains little difference between appetitive and rational desire. He does not, for example, distinguish reasoning from other kinds of desiderative cognition: "The whole sum of desires, aversions, hopes, fears, continued till either the thing be done or thought impossible, is what we call deliberation."[91] And just as Hobbes denies the power of reason any special status, he likewise denies it to the power of volition: "The last appetite, or aversion, immediately adhering to the action or to the omission thereof, is what we call the will; the act, not the faculty, of willing" (1.6.53). The only thing special about the desire that carries us into action is its timing, not its status as a distinct faculty of will.

Unlike Descartes, Hobbes has a theory of personification, but it is one that ends up drastically revising the premodern model. Hobbes develops his account with the intention of explaining the conditions on which people assert authority over each other. When one person "personates" another (Hobbes borrows the term for theater performance that emerged in the 1590s), the first is the *actor* of the words or actions, whereas the second, "he that owneth the words and actions, is the *author*, in which case the actor acteth by authority" (1.16.4).[92] Political or legal authority, according to Hobbes, travels only from author to actor, and an author may deny responsibility for things done by an actor who lacks proper authority. How different from traditional premodern personification, which implies that one potentially cedes complete control over one's agency when one exerts that agency. The figure of Joy extends the delight you feel into action or speech, but this figure therefore becomes partly independent of you, her own master and not fully your instrument. Not so for Hobbes, who insists that personifier and personified do not mutually share agency. In his formulation, nonhuman things also can be personified—a rector can personate a church, for example— but they remain inert and lack agency: "Things inanimate cannot be authors, nor therefore give authority to their actors" (1.16.9). The authority entailed by personation takes place only between people living in civil society, and Hobbes's account limits the commerce between humans and nonhuman things that personification long cultivated.

In premodern literary personification, the figure of Joy personifies a part of you by assuming an agency that you do not authorize. Yet Hobbes's account regards personation as valid only if you authorize the actor who personates you. Hobbesian personation thus involves a more carefully managed expression of will—namely, consent—than does literary prosopopoeia. It may be appropriate, then, to read the famous cover illustration of the *Leviathan*, the figure of the sovereign made up by hundreds of individual consenting citizens, as closer to the modern notion of corporation than to the premodern notion of personification.[93] When Lucan has the figure of Rome reprimand Caesar as he crosses the Rubicon, for example, this figure personifies a specific aspect of the city's inhabitants: their outrage.[94] Yet Hobbes's prosopopoetic Leviathan does not personify anything in particular, merely the people's authority, the authority to express their will. It has rights, prerogatives, and duties, but it does not represent a content, such as a human passion, an ideational concept, or a feature of the natural landscape.

As the foregoing remarks suggest, there is no denying that seventeenth-century philosophy proposes substantial alterations to the premodern notion of the will, alterations that are potentially less congenial to a practice of literary prosopopoeia that assumes some degree of a gap between agency and the self. For Descartes, the will is a verb—the action of a unitary soul—more than it is an isolatable faculty. For Hobbes, *will* is simply the term we apply to the desire that happens to precede an action. Such formulations make it difficult to specify what kind of independence the will might have from the other cognitive capacities of the self. As we shall see, seventeenth-century literary personifications of sin—most famously in the second book of Milton's *Paradise Lost*—struggle to distinguish the willed act of evil from both an idealist nonmaterialism and a cause-and-effect process of determinism.

Yet despite the importance of these philosophical revisions we should note two things. The first is that the faculty model of the human psyche, although challenged, continues to flourish through the seventeenth century. Indeed, although scholars have often treated Cartesianism as the crucial event separating the premodern and modern self, the range of Descartes's writings includes notions of the pineal gland (which links body and soul) and the humoral orientation of the body, ideas that significantly qualify the dualist dimension of his thought. As Susan James has observed, "By treating the *Meditations on First Philosophy* as Descartes's philosophical testament, scholars have created a one-sided interpretation of Cartesianism in which the division between body and soul is overemphasized and sometimes misunderstood."[95] The seventeenth century did not suddenly abandon faculty psychology for the unitary consciousness. In diverse writings by poets, political theorists, English divines, and natural scientists, the will remains a faculty partially independent from the other capacities of the self.

The second thing to note is that Descartes and Hobbes, despite their redescription of the human psyche, postulate no special relationship between the essential self and the will, such as emerges over the eighteenth and nineteenth centuries. Although Descartes posits a concept of ego, he does not imagine the will as the essential expression of this ego. Instead, rather like his predecessors, he sees the will as alternatingly coinciding with and breaking with reason. On the one hand, "The will by its nature is so free that it can never be constrained," whereas, on the other hand, reason's judgment produces "a great inclination in the will. . . . If we see very clearly that a thing is suitable for us, then it is difficult for us (I think, even impossible) . . . to stay the course of our desire."[96]

Likewise, although Hobbes limits the circulation of agency in his account of personation, he does not ground the authority of the "author" on a concept of personhood. Indeed, Hobbes's definition of a person tends to strike modern readers as a bit counterintuitive. The instance of a "natural person," representing himself, implies no more personhood than does an instance of an "artificial person," who represents someone else.[97] All personhood is comparable to theatrical presentation, "so that a person is the same that an actor is, both on the stage and in common conversation; and to personate is to act, or represent, himself or another" (1.16.3). Thus, although Hobbesian personation differs importantly from traditional premodern personification, it does not predicate political consent or authority on a special notion of self or will. Consent and authority produce, rather than derive from, personhood as Hobbes conceives it. Hence, although seventeenth-century philosophy changes the psychological and political context, it does not associate the will with anything like Kant's transcendental ego, Mill's permanent me, or Bergson's fundamental self.

The humanist, the late Renaissance philosopher, and the Reformer: all these thinkers place their distinctive mark on the notion of volition, but none of them dislodges the basic medieval sense of the will as a faculty that seems partially to slip free of the causation of other cognitive activity. That is to say, the Renaissance conception of the will continues to offer fertile ground for prosopopoetic literary writing. The disappearance of this faculty model of will in the eighteenth and nineteenth centuries coincides with the passing of personification as an admired and intuitive literary expression. Once the will expresses the self, rather than just a part of the self, personification depletes or freezes human agency instead of affirming it.

Will Personified and the Modes of Volition

As I noted in the Introduction, this is not a book about literary personifications of the will but instead a book about personification as a literary expression of will. Nonetheless, it is instructive to glance at a few Renaissance examples of the personified will because they illustrate quite keenly the problem of causality that has concerned this chapter. The question these examples raise is *why* the will does what it does. Thomas Wright explains that the will "hath engrafted in her two inclinations, the one to follow Reason, the other to content the Senses."[98] The will's position between the impulses of Reason and Appetite was a standard feature of faculty psychology, as we have seen, but also standard was the assumption that volition did not receive these impulses as a passive or automatic instrument. As Pierre de la Primaudaye makes clear, "If it so fall out that the Will give place to the appetite, it is always with her consent, and that because she agreeth rather unto the sensual appetite than unto Reason."[99] The will must consent or agree to one influence rather than another. But *why* does she agree the way she does?

The ambiguity of will's behavior in Renaissance faculty psychology has recently been taken up by Kathryn Schwarz in a fascinating study about female consent in Shakespearean drama.[100] The notion of consent blurs the categories of active and passive, implying both submission to an external pressure and the potential to resist this pressure. Schwarz argues that this blurring troubled the traditional domestic hierarchy of husband and wife: women affirmed this hierarchy only under the tacit condition that they could refuse it if they wanted. Schwarz finds it significant that the personified figure of Will in Renaissance faculty psychology often took the form of a wife, wedded to her husband Reason but tempted by seducers such as Appetite, Desire, or the Senses. The competing solicitations on the will in this "vocabulary of personation" produce a model of self that recapitulates the unstable mechanisms of domestic patriarchy: "Such qualities as reason, will, passion, judgment, fantasy, imagination, and wit appear less as fragments of a unified whole than as contentious citizens of a community, who may or may not conform to rules of behavior, function, and place"(28). The will that both asserts and submits analogizes the wife whose consent implies refusal.

Schwarz's interest in consent as a social practice naturally leads her to emphasize the link between faculty psychology and the political arrangements of patriarchal authority. When one moves outward in this way, from microcosm to macrocosm, one encounters questions of normativity: "Faculty theory . . . extrapolates social principles from the fluctuations of rebellion and restraint. . . . Microcosm both predicates and imitates macrocosm: the role played by will within the psyche prefigures and echoes the question of how to act in the world" (28). Personifications of the will are, in this view, disciplinary: they offer models of proper behavior for men and women while also intimating the problems that make such models urgent. This is a crucial aspect of prosopopoetic faculty psychology. Yet when one travels in the reverse direction, from macrocosm to microcosm, one encounters not so much problems of normativity as puzzles of causation. The central difficulty of the will, from this perspective, turns out to be, not what Schwarz calls "autonomous mediation" (38)—what we might think of as the paradox of the political agent—but instead underdetermination. Faculty psychology tries to explain why the will does what it does but instead ends up positing an infinite regress of causes. This is the legacy of the medieval habit of calling the will free.

The personification of the will in Phineas Fletcher's *The Purple Island* offers a useful illustration of this causal regress. In the poem's allegory, the various features and personages of the island signify the parts and aspects of the human body and soul. Canto 6 describes the court of Prince Intellect and his various counselors and likewise describes the court of Queen Voletta, Fletcher's figure for the will, a queen who once "stain'd her beautie with most loathsome spot."[101] This bit of prosopopoetic faculty psychology refers to Adam's original sin but also promises to explain why any given human agent would choose evil over good. The canto implicitly moves us from the sphere of human action—an agent is choosing between two options—to the microcosmic sphere of human faculties: the will inclines to one option or another on the basis of its interaction with the intellect and with other moral and psychological faculties.

What is the nature of this interaction in the fiction? Fletcher tells us, on the one hand, that Intellect presents his wife with his various reasoned judgments for her to act upon (6.57), but on the other hand he tells us that "though Voletta ever good intends, / Yet by fair ills she oft deceived is" (6.61). It would seem to be Intellect's job to protect Voletta from deception, but perhaps the "fair ills"— whoever they are—outmaneuver him. The poem thus prompts us to ask about the nature of these deceptive ills, and we learn that

Voletta's first wicked choice occurred when she was "entic'd by her own worth and pride" (6.60). Keeping to the faculty personification, we might imagine two figures—Intellect and Pride—each soliciting the Will for attention. But Fletcher also depicts Voletta as a character with internal motivations—"her *own* worth and pride"—which prevents the interactions of the personified faculties within the fiction from explaining her action. Instead, we need to look inside Voletta to understand her will.

Voletta represents a special kind of problem that sometimes emerges when one personifies the will. Of course, all of the personifications in the fiction possess wills, insofar as we think of them as literary characters. Prince Intellect, for example, must actively and willingly fight against the irrational aspects of the soul lest he "neglect his Masters law" (6.36). Intellect thus might fail to will hard enough, but there is no question about what sort of thing he will try to will. Intellect is reasonable; if we looked inside him, we would find reasonableness. Yet Voletta is not like that. To say that we would find willingness or willfulness inside her does not explain anything about why she does what she does. As Fletcher tells us, she does "oft good, oft ill, oft both; yet ever free remains" (6.57). Voletta illustrates the problem of the will we have been tracking throughout this chapter: its freedom from external causation simultaneously gives it an executive function but also renders the motivations for its various actions—good, bad, or both—rather elusive. As Augustine and Scotus argue, the cause of the will is the will.

Indeed, Fletcher's efforts to account for Voletta's behavior through her relationships with her fellow personifications only exacerbate the impression of causal regress. He gives her Synteresis (the common Renaissance mistake for *syneidesis*, or Conscience) as a counselor and Repentance as a lady-in-waiting. Both of these characters seek to draw Voletta to the good: Synteresis uses her "nimble sight" to guide the queen, while Repentance washes her lady's sinful stains "with ever-falling tears" (6.62). Again, if we imagine these figures to describe the psychology of a human agent, they explain how the interplay of various mental faculties leads to certain kinds of actions. Yet in the fiction it is not some character on the macro level (say, the Purple Island itself) who wills to repent, but Voletta herself: "She sees, loathes, mends her former waies" (6.64). This implies that Synteresis and Repentance reside *within* her instead of only alongside her. We thus must imagine a whole cast of characters populating Voletta's psyche—Pride, Intellect, Conscience, Repentance . . . and, of course, Will. And then within this micro-Will we could imagine a similar cast of nano-characters, including a nano-Will, who in turn would house a cast of pico-characters, and so on.

Causal regress is not a feature of literary prosopopoeia in general, and the personified Will does not represent a special paradigm of the trope. Nonetheless, the regressive iteration that characterizes Fletcher's Voletta does point to a general function of personification, namely, the translation of passions and concepts into acts of will. Translating the will into an act of will is a strange thing to do, suggesting why the effort to specify the motives behind Voletta's will produces tautology. The will wills as it does because of the will: this is a deep truth about the medieval and Renaissance notion of volition. Literary personification seeks to capture this truth by converting aspects of the human soul and of the natural landscape into blasts of volition that become partly independent of their origin.

This conversion always derives, more or less, from the peculiar causality of the premodern will. Yet it makes a difference, as the chapters that follow will assume, whether the quality being personified is despair or love or wrath. Differing affects call for differing permutations of the will. I will conclude this chapter with a brief outline of some of the typical modes of prosopopoetic volition. It will be convenient to return to Spenser's personification of rage, Furor, as an example of these modes.[102] To recall the basic story, some of which Spenser borrows from Ariosto: Sir Guyon and his Palmer come across an old hag (Occasion) egging on a madman (Furor) who is dragging by the hair a young man (Phedon). Guyon in a rage is able to force Furor back but not to subdue him until, at the Palmer's advice, he first subdues Occasion. The rescued Phedon then explains that he was affianced to a lady (Claribell) but that his friend Philemon, aided and abetted by Claribell's handmaiden

Pryene, tricked Phedon into believing that Claribell was unfaithful. Enraged, Phedon murdered Claribell, only to learn shortly after from a repentant Pryene that Claribell was innocent. In revenge, Phedon poisons his friend Philemon and then pursues Pryene through the woods with the intention of murdering her. In the course of the pursuit, Phedon is overtaken by Furor, who traps him and is abusing him until Guyon intervenes.

Exteriority

Personification assumes that passions and inclinations operate within the human soul but also, in some sense, reside in the external landscape. What is inside us is also on the outside. The self is porous, passible, and composed of the same materials and energies that compose the outside world. As exteriority, personification implies a causal link between inside and outside, whereby the energies of the landscape transact with the energies of the self. As Phedon pursues Pryene through the woods he is filled with a murderous rage, and his rage calls forth, and is completed by, the external figure of Furor: "And with my heat kindled his cruell fyre."[103]

A paradigmatic case of exteriority might be found in the personification of Conscience, a faculty that commentators long understood to reside within the soul but also to speak to us as if from the outside.

Transmission and Enactment

Personifications express their inner daemon in two ways that, if we were thinking grammatically, we would call transitive and intransitive. In some cases, a personification will transmit its daemonic quality onto another character, obliging that character to take on this daemonic energy. One of the effects of Furor's assault on Sir Guyon is that it fills the knight with a tremendous fury and sets him "emboyling in his haughtie hart" (3.4.9). In other cases, the personification will itself enact the daemonic quality that drives it. Furor is so consumed by rage that he can scarcely control himself: "His force was vaine, and strooke more often wide" (3.4.7). Most personifications involve a mix of transmission and enactment, but it is entirely possible for extreme instances of one mode or the other to occur.

An illustrative instance of an extreme alternation between these modes is the personification of Despair, who traditionally seeks either to kill himself out of spiritual hopelessness or to cheerfully go about his business of inflicting despair onto others.

Possession

A transmissive personification imbues another character with the daemonic quality it represents. The character then wills the quality that has possessed him: something gets into him, and he takes action. Possession can have the effect of inspiring the character to this action, augmenting and focusing his power. Furor enrages Sir Guyon, which initially allows him to hold down his attacker: the knight, "more enfierced through his currish play, / Him strongly grypt" (3.4.8). Possession can also dispossess the character, concentrating his attention so narrowly on the quality that it consumes him and deprives him of self-control. Furor's possession of Phedon makes the young man the victim, rather than the agent, of rage. Possession, in other words, activates a continuum among will, willfulness, and compulsion.

There is perhaps no more striking example of possession than the personification of Love, a figure that both assaults victims against their will and also inspires them to pursue the object of their desire.

Agent or Sign?

This distinction recalls the distinction between example and sign that we considered in chapter 1, but rethought in terms of this chapter's concern with causation. As an external agent, a personification literally and causally imbues another character with the quality it represents. The agency of the personification precedes in time the passion transmitted to the character. Furor enrages Sir

Guyon as an agent: the knight feels wrath only *after* the personification has beaten and humiliated him. Yet as a sign a personification reflects the quality the character already feels or wills. The character's agency precedes in time the appearance of the figurative personification. Furor does not appear on the scene until Phedon is already raging: Furor signifies—is a figure for—the murderous act that Phedon has willed. Personification hovers between agent and sign. Insofar as personification partakes of agent-hood, it maintains a daemonic interaction with the literal narrative; insofar as it partakes of sign-hood, it remains heterogeneous to the literal narrative.

The ambiguity between agent and sign finds one of its most powerful expressions in the personification of Sin, where it is often hard to be sure if she has caused the wicked action to occur or if she metaphorizes it after the fact.

"Conscience." Detail from Caesar Ripa, *Iconologia, or Moral Emblems* (1603; repr., London, 1709), 19. Reproduced with permission of the Folger Shakespeare Library.

Chapter Three

CONSCIENCE IN THE TUDOR INTERLUDES

In writing an account of the daemonic basis of personification, one could not start more conveniently than with Conscience. The Christian faculty of conscience was born from the Greco-Roman figure of the daemon. The daemon I speak of here is not the kind one finds in Greek tragedy, those who have charge of particular energies such as Health, Madness, or Discord. Instead, it is the daemon that the Romans translated with the word *Genius*, the unseen guardian of a person's moral integrity and physical welfare. Socrates famously attributed his ability to abstain from improper actions to his personal daemon, and Plato's myth of Er, discussing the reincarnated soul about to enter a new existence, describes the daemon as "the guardian of the soul's life and the fulfiller of his choice."[1] Plato's most influential expositor, Plotinus, explained that this guardian spirit resided just above us on the cosmic hierarchy, watching over us and leading us, when possible, to a better life.[2]

The New Testament, however, has little use for the daemon, a term it always uses to denote wicked spirits. Paul's version of a sinner's personal instrument of moral guidance is conscience, or *syneidēsis*, stemming from the future infinitive of *eidō*, to see or know. Conscience is a joint seeing or knowing shared between the sinner and the moral consciousness planted in us by God. Paul emphasizes the truth-telling quality of conscience and its power to excuse or accuse our actions.[3] Like the guardian spirit of the ancients, Pauline *syneidēsis* instructs and chastises the mind in order to activate the will. Yet commentators have noted that Paul's usage appears to combine the Hellenic daemon with the Hebraic notion of the guilt-imposing accuser, redefining them from external figures to an internal moral faculty.[4] The daemon is no longer a good spirit invisibly guiding us from the outside: Paul turns it into the strictly interior affair of conscience.

In the centuries that followed, some Platonic philosophers, although still insisting on the objective existence of daemons, were increasingly willing to align them with the mental processes of moral scruple and remorse. Apuleius, in his influential *De Deo Socratis*, suggested that when a human life ends, the daemon in charge of that life seizes the soul and brings it to an afterlife judgment, "and there stands beside us in the trial of our case, refuting any lies we make and supporting any truths; and it is on his testimony that judgement is pronounced."[5] This is remarkably close to Paul's sense that conscience prohibits any dissembling and that it passes judgment—"accusing or else excusing" (Rom. 2:15)—on our deeds and thoughts. Furthermore, at one point in his exposition Apuleius suggests that the daemon not only has knowledge of things inside the mind but in fact lives there: "The daemon . . . dwells in the inmost sanctum of the human mind in the function of consciousness itself [*in ipsis peritissimis mentibus vice conscientiae diversetur*]."[6] Another way to render *conscientia* here, of course, would be "conscience."

Apuleius's identification of the daemon with conscience did not satisfy Christian commentators: Augustine singled out *De Deo Socratis* for aggressive attack in *The City of God*. But Apuleius had stopped only just short of saying that daemons could be understood as metaphors for mental dispositions. As late as the sixth century, the pagan philosopher Olympiodorus, discreetly teaching Platonism to his Christian students, makes a direct equation between daemons and conscience:

It must be said, therefore, that the allotted daemon [*eilēchota daimona*] is conscience [*syneidos*], which is the finest flower of the soul, is sinless in us, is an inflexible judge, and a witness to

Minos and Rhadamanthus of the happenings of our life here. The daemon also becomes the cause to us of our salvation, as always remaining in us without sin, and not assenting to the errors of the soul, but disdaining them, and converting the soul to what is proper. . . . The allotted daemon . . . and conscience are of one and the same kind [*homōnumōs*].[7]

If the daemon is conscience, and conscience is the finest flower of the soul, then it seems in this passage that daemons are inherent aspects of our souls. To go from this passage to reimagining the daemon as an external figure would smack of personification, as if the internal Pauline faculty of conscience were presented in a fiction where an antagonist named Conscience confronted the sinner.

The ambiguity between internal faculty and external spirit continues into the Middle Ages, where writers sometimes associate conscience with the daemonic figure of Genius.[8] This figure is sometimes imagined as a special agent or aspect of nature, with particular charge over the human function of reproduction. In Alain de Lille's *Complaint of Nature*, for example, Nature sends Genius a letter by way of the figure of "Hymen," and she calls him her "other self."[9] Yet writers also describe the figure as a tutelary spirit and moral guide, reminiscent of the guardian daemon of Apuleius and Olympiodorus. Bernardus Silvestris explains that "when . . . the new creation of man has taken place, a genius will be assigned to watch over him."[10] This Genius is an external spirit, to be sure, but it also seems to be partly built into us: "The Genius . . . is joined to man in the first stages of his conception, and shows him, by forebodings of mind, dreams, or portentous displays of external signs, the dangers to be avoided."[11] Genius maintains all of these various qualities into the late Middle Ages. In John Gower's *Confessio amantis*, for example, Genius is a priest of Venus (recalling his reproductive function), but he also counsels the protagonist Amans on the correct attitude to take toward love. As a counselor, he operates both outside and inside the psyche. He is an external figure teaching Amans moral understanding, but also a figure internal to the human soul, in which he represents the imagination and Amans represents the will, as James Simpson has recently argued.[12]

I want to suggest that conscience and daemons (in the guise of Genius or otherwise) have a shared prosopopoetic resonance because personification, as we discussed in chapter 1, is the trope that allows intercourse between the external energies of the landscape and the internal inclinations of the soul. Both the daemon and conscience are defined by this intercourse. Daemons are not simply an extension of our selfhood but influence us from the outside, prompting, guiding, and sometimes possessing us—the guardian daemon "is ours . . . but not ours," as Plotinus puts it.[13] Edmund Spenser says something analogous about the figure of Genius: "That is our Selfe, whom though we do not see, / Yet each doth in him selfe it well perceive to bee."[14] Genius *is* the self but, by virtue of residing *in* the self, does not exactly coincide with the self. In a similar fashion, a Christian conscience belongs to us but is a special gift (or constraint) bestowed by God that retains its otherness in relation to us. Few psychic faculties in premodern writing are so readily described as *doing* things to us: advising, rebuking, accusing, affirming, stinging, torturing, dissuading, and persuading us. Conscience, like the guardian daemon, is ours but not ours.

Indeed, the notion that conscience enjoyed a daemonic independence from the judgment and will of the sinner was not an alien proposition to Renaissance theologians. The puritan divine William Perkins writes about our faculty of moral scruple in terms unexpectedly reminiscent of Apuleius and Olympiodorus:

Hence we may observe God's goodness and love to man. If he do anything amiss, he sets his conscience first of all to tell him of it secretly. If then he amend, God forgives it; if not, then afterward conscience must openly accuse him for it at the bar of God's judgment before all the saints and angels in heaven. Nay, it is (as it were) a little god sitting in the middle of men's hearts, arraigning them in this life as they shall be arraigned for their offences at the tribunal seat of the ever-living God in the day of judgment.[15]

For a moment in Perkins's discourse, conscience operates just like the daemon of late antiquity, a subordinate deity living inside us, rebuking our sins, and testifying against us to the Christian Minos and Rhadamanthus. The parenthetical "as it were" asserts the limits of this comparison: literally, there are no little gods, only one big god. But with "as it were" Perkins suggests that we can understand his discourse better by means of a miniature prosopopoetic fiction, wherein conscience becomes Conscience.

Scholarship on the role of conscience in Renaissance literature has often focused on the complex interplay between the commitment to one's personal convictions and the public demands of self-representation. How much external pressure can a believer accommodate while maintaining a good conscience? This tension can be traced back to Aquinas, who divides the Pauline instrument of moral scruple into *syneidēsis* (the theoretical knowledge of moral principles) and *conscientia* (the practical application of principles to specific cases).[16] The gap between these two things opens up the practice and institution of casuistry, whereby the believer seeks in good conscience to negotiate competing moral demands in particular, difficult cases. Casuistic theory and practice bloomed in the Counter-Reformation period, and a number of studies have examined the role of conscience from this perspective.[17]

But the daemonic basis of conscience in Renaissance literature has been less examined. An exception is the suggestive, if difficult, study by Ned Lukacher on daemonic figures in Shakespeare. Lukacher reads the shift from the Greek *daimōn* to Pauline *syneidēsis* to medieval *conscientia* in terms of the Heideggerian history of being. In this history, the early Greeks held open the ambiguity between things and their elusive origin in Being. Daemons, neither damned nor sacred, neither entirely outside us nor inside us, exemplify this salutary ambiguity. Starting with Plato, the Western conception of Being becomes increasingly narrow, and individual things are increasingly isolated from the otherness of Being. The Christian translation of daemon to conscience represents, for Lukacher, a crucial event within this Heideggerian history, "the victory or dominance of Christian and Latin subjective certainty over the irresolvable undecidability of the *daimon* of Greek antiquity."[18] In Lukacher's reading, Shakespeare's drama hints at the daemonic uncanniness still lurking within the modern concept of conscience.

My interest here is not to pronounce this thesis right or wrong: Lukacher's history of conscience is so massive in scope that it is unclear what would constitute "evidence" to confirm it or disprove it. But I do want to suggest that if one is pursuing a specifically daemonic history of conscience in Renaissance imaginative literature, then the place to look might be, in the first instance, not Shakespearean drama, but rather the early modern heir of the daemon—personification. And the personification of Conscience appears nowhere more frequently than in the moral interludes of the Tudor period.

The sixty or so extant moral interludes—spanning the period from the late fifteenth century to the 1580s—usually share a basic plot: a protagonist, often a young man, falls into bad company and lives a life of sin; the forces of good try to persuade him to repent; sometimes they succeed, sometimes they fail. Over the course of the sixteenth century, this basic plot was elaborated in a number of ways. The interlude sometimes features overt topical allegories and satires about well-known political and religious figures.[19] They often include a great deal of humor, much of it based on the linguistic curiosities of foreign or regional dialects. Personifications of virtues and vices populate these plays, distinguishing themselves from their morality play ancestors by frequently disguising or changing their names. Although one commentator has understood this practice of name changing to challenge the plays' allegorical nature, the fact that only the evil personifications do this suggests, rather, that the practice indicates a sixteenth-century concern with the sin of hypocrisy.[20] As Sarah Beckwith has argued, the actor's mask in medieval liturgical drama functioned as a sign of supernatural reality, whereas the Protestant plays instead operate within a "theater of disguises" whereby the mask calls attention to the misleadingness of appearance.[21] This crucial religious dimension of the plays should cause us to qualify the recent scholarly inclination to see a shift from sacred to secular in the moral interludes: the basic repentance plot continues to drive this genre until the end of the Tudor period.

Indeed, these plays differ from other religious literary forms in that repentance is not simply one event among others in their narratives. Rather, the sinner's repentance (or failure to repent) is the point of the interlude, the telos toward which the story travels. In pursuing this emphasis, this drama does not imply what Lukacher calls the "Christian and Latin subjective certainty" of Christian conscience. Instead, it embraces the simultaneously interior and exterior nature of daemonic energy. As in much personification literature, the reader alternately experiences the personified figure as external to the protagonist and as a projection of his inner passions and faculties.

This Christian drama does not, of course, posit that conscience is actually a pagan deity any more than Perkins does. Instead, it assumes that we must understand *vice conscientiae*, "the place of conscience," to borrow Apuleius's phrase, with a divided attention to inside and outside. To heed conscience always amounts to simultaneously talking to oneself and listening to someone else talk. For example, in the anonymous Catholic play *The World and the Child* (1522) the figure of Conscience comes to the sinful protagonist as a fully external figure, a counselor dressed as a friar who preaches the discipline of the Catholic Church. Yet the protagonist, Manhood, eventually eschews these teachings and listens to Folly, in part because "the World and Folly counselleth me to all gladness, / Ye, and Conscience counselleth me to all sadness, / Ye, too much sadness might bring me in to madness."[22] The end of the play finds Manhood, now named Age, in deep sadness as he echoes the teachings of Conscience that he abandoned.

But does his sorrow derive from Conscience's absence or presence? Age is sad because his guide has departed from him, but it is the inner prompting of conscience, whose doctrine he echoes, that teaches him remorseful sadness in the first place. The laments of conscience call forth Conscience's "brother" (813), Perseverance. This extension of Conscience gives Age a new name, "Repentance" (854), a renaming that prompts the hero finally to voice his contrition for his sinful life. This plot yields what could be taken as an allegory of the internal mechanisms of contrition. Conscience is moral awareness, Perseverance is the continued application of that awareness in one's life, the fruit of which is Repentance. Conscience was always inside the sinner, but also outside in the form of the institutions of the church.

This depiction of Conscience possesses a number of qualities deriving from earlier medieval depictions of the figure. For example, the opposition between Conscience and World in *The World and the Child* at least partly recalls the opposition between Conscience and the worldly Meed in William Langland's *Piers Plowman*. Furthermore, both texts assume that the faculty of conscience ideally prompts the will into action. In the interlude, Perseverance is the extension of Conscience into action. Manhood makes explicit the equation between knowledge and action:

> For Conscience clear I clepe my king,
> And am his knight in good doing,
> For, right of reason as I find,
> Conscience teaching is true.
>
> (502–5)

In these lines, good knowing amounts to good doing. Likewise, in Langland's poem Conscience's victory over Meed and Wrong at the end of passus 4 arguably leads to the work of Repentance at the beginning of passus 5, where, as the poet relates, "Thanne ran Repentaunce and rehersed ys teme, / Ant gart Wille to wepe water wyth hise eyes" (B:5.60–61).[23] There is a suggestive connection here between conscience, repentance, and will. The poem and the interlude both also assume that Conscience, although inducing a salutary sadness, is the natural opposite of Wanhope, or Despair, which seeks to drive the sinner deeper into sin.[24] Finally, both texts imagine conscience to operate within and outside the sinner. Much as Conscience simultaneously represents Manhood's moral scruples and the institutions of the church, so Conscience in *Piers Plowman* functions as a member of the king's council and as the mental faculty by which God monitors us, as the poet warns sinners: "For God knoweth thi conscience and thi kynde wille" (B:3.67).

The interlude's depiction of the figure of Conscience, then, plays on a number of themes that can be found in earlier Catholic literature. In particular, it assumes that Conscience functions by activating the will, either directly or via other prosopopoetic agents. It also assumes that Conscience, although imposing painful remorse on sinners, also intimates the future joy of repentance and so stands as a natural opposite to despair. The Protestant interludes, by contrast, share neither of these assumptions: Conscience does not prompt the will to do anything, and it is often all but indistinguishable from despair. These crucial revisions of the personification of Conscience illustrate the changed role of the will, regarding the act of repentance, in Reformed theology. To explain these revisions, the next section will discuss the source of the will to repent in Reformed thought. Then the remainder of the chapter will return to the altered role of conscience as a faculty in Protestant moral psychology and as a personification in the Tudor interludes.

The Protestant Asymmetry Thesis

I borrow the term *asymmetry thesis* from modern commentators on Plato. When people set out to do something, Plato claims, they assume that their intended action is, in some way, a good one. Everyone acts for the sake of the good—at least, their understanding of the good. This means that no one chooses to do evil acts *qua* evil; instead, they do evil by mistake. Plato is stricter about this than Aristotle, who says that although we cannot rationally choose evil we nonetheless do it voluntarily. Plato insists in the *Meno* that wrongdoers "don't desire evil but what they think is good, though in fact it is evil; those who through ignorance mistake bad things for good obviously desire the good."[25] In the *Laws* he suggests that the city should punish wrongdoers, not for the sake of their evil intentions (they intended what they thought was good), but for the sake of the damage they cause.[26] This state of affairs is what modern philosophers call asymmetrical in Plato's philosophy of action: he claims we can choose virtue but not vice, which we commit only through error. For this reason, Plato expresses confidence that acquiring moral knowledge will result in performing virtuous actions.

Reformation theology produced its own version of the asymmetry thesis, but produced it in reverse. Plato assumes that our desires take their direction from the orientation of our reason and that reason wants the good. Martin Luther, John Calvin, and their followers assume that our desires take their direction from the orientation of our corrupted nature and that this nature wants the bad. Because of this innate corruption, everyone acts with wicked intentions. If we happen to do something virtuous, we do it for the sake of gratifying our pride or conforming to civil law—do the good, as it were, incidentally—which means it is not truly the good. We can genuinely behave virtuously only if God intervenes by granting us grace, which reverses our desires so that we begin to want the good. This model is fundamentally asymmetrical: sin is something we do, whereas grace is something that happens to us. As historians of theology often note, versions of the asymmetry thesis were espoused by a wide variety of Catholic thinkers in the Middle Ages, but early modern Protestants distinguished themselves by making it an uncompromising centerpiece of their faith's moral psychology. This is why repentance is such a radical act of will in Protestant thought, compared to the exercise of virtue in the Platonic scheme. The Platonic agent does the good naturally, so to speak, simply following reason's direction. Protestant repentance, by contrast, is in a sense unnatural: the agent wills a reversal of the corrupt character that heretofore has determined how the agent wills.

This means that the act of repentance is the consequence, rather than the cause, of divine forgiveness. The Protestant Tudor interludes regularly affirm this counterintuitive causality. In these plays, the virtuous personifications don't say (as Conscience says to Manhood in *The World and the Child*): repent so that God will forgive you. Instead, they say: try to repent in order to find out whether God has already forgiven you. A few examples will stand for a general tendency:

> If thou hast grace, for mercy now call,
> Yet thy soul perchance thou mayst save;
> For his mercy is above his works all,
> On penitent sinners he is wont mercy to have.[27]

Although thou see nothing now but thy condemnation,
Yet it may please God again to open thy eyes.[28]

Now near he is to the fount of perdition:
God grant him repentance, or it be too late,
That of his sins he may have remission.[29]

God will all their sins for [Christ's] sake forgive,
So that they can be contrite and repent.[30]

Even out of context, these passages express the counterintuitive cause-and-effect relation between divine forgiveness and contrition characteristic of the Protestant asymmetry thesis. Now, it is true that if one digs into the dialogue of these plays one can find examples of the more intuitive scenario in which God forgives sinners *because* they repent.[31] These alternate examples persist, presumably, because the interlude authors want to offer moral instruction whereby sinners amend their lives in order to win God's approval. Nonetheless, the interludes by and large stick to their theological mission, maintaining the asymmetry thesis whereby the will to sin comes from us and the will to repent comes from God.

This state of affairs gives rise to a host of familiar questions that have exercised skeptics from Erasmus to Alan Sinfield. If sinners cannot repent on their own, why blame them for their sin? If the ability to repent rests entirely in God and not at all in us, why bother to try to repent? Does an act of will even count as will if divine grace irresistibly prompts it? This line of thought has inclined many modern scholars to assume that the human will per se plays little or no role in the Protestant notion of contrition. The philosopher Jennifer Herdt comments disapprovingly that, in Reformed thought, "human goodness . . . requires human passivity."[32] The literary critic Angus Fletcher similarly argues that the Protestant notion of predestination amounts to "the destruction of an individual will by the arbitrary power of the Calvinist God."[33]

These views derive, at least indirectly, from two ostensibly reasonable but finally mistaken intuitions about predestinarian theology. The first is that divine predestination takes over the human will, forcing humans to sin and then unfairly damning them for sinning. This impression has long aroused the ire of Calvinism's critics. In 1584 Samuel Harsnett sermonized in disgust, "This opinion saith that not one or two, but millions of men should fry in Hell, and that [God] made them for no other purpose than to be the children of death and Hell, and that for no other cause, but his mere pleasure's sake."[34] Yet as we discussed in chapter 2, Luther, Calvin, and their followers treat the human will as operating in a different register from the fatality that divine omnipotence logically imposes on all events. God doesn't make us sin against our will; we *want* to sin. We are punished for the sake of those sins, not for the sake of God's sadistic pleasure. Our will to sin belongs to us and to our morally depraved character, which prompts our will.

I don't deny that one might still find this state of affairs unsatisfactory: the moral character that prompts our will inclines us to want only one kind of thing (sin). Luther and Calvin concede that this doesn't amount to what we ordinarily call free will; it merely amounts to the absence of compulsion.[35] But if the asymmetry thesis is unfair, its unfairness has nothing to do with divine fatality or with the abrogation of the human will. The cultural historian John Stachniewski is missing the point when he claims that, in Calvinist drama, the literary device of personification can only "invade the mind [of the protagonist] and take over his will."[36] On the contrary, personifications such as Infidelity, Hypocrisy, Pride, and Flesh *express* and *prompt* the will of sinner. They never take over that will, which belongs to the sinner.

The second mistaken impression is that the act of repentance has nothing to do with the agent's will because it comes from God's grace, not from the efforts of the repentant sinner. This is a more difficult impression to counter. Ordinarily when we change our minds we make sense of the change by pointing to earlier thoughts, feelings, and inclinations relevant to our new outlook. Even when we discover that our minds have changed without our having deliberately intended it, we can still adduce earlier mental states as a means of affirming that we *own* our change of heart: it didn't just happen to us. This intuition about the importance of the mental history leading to a change of heart offers a major stumbling block to understanding repentance, in Reformed thought, as an act of will, insofar as acts of will are active. Prior to grace, our sinful disposition prevents us from genuinely wanting to be atoned with God. Since grace comes to the sinner out of the blue, irresistibly reversing her disposition to sin, we might be tempted to conclude that repentance happens *to* us, an event that we passively experience. This line of thought seems, at first glance, to lend credence to Herdt's view that in Reformed thought, "human goodness . . . requires human passivity."[37]

Yet, in fact, the reformers almost never speak of our response to salvation in this manner. When we repent, we will a new life for ourselves, a "real conversion of our life unto God," as Calvin puts it, occurring when the believer, according to William Perkins, "doth purpose, will, desire, and endeavor to relinquish his former sins, and to become a new man."[38] This sounds like the active effort of a deliberate agent. Perkins elsewhere insists that "man's will is not passive in all and every respect, but hath an action in the first conversion and change of the soul. When any man is converted, this work of God is not done by compulsion, but he is converted willingly: and at the very time when he is converted, by God's grace he wills his conversion."[39] This perplexing mix of passive and active voice certainly sounds contradictory at first glance. But Perkins is trying to coordinate the fact that God is the efficient cause of repentance with the fact that believers experience repentance as an act of will. In the above passage, even as God pushes the agent over the threshold between sin and salvation, the agent feels the need to make an effort to cross.

Again, the skeptic can ask: Why bother to try to repent, since the success or failure of the effort does not lie in the agent? Yet when it comes to the subjective experience of the sinner, Reformation divines sometimes concede the impression of contingency in a process that otherwise proceeds as a matter of necessity. Perkins offers King David as an example of those who "despair of God's mercy for a time . . . a dangerous sin,"[40] suggesting that David is not truly safe until he actually repents. The danger of this sin appears to come from the sheer difficulty of moving from guilt to repentance: "What a wonderful hard thing it is at the same instant when a man is touched for his sins, then to apply God's mercy to himself. . . . When a man is in this perplexity, he shall find it a most hard matter to be freed from it, without the marvelous power and strength of Christ Jesus" (31–32; 41). Strictly speaking, moving from guilt to repentance without the power of Christ is not hard but impossible. Likewise, David's sin of despair cannot objectively be "dangerous" to him, because his election guarantees his repentance.

The language of danger and difficulty appears to grant the guilty sinner an agency in the midst of his entirely passive reception of grace. This view of volition challenges the common assumption that acts of will must amount to *self-mastery*, whereby we assert dominion over ourselves in order to become the origin of our actions. Reformation moral psychology suggests, by contrast, that acts of will need only amount to *self-identification*: as we sense one inclination within us overriding contrary preferences, we endorse that inclination as it carries us into action. We will it by committing ourselves to it, not worrying much about its origin. This is the implicit logic, I would argue, of a great variety of Protestant theological, homiletic, and literary writings. We could put the matter in this way: the sinner cannot will himself to repent (self-mastery), but he does will his repentance (self-identification). The asymmetry thesis yields this peculiar formula, and Protestant commentators made sense of it through the faculty of conscience.

THE PROTESTANT CONSCIENCE, OR, WANTING TO WANT TO REPENT

To call the early Protestant notion of conscience "daemonic" is to note, among other things, its extraordinary moral ambiguity at the moment of spiritual crisis. Conscience doesn't lie, of course. God has designed it to impress upon us our responsibility to the Law and our failure to live up to that responsibility.[41] This is why people say that conscience "stings" more often than they say it lashes or tortures: a sting unexpectedly startles its victim from inattention to awareness. But the sting of the Protestant conscience does not prompt the sinner to live a better life. Instead, it tells the terrible truth of our moral inadequacy and the deadly peril in which we live. This is why Luther warns that at the moment of spiritual crisis conscience becomes demonic, a tool by which Satan drives away hope of forgiveness.[42] Luther goes so far as to insist that the sinner stop listening to conscience at this point, but for Calvin, and for the English divines he influenced, the sinner must continue to heed the accusations of conscience, no matter how deeply they may wound.

The Protestant conscience, unlike its Catholic predecessor, cannot push the sinner to will his repentance; at times it even seems to dissuade the sinner from repenting. Given this condition, what difference does conscience make? We can begin to answer this question by contemplating the absence of conscience. When conscience is dulled or sleeping, the sinner's depraved character determines that he wants only to sin, and wants it with his whole heart. This kind of sinner has "no power, no not so much as once to desire to give one little sob for the remission of his sins," as Perkins puts it.[43] Not only does such a one lack the power to repent, but he does not even want the power.

However, an awakened conscience produces certain kinds of aversions about one's sin. To illustrate, let us distinguish among three different cases of conscience. In the first, conscience plays little or no role because the conversion arrives so abruptly. This is the case of Saul, who, cheerfully and voluntarily going about his sinful work, is suddenly struck by grace and converts into the repentant Paul. In the second, conscience produces an aversion to one's sin but not the desire to renounce this sin. This is the case of Judas (at least in some accounts of Judas), who, becoming aware of his egregious sinfulness, despairs of God's mercy and commits suicide while cursing God's justice. Paul repents and is saved, Judas despairs and is damned, but neither of them *wants* to repent beforehand. This is what distinguishes the third case of wanting to repent prior to willing repentance, illustrated by King David, who sins, despairs of God's mercy, but wants to repent and prays for help in doing so. Here we have a genuine case of conscience.

Notice two crucial things about this case. First of all, unlike the first two cases, this third case encompasses both elect and reprobate sinners. David, it turns out, was saved, but popular histories of reprobate sinners like Francis Spira and Johann Faustus feature at length their plaintive desire to be moved to ask forgiveness for their sins. They seem similar to David in their wish that they might repent. Now, Reformed theology would officially contest the thesis that Spira, Faustus, and David share any kinship. Since David is elect, his desire to repent represents the work of grace, which can be read backwards into mental states anterior to the actual will to repent.[44] Conversely, Reformed theology would say that since grace does not underwrite Spira's and Faustus's feeling of contrition, they do not *really* want to repent. Along these lines Perkins distinguishes between legal contrition (remorse that our sins merit punishment) and evangelical contrition (remorse that we have offended God).[45] Although prior to repentance itself Spira and Faustus appeared to resemble David, in fact they always belonged with Judas.

However, the distinction between legal and evangelical contrition pertains to outcome, not to genesis. Guilt will lead David to salvation, whereas it will lead Spira and Faustus to despair. Yet for all of them the guilt *started* with conscience, which prompted in them the desire that they might repent. Again, this speaks to the daemonic ambiguity of conscience in Protestant thought. In the case of evangelical contrition, "God in mercy makes it to be an occasion going before, of grace to be given." For the elect, then, conscience can be a kind of angelic forerunner of God's love. But in the case of mere legal contrition, "remorse of conscience for sin is no beginning of repentance . . . but rather . . . the beginning of unspeakable horrors of conscience, and everlasting death."[46] For the reprobate, conscience is a torturing devil. Yet be it angel or demon, conscience provides the common means by which David, Spira, and Faustus come to want to repent.

The second crucial thing to note about the case of wanting to repent prior to repentance is that desire still falls short of willing.

This statement risks some ambiguity, as it might be objected that, in ordinary usage, when we "want to repent" we repent. But David, by his own admission, still harbors the desire to persist in sin. In this conflict, the desire to repent fails to overcome the desire to sin, so his repentant inclination does not effectively move him to the act of contrition. To speak as precisely as possible, then, David does not yet want to repent, but he *wants* to want to repent; he wishes he had the effective desire to repent. I realize that this is a peculiar way of putting the matter, but it calls attention to the degree to which David has a *perspective* on his conflicting desires, even if he cannot control which desire carries the day. Only God can control that.

This is precisely how the Protestant conscience works: it creates a perspective on one's spiritual conflicts such that the sinner can identify with some desires and not others. Conscience does this by rapaciously laying bare all the sinner's secrets. James Dougal Fleming has recently discussed conscience's panoptic capacity to see everything, even itself.[47] He quotes Jeremy Taylor's remark that by calling on God we show that "our conscience is right, and that God and God's Vicar, our conscience, knows it."[48] If conscience is both the subject and object of knowledge, then the sinner's mind is never fully sealed. Such a mind can hold no fundamental secrets, since conscience allows neither itself nor the mind it is part of to stand as an unobserved viewpoint. We check our conscience, but conscience itself does the checking, starting, as Fleming puts it, "down the road of infinite regress (as the checking must be checked, and that checking must be checked, etc.)."[49] For Fleming, this anti-secret regress ideally moves the Puritan believer to confess his interior state and represent himself publicly according to a right conscience. In the desire to repent, however, the regress takes a rather different form: conscience prevents the sinner from being neutral about his desires by prompting what modern philosophers call second-order desire.

In purely formal terms, a first-order desire is a desire for an object, while a second-order desire is a desire about a desire. Out of this formal distinction the philosopher Harry G. Frankfurt has sought to make a substantive claim about free will.[50] At any given time an agent may have competing desires such that she does not know which one will motivate her into action. In the immediate term she cannot control which will be effective desire and emerge as her will. Over time, however, this agent may come to wish that one desire rather than others prove decisive. This second-order desire, concerned with which first-order desire is to be her will, is properly called a *second-order volition*. A second-order volition cannot simply compel the course of the first-order, but if the two correspond—if the agent wants what she wills—then, according to Frankfurt, the agent enjoys free will.

Frankfurt considers the example of drug addiction (which has suggestive affinities with early modern sin, since both phenomena produce behavior that cannot be reversed by a direct act of will). Addicts may have competing desires about taking drugs stemming from a variety of reasons: physiological impulses urge the taking of drugs, but a fear of self-destruction urges refraining from the same, et cetera. In a given case an addict may have no second-order volitions about which desire wins out—he goes with the flow—and Frankfurt calls such an agent a *wanton*. A wanton can rationally deliberate about how to do what he wants to do, but he does not care which of his inclinations are the strongest or what his will is to be. (In the terms of my discussion, he has no perspective on his desires.) In another case, however, an addict may deeply wish that her desire to avoid self-destruction trump her craving for the drug. The craving may win out, and the addict then takes drugs because she wants to take them, but, unlike the wanton, this addict can meaningfully claim that the craving moves her against her will. Through the formation of a second-order volition, she has identified herself with a first-order desire (to refrain from drug use) and has withdrawn from another (to indulge in drug use). Regarding her addiction, the unwilling addict has the potential for free will but fails to achieve it; the wanton's will is neither free nor exactly unfree.

In Reformed thought, conscience prevents the sinner from being a wanton with regard to his sinful desires. When conscience is dulled or sleeping, the sinner's dispositional depravity determines that he wants only to sin and that he wants it with his whole heart. A functioning conscience intervenes, however, by forcing the formation of second-order knowledge about one's first-order desire to sin. Calvin observes that conscience takes the sinner's "simple knowledge" of his sin and obliges him to reflect on it, "that nothing may remain buried in darkness."[51] Perkins likewise draws out this inference of the knower knowing that he knows:

> For there must be two actions of the understanding: the one is simple, which barely conceiveth or thinketh this or that, the other is a reflecting or doubling of the former, whereby a man conceives and thinks with himself what he thinks. And this action properly pertains to the conscience. The mind thinks a thought, now conscience goes beyond the mind, and knows what the mind thinks . . . and from hence also it seems to borrow his name, because conscience is a science or knowledge joined with an other knowledge; for by it I conceive and know what I know.[52]

If you know what you know, then you have a perspective on what you know, and you can form desires or aversions about it. Conscience makes the sinner see both that he ought to repent and that he does not merit forgiveness. This perspective does not activate the will but instead imposes stasis. Yet in this self-reflective stasis, the sinner may form the second-order volition that his desire to repent trump the desire to persist in despair. This is, in fact, precisely what King Claudius does in *Hamlet*, once the "lash" of "conscience" has rendered the king remorseful:

> Pray can I not,
> Though inclination be as sharp as will.
> My stronger guilt defeats my strong intent,
> And like a man to double business bound
> I stand in pause where I shall first begin,
> And both neglect.
>
> (3.3.38–43)

Whether Shakespeare is drawing on a technical account of Reformation contrition psychology is hard to say, but the passage clearly follows the spirit of this psychology. Conscience gives Claudius a perspective in which he "stand[s] in pause," contemplating his competing desires. He would like to repent, he *wants* to want sincerely to repent, but he cannot push his inclination into will by his own effort.

The outcome of this second-order volition does not, then, lie in the control of the sinner. Prior to grace, in the interval between wanting and willing repentance, conscience can at best pose questions of higher and higher orders: Is my contrition sincere? Have I asked myself that question sincerely? Have I sincerely asked myself about the sincerity of my questioning (etc.)? Rechecking the checking, conscience occasions either the angelic "doubtings" that lead to repentance or the demonic "perplexities" that plunge the sinner deeper into despair.[53] Frankfurt imagines a similar process occurring in his addicts, who might have two conflicting second-order volitions about first-order desires, and so might form a third-order desire about these second-order volitions. Third-order desires could themselves become the objects of fourth-order desires, and so on: "There is no theoretical limit to the length of the series of desire of higher and higher orders. . . . The tendency to generate such a series of acts of forming desires . . . leads toward the destruction of a person."[54] Higher-order regression does not make us more profound, merely more scattered. The agent can forestall this destructive regress, Frankfurt suggests, through an act of self-identification: "It is possible . . . to terminate such a series of acts without cutting it off arbitrarily. When a person identifies himself *decisively* with one of his first-order desires, this commitment 'resounds' throughout the potentially endless array of higher orders. . . . The decisiveness of the commitment he has made means that he has decided that no further question about his second-order volition, at any higher order, remains to be asked."[55] This self-identification characterizes the free will that persons, but not wantons, can potentially exercise.

Frankfurt does not claim that we can specify how an agent succeeds or fails to realize her second-order volitions; he would presumably admit that he has no idea, ultimately, why some unwilling addicts manage to stop using drugs while others fail to do so. Gary Watson has complained that Frankfurt's reticence in this regard makes it impossible to say what gives a second-order volition a non-arbitrary relation to "oneself": "It is unhelpful to answer that one makes a 'decisive commitment,' where this just means that an interminable ascent to higher orders is not going to be permitted. This *is* arbitrary."[56] Indeed, it does seem counterintuitive to say that freedom is the *consequence* of a first- and second-order correspondence instead of the *condition* of this correspondence. Yet Frankfurt's disinclination to say that the agents can simply will the act of identification (he thinks such libertarian claims are hopelessly confused) gives his account a powerful affinity with Reformation theology's sense of the act of repentance. The sinner, prompted by conscience to want the will to repent, does not *effect* the transition from wanting to willing; rather, he *endorses* it as it happens to him. The repentant man, as he finds himself able to will repentance, approves of this will: he finally wants what he wanted to want. In doing so, the new man gains what Luther calls "a royal freedom,"[57] despite the fact that the cause of repentance remains outside the agent.

Thinking of second-order volitions as endorsements rather than causes of first-order desires, we can describe the shift from despair to repentance as an act of self-identification but not an act of self-mastery. Endorsing the will we have does not mean that we create the will we have. This allows us to locate Luther's "royal freedom" phenomenologically outside the fatalist implications of divine election, yet still to distinguish it from Erasmian free will. The freedom of the repentant man, for example, does not allow him simply to will himself to forgo wickedness. Even though the gradual process of sanctification permits the godly to live increasingly perfect lives, sinning remains a condition of being in the world. Yet when the godly sin, "they never give full consent, for they are in their minds, wills, and affections partly regenerate, and partly unregenerate, and therefore their wills will partly abhor that which is evil. . . . For not only their consciences prick them and reprove them for sin, but also their hearts are so renewed, that they rise in hatred and detestation of sin."[58] The godly still want to sin sometimes, but they no longer want to want it. Prompted by their renewed conscience, they have formulated an explicit second-order volition eschewing sinful

desire. Through this second-order volition, the godly identify themselves with the desire to do good and withdraw themselves from the
fleshly desire to sin—which is to say, they endorse the one and not
the other.

The distinction between godly and reprobate thus lies, not in
the will to sin or not sin, but rather in their attitude toward this will.
When the wicked man sins, "his conscience accuseth, checketh and
controleth him . . . and thereupon he is very often grieved for his
sins, yet for all that he liketh his sins very well, and loveth them, and
could find in his heart to continue in them for ever."[59] Conscience
creates two orders of preference in the sinner: in the first order (his
heart) he wants to sin, whereas in the second order (his conscience)
he reflects on his sin and is grieved by it. He likes his sin but dislikes
his guilt. To some extent, then, Perkins suggests, some sinners have
an implicit second-order *desire* to stop wanting to sin, but they do
not formulate an explicit second-order *volition* that wanting to sin
not be their will. This kind of sinner is not Frankfurt's wanton (he
doesn't have it that easy), but neither is he Frankfurt's unwilling addict. He can neither fully endorse nor withdraw from his will to sin,
so he never truly wants what he wants.

Conscience and the Timing of Repentance

Let us now shift from conscience the psychological faculty to Conscience the literary character. As this character makes a sixteenth-
century transition from Catholic to Protestant, the manner in which
it prompts repentance in the dramatic plot alters significantly. English Catholic interludes offer a rich variety of ways in which the
protagonist comes to repent. In some plays, such as *Youth* (1513–14)
and *Hick Scorner* (1513–16), the sinner stubbornly resists the appeals of the Conscience personifications until a certain point at
which, suddenly, he voices his conversion. In other plays, such as
Mankind (1465–70) and *The World and the Child* (1522), the sinner,
realizing the deadly peril of God's judgment, falls into a relentless
despair that he slowly overcomes only through the prolonged ex-
hortation of Mercy personifications. (The story of the despair and

contrition of Mankind is one of the most moving examples of spiritual crisis in English drama.) In still other Catholic interludes, such as John Skelton's *Magnificence* (1520–22), the just-in-time arrival of a Grace personification interrupts the sinner in the process of committing suicide, yielding an abrupt reversal of despair to joy.[60]

In all these variations, the desire to ask forgiveness corresponds to the act of asking. That is, as soon as the protagonist wants to repent, he repents. The godly personifications of Charity, Contemplation, Mercy, Perseverance, and Good Hope (in the above plays) surround the sinner before and after his moment of contrition, but they don't trespass on the moment itself. As far as the audience can tell, that moment of volition belongs to the protagonist. This distinguishes the Catholic interludes from the Protestant ones, which add another dimension to this experience: they make the protagonist wait. When Conscience makes sinful Catholics become aware of the desire to repent, they repent; when Conscience makes sinful Protestants become aware of this desire, they still have to wait for repentance to come to them. This waiting, imposed by a fatalistic timing outside their control, prompts them to voice second-order volitions about their will. The personification of Conscience, as we will see, is the mechanism through which this second-order consciousness emerges.

George Wapull's *The Tide Tarryeth No Man* (1576) offers a good place to start. The despair of Wastefulness begins as does Magnificence's, with the loss of his worldly fortune. Wastefulness expresses certainty that his sins do not merit divine forgiveness: "I know it is folly unto God to call: / For God I know my petition will shun."[61] Yet in the midst of his spiritual trial, Wastefulness suddenly asks himself: "Why should I despair, since God doth behold / The sinner with mercy, as the Scripture doth say" (sig. G2r). Uttering this sentiment does not amount to repentance: Despair, standing over his shoulder, immediately persuades Wastefulness to give up hope and kill himself. He is saved in the nick of time only by Faithfulness, the Grace figure whose appearance immediately reverses Wasteful's despair and who leads him, line by line, through a formula of repentance. The protagonist's ability to repent, it appears, very much depends on God's prior forgiveness.

Yet although short of the will to repent, Wasteful's utterance — "Why should I despair?" — does imply the desire to repent. Despairing of God's mercy, he imagines repenting, and the inclination to do so suggests that he perceives despair and contrition as two competing desires within him, one of which might become his will. This perception does not grant him the power to choose his will — he still has to wait for Faithfulness — but while waiting he briefly has a perspective on his conflict. This is not self-mastery, but neither is it pure passivity. He cannot will himself to repent in the way Mankind, Youth, and Free Will appear to do in the Catholic interludes, but with Faithfulness's influence he wills the repentance that he wanted. Indeed, Wapull's dramatic presentation of the despair episode invites us to understand Faithfulness appearance as a response to Wasteful's despairing desire to repent. The Grace figure simply reasserts the availability of divine forgiveness — "God's mercy so free" — that that the protagonist himself earlier intimated ("God doth behold / The sinner with mercy"). Faithfulness does not compel or constrain Wastefulness; rather, he sets the protagonist free by giving him the power to do what he wanted to do. In prosopopoetic terms, the desire inside him to repent summons an external agency that provides him with the will to repent.

But how, given his corrupt disposition, was he able to want it in the first place? Wapull hints at the answer by having Faithful ask the newly repentant Wasteful, "How feelest thou now, thy conscience and mind?" (sig. G2r). Protestant despair interludes operate according to the protocol of conscience that we examined earlier in the homiletic writings of Perkins and others. Conscience appears repeatedly in these dramas, sometimes so named as a personification, sometimes closely approximated under names such as Good Counsel. Its primary function is to create spiritual conflict for the protagonist by forcing a knowledge of sin. In Wapull's play, the villain Greediness complains that a preacher's rebuke "did my conscience prick," briefly depriving him of the savor of his wicked work: "My conscience doth tell me, I have done amiss, / And of long time I have gone astray, / And a thousand witnesses the conscience is" (sig. B3r). Greediness returns to his avaricious ways, but only after conscience sees his sin and thus obliges him to see it. This is precisely the observation of Virtuous Life in Ulpian Fulwell's *Like Will to Like* (1562–68), who remarks (somewhat smugly), "How clear in conscience is the virtuous life? / The vicious hath consciences so heavy as lead: / their conscience and their doings is always at strife."[62]

As I have suggested, scholars have underestimated the degree to which the Tudor interludes represent the most sustained example of early Protestant moral psychology in a popular literary form. Too often critics reduce these plays to a simplistic background against which to appreciate the complexities of later plays, such as Marlowe's *Doctor Faustus* or Shakespeare's *Macbeth*. The single sustained examination of the role of conscience in these interludes is a chapter in a book about Renaissance tragedy by John S. Wilks, who concludes that these plays show "the hopeless ineffectuality of conscience upon the will of man, in turn Calvinistically enslaved to sin."[63] But the Protestant conscience is not supposed to effect acts of will. Rather, it posits a revised understanding of how the will works, according to a protocol of self-identification rather than self-mastery. The personification of Conscience in the Protestant interludes foists the fact of sinfulness onto the sinner to force an awareness of culpability.

Here the daemonic moral ambiguity of conscience is most evident. Often in these interludes Conscience itself precipitates the onset of despair. In Nathaniel Woodes's *Conflict of Conscience* (1581), the character Conscience warns of the imminent appearance of Horror, who when he arrives afflicts the protagonist with "confusion and cursing."[64] Horror does not oppose Conscience but fulfills it: among the sufferings he brings is "torment of conscience" (line 1972). The faculty of conscience drives the psychological despair plot of Lewis Wager's *The Life and Repentance of Mary Magdalene* (published posthumously in 1566): Infidelity, preparing to corrupt Mary, boasts that "the conscience is where I dwell"; the play's Conscience figure, Knowledge of Sin, describes how he acts to "fret and bite the conscience within"; Mary reports that because "in my conscience I am so grievously perplexed" she finds herself "in despair."[65] Sometimes the interlude will even combine the Conscience figure with the Despair figure: in Richard Wever's *Lusty Juventus* (1550?), Good Counsel, having failed to dissuade Youth from sin, suddenly confronts him with divine wrath, telling him that "this blasphemy, / Shall never be pardoned nor forgiven, / In this world, nor in the world to come," at which point Juventus falls into despair.[66] (Remember, this is "Good Counsel" speaking.)

The Protestant personification of Conscience, then, does not inspire a will to repent; in fact, it does not directly engage the will to do anything. Instead, it requires the sinner to exercise self-reflection. In this fashion the interludes dramatize the tautological language of Reformation homiletics: Conscience requires the sinner to check his conscience. The Protestant suspicion of insincere contrition differs markedly from the presentation of contrition in the Catholic interludes. Once their protagonists repent, the Catholic plays assume or demonstrate absolute confidence that the repentance is sincere and efficacious. *Mankind* simply has its protagonist leave the stage (line 902). *Magnificence* raises the question of sincerity, but in such a way as to show that the question need not have been raised:

> REDRESS: Yea, but have ye repented you with heart contrite?
> MAGNIFICENCE: Sir, the repentance I have no man can write.
> REDRESS: And have ye banished from you all despair?
> MAGNIFICENCE: Yea, wholly to Good Hope I have made my
>   repair.
> GOOD HOPE: Questionless he doth me assure
>   In good hope always for to endure.
>
>   (lines 2392–97)

"Questionless": there is no uncertainty about Magnificence's will after his repentance, just as there was no question about his having any desire to repent prior to it.

The Protestant interludes express no such confidence. In these plays, Conscience triggers an almost obsessive checking on the sincerity of the protagonist's claim to repent. The plot sometimes justifies this checking, since the protagonists of these plays (as in some of the Catholic plays) tend to publicly reform their lives early in the story, only to backslide into sin soon after. Furthermore, the Protestant interludes maintain a constant background suspicion about repentance by emphasizing the human disposition toward moral depravity, often invoking the book of Ecclesiastes to encourage harsh discipline for vain youth.[67] When Worldly Man repents of his acquisitive ways, in William Wager's *Enough Is as Good as a Feast* (1570?), Contentation checks his sincerity: "Do you speak as you think, and as you mind do you say?"[68]—an appropriate skepticism, as it happens, since Worldly Man returns to his worldly habits later in the play.

Yet more often than not, the checking of conscience proceeds beyond the explicit writ of either plot or unreliable character. These plays, it seems, check for the sake of checking. In *The Tide Tarryeth No Man*, Wastefulness answers Faithfulness's question about his conscience with assurance: "Despair is now fled, I perfectly know, / And in God's mercy I firmly do trust." Yet Faithfulness, with no apparent cause, remains dubious: "That is all very well said, if so thou do think" (sig. G2v). In *Nice Wanton* (1547?), the contrite sinner Dalila says forthrightly of her physical afflictions, "All this I have deserved for lack of grace, / Justly for my sins God doth plague me."[69] We have no reason to doubt her sincerity. Yet her virtuous brother Barnabas nonetheless finds it necessary to say to her, "Ye seem to repent, but I doubt whether / For your sins or for the misery ye be in."[70] It is as if the mechanism that brings Dalila to self-knowledge—"the worm of conscience that shall never die"—creates a state of affairs in which checking is good in itself, whether or not it brings the sinner closer to genuine repentance.[71] This would help make sense of the gesture of Jesus Christ, in *Mary Magdalene*, to double-check the sincerity of Mary's repentance: the dialogue gives us no reason to suspect Mary's earnest contrition, and Jesus presumably does not ask in order to satisfy his curiosity.[72]

The checking of conscience is indeed good in itself, not because it makes the sinner repent (it may instead make the sinner despair more deeply), but because it produces second-order knowledge about one's desire to repent. As theological and homiletic writing of the period would lead us to expect, conscience gives the protagonist a perspective on his or her desires, preventing the protagonist from being a wanton regarding these desires. Sixteenth-century writers never use the word *wanton* directly to mean a lack of perspective on one's desires, yet neither is their use of the word completely alien to Frankfurt's use of it. The substantive sense of "a spoiled child" (*OED* 3) and the adjectival sense of "free from care" (*OED* 4a) more than obliquely imply the notion of a lack of concern with the outcome of one's desires.[73]

It often appears in the Protestant interludes that the chief sin is a lack of concern about one's sin. These plays are designed to represent and to punish wantonness. Dalila and Ismael, the wantons of *Nice Wanton*, play their title roles in the Tudor sense of spoiled, careless children, but they also play them in Frankfurt's sense, as Ismael boldly declares at the play's beginning: "I will set my heart / On a merry pin, / Whatever shall befall."[74] To the degree that a "pin" indicates an insignificant or varying desire (*OED* n.¹, 8), setting one's heart on it sounds less like identifying oneself with it and more like going with the flow. Likewise, Wapull names one of his characters Wanton, a fourteen-year-old girl who leads herself and her husband to ruin by ignoring her parents' advice that she plan for the future: "I care not what my mother do say" (sig. D2v). Mary Magdalene in Wager's play calls Infidelity "a merry man indeed . . . a wanton," and once Knowledge of Sin begins to afflict her conscience Infidelity actively tries to keep her in wantonness: "Follow my counsel, and put care away." Yet Mary replies that Knowledge of Sin is "evermore before the conscience sight" and she "cannot be merry."[75] Conscience paralyzes Mary's will but also forces her to acknowledge that she needs to will something she is not yet able to will. Another way to put this: it makes her wait.

Conditional Agency and Nathaniel Woodes's *Conflict of Conscience*

Mary has to wait because she faces an asymmetrical set of options: to continue to sin, which is under her control, or to repent, which is not under her control. This asymmetry, as we have seen, bars Conscience from exercising its traditional role of prompting the sinner's will. Instead, Conscience obliges the sinner to become aware of the conflict within her between her sinful and remorseful inclinations. This awareness, in turn, prevents the sinner from indulging in a wanton indifference about what her will is to be. She knows she *should* repent, and even wishes she *could* repent, but in her present state of sin she *cannot* repent. She imagines a future she would like to have, but can only imagine it modally, so to speak, since this future is in a crucial sense not up to her volition. The Protestant asymmetry thesis denies the sinner the future indicative *will*, leaving her instead with the conditional or modal *would*. The final section of this chapter will consider the characteristic grammar by which interlude protagonists voice second-order volitions about their will. It also examines, as an extreme example of this grammar, Nathaniel Woodes's *Conflict of Conscience*.

At first glance it may seem unlikely that matters of salvation and reprobation would hinge on a grammatical mood, but, as Brian Cummings has recently demonstrated, religious polemicists of the period understood even the most abstract theological problems in terms of linguistic questions. He notes in particular that the interpretation of conditional statements in scripture played a crucial role in theological disputes.[76] In their debate about free will, for example, Erasmus and Luther devote a great deal of space and energy to arguing whether the conditional or hortatory moods signify the human *capacity* to do something or simply the human *duty* to do it. A similar ambiguity was featured in sixteenth-century English, in what Tudor grammarians were calling the "potential" mood, an emerging verbal form that translated a wide range of Latin grammatical moods. Lynne Magnusson, in a discussion of the potential mood in Renaissance drama, quotes a drill for students proposed by John Brinsley in 1612:

> Q. How know you the Potential Mood?
> A. It showeth an ability, will, or duty to do any thing.
> Q. What signs hath it?
> A. May, can, might, would, should, ought or could: as, *Amem*, I may or can love.[77]

The potential mood stretches over the ambiguous linguistic terrain between *can* and *ought*, leaving uncertain whether or not modal auxiliary verbs such as *might*, *would*, and *should* signify either the agency or the obligation to do something. Magnusson suggests that modals flourished in Renaissance drama to express a character's perplexed sense of action in the face of an uncertain future, what she calls "a psychology in the potential mood."[78] We find a version of this psychology in the Protestant interludes, which depict their protagonists wanting a certain future but unable to will it. Their agency is conditional or potential, not indicative.

Reformation theology implicitly demands that reprobate and elect share a common conditional grammar: if God forgave me, I would repent. This grammar denies both sorts the agency to will their repentance prior to the arrival of grace. Up until that point, "I *would* repent" conceals the trajectory of its future linguistic resolution into either "I *do* repent" or "I *do not* repent." Protestant writers commonly express the disjunction between wanting and willing with modal auxiliary verbs of this sort. One sees this grammatical effect in Protestant homiletics. Perkins notes, for example, that God in his mercy calls to both the elect and the reprobate, but whereas the elect respond with alacrity, the reprobate man, even "if he *would*, yet *could* he not answer and be obedient to the calling of God."[79] Perkins here avoids the impression of symmetrical options. He does not say, "If the reprobate repented, he would be refused"; he says instead, "Even if he wanted to repent, he couldn't do it." Protestant despair interludes likewise use this grammar to signal unrealizable reprobate remorse. In Wager's *Enough Is as Good as a Feast*, Worldly Man, shocked into awareness of his sin by the Conscience figure of God's Plague, falls asleep and dreams that someone urges him to repent. "O, I *would* if I *could*, but now it is too late,"[80] he moans, a reply that accurately predicts the end of the interlude, when a gloating Satan carries Worldly Man to hell on his back. Worldly Man cannot will repentance, but he wants to will it. The conditional "I would" signals his awareness of his predicament through an unrealized second-order desire to have a particular will.

This is perhaps a bit hard to take: Does God use Conscience to make sinners want to ask forgiveness and yet deny them the power to do so? This is the kind of outraged question that a minority of Tudor divines asked and that nearly all modern readers ask. As we have discussed, Protestant writers work hard to make the experience of sin and contrition seem coherent on the ground, even if divine fatality is calling the shots from above. Both Perkins and Wager would insist that their reprobates do not *sincerely* want to repent, thus easing the impression of divine cruelty in their damnation. After Worldly Man's expression of conditional contrition, for example, Wager immediately has him voice a return to wantonness: "Hold thy peace I pray thee, and do me no more rate!"[81] If there is any difference, prior to repentance, between the "psychology in the potential mood" of reprobate and elect, it involves the elect's readiness to remain in the painful conflict that conscience has imposed, to embrace the terms of the conditional. This is perhaps why suicide, that late medieval staple of the despairing sinner, represents a chief temptation in the Protestant interludes. Suicide is the willful means by which the sinner might try to escape the period of waiting that God has set for him.

The interludes, then, ask us to understand the conditional grammar of contrition as part of the mental process through which the elect man comes to feel he owns his eventual repentance. "I would repent" does not produce "I do repent"; instead, the former provides an affective context by which the latter can be understood. In Wever's *Lusty Juventus*, as we have discussed, Good Council's admonitions briefly send Juventus into a suicidal despair. The Conscience figure cannot, on his own, prompt Juventus to repent, but he does urge him to wait, telling him that God's Merciful Promises might soon arrive. The protagonist responds, "I *would* believe if I might them hear, / With all my heart, power, and mind."[82] Juventus acknowledges that he cannot simply will belief in mercy, but he is ready to identify with such a belief should it come to him. He embraces the terms of the conditional. The play maintains this interval between wanting and willing for the next few lines, until God's Merciful Promises enters onstage, giving Juventus the power to repent.[83] Before this happens, he wants to will it; he imagines shifting from painful waiting to active affirmation.

Nonetheless, it remains hard to distinguish *embracing* the terms of the conditional from *resigning oneself* to these terms. The pregrace psychologies of the reprobate and the elect share similarities intended to remind readers that the difference depends on God's will. "I would repent" encompasses both reprobate and elect desire, the sincerity of which cannot be known until salvation or damnation occurs. To see an extreme example of the overlap between elect and reprobate psychologies, I will conclude this discussion by considering Nathaniel Woodes's *The Conflict of Conscience* (1581).

The despair of Francis Spira, the Italian lawyer who recanted Calvinism to protect his family from punishment, had gained popular currency in the 1549 account of Matteo Gribaldi and others, which included a preface by Calvin. In the following year Edward Aglionby translated this Latin text into English, and his translation was republished in 1569. In his own 1581 play Woodes renamed his protagonist Philologus and drew on examination scenes from John Foxe's *Acts and Monuments* to depict Philologus's tribulations before Catholic officials. Francis Spira, along with Johann Faustus, was for Tudor readers one of the great contemporary examples of the phenomenon of wanting to want to repent.

Woodes takes the Calvinist message of the story very seriously. To a degree unprecedented in earlier Tudor interludes, *The Conflict of Conscience* explicitly dwells on the dictates of predestination. The Prologue explains that conscience, constrained by the flesh, deprives the sinner of the power to ask forgiveness: "Then (wretch accursed) no power hath, repentance to begin."[84] Once Philologus falls into despair, he asserts his certainty that "my name within the book of life, had never residence" (line 2033). When Eusebius tries to comfort his friend by observing that God forgave the repentant David, even after so many sins, Philologus responds, "King David always was elect, but I am reprobate" (line 2304). Shortly before his death, his friend Theologus grimly concurs with Philologus's assessment of the limitations of his will: "Do as you can, no more than might, we can ask at your hand" (line 2349). This play not only dramatizes depraved human nature preventing the will from repenting but also has its characters refer explicitly to the theology that explains this dynamic. Philologus on his own wills his apostasy, but Woodes keeps the operations of fatality close at hand.

To title the play *Conflict of Conscience* comes close to announcing that this is a play about what Conscience does to sinners: it puts them at variance with themselves. Woodes repeatedly dramatizes the manner in which conscience prevents Philologus from wholeheartedly enjoying his inclination to sin. When pressed by the Cardinal to recant, Philologus responds that he would do so if his conscience would permit it:

> I would gladly to your doctrine consent,
> If that I could so my conscience content.
> But my Conscience crieth out and bids me take heed
> To love my God above all earthly gain,
> Whereby all this while, I stand in great dread,
> That if I should God's statutes disdain,
> In wretched state then I should remain:
> Thus cryeth my Conscience to me continually,
> Which if you can stay, I will yield to you gladly.
>
> (lines 1380–89)

That Philologus is willing to "consent" and "yield" to the Cardinal's doctrine suggests not so much a strong conviction in Catholic sentiment as a readiness to follow the path of least resistance. Philologus would like to be a wanton ("hap what hap will" [line 1722], he suggests at one point), but his conscience will not let him. Yet neither does conscience enable him to make the virtuous choice. Instead, it foists a painful awareness of his conflict on him, producing stasis rather than will: "For I am but dead, which ever side I take, / Neither to determine herein am I able / With good advice mine election to make" (line 1488–90). In this stasis, he can only imagine hypothetically willing one way or another: "I *would* . . . consent," "if I *should*." Even after Philologus has "fully resolved" (line 1601) to side with worldly pleasures, the figures of Spirit and Conscience continue to oblige him to reflect on his spiritual error, eventually sending in Horror to drive him to despair.

So far I have noted qualities of the play that offer more intense versions of the topoi we have discussed in earlier Tudor interludes. Yet when he comes to the despair episode, Woodes does something that other interludes authors avoid: he places the Protestant asymmetry thesis in explicit opposition to the didactic and consolatory impulses that otherwise constitute an essential part of the interlude genre. Whatever their theological convictions about unmerited grace, the interludes also say to the audience: live right; trust God, not the world; eschew pride; pray for forgiveness; abstain from lust; and so on. *Conflict of Conscience* has some of these same gestures. After the despairing Philologus exits the stage, for example, Eusebius comments, "Here may the worldlings have a glass, their states for to behold, / And learn in time for to escape the judgments of the Lord" (lines 2391–92). Citing these lines, David Bevington has recently suggested that "the story of Philologus, as of Spira, is an object lesson. . . . Philologus has failed, but others may learn from his example to turn to God."[85] This is a reasonable description of much Tudor sacred literature, but it runs completely counter to the tenor of this play's despair episode. At its heart, the play alerts us that no one can rightly learn from an example and say, "I will repent"; the best we can ever do prior to grace is say, "I would."

And it turns out to be the best Philologus can do, as well. Upon the advice of his friends, for example, Philologus utters a version of the Lord's Prayer, pleading for divine help (lines 2128–34). His friends rejoice, but Philologus interrupts their congratulations to say that he prayed merely with "lips," whereas in his "heart" he continues to deny God (line 2146). The lips/heart distinction exemplifies a conventional Protestant emphasis on sincerity, but in dramatic terms this is rather shocking and all but unprecedented on the interlude stage.[86] A sinner has uttered a genuine-sounding prayer—the recourse that divines always counsel sinners to take—has, in fact, performed what looks like repentance, only to reveal that it did not count as a repentance. (Even Shakespeare, when he stages Claudius's ineffectual prayer, does not allow the audience to hear words addressed to God that sound like genuine contrition.) Theologus and Eusebius then take the next logical step, counseling their friend to try repenting again, but this time sincerely. Eusebius reminds Philologus of the promise in scripture: "God hath said (who cannot lie), at whatever time / A sinner shall from heart repent, I will remit his crime" (lines 2157–58). Eusebius implies the same conditional statement that Catholic Mercy figures offer to their protagonists: if you repented, God would forgive you.

At this point Philologus plays Luther to Eusebius's Erasmus. Lecturing his companions on the correct causal relation between faith and divine forgiveness, he replaces Eusebius's conditional with the conditional required by the Protestant asymmetry thesis. *Should* does not mean *can*:

> You cannot say so much to me, as herein I do know,
> That by the mercies of the Lord, all sins are done away,
> And unto them that have true faith, abundantly it flow.
> But whence do this true faith proceed to us, I do you pray?
> It is the only gift of God, from him it comes alway.
> I *would* therefore he *would* vouchsafe one spark of faith to plant
> Within my breast: then of his grace I know I *should* not want.
>
> > (lines 2160–66, my emphasis)

If God forgave me, I would repent. He wants it but cannot will it. This is the conditional grammar of repentance voiced (explicitly or implicitly) by Philologus's fellow Reformed interlude protagonists, including Juventus, Wastefulness, Dalila, and Mary Magdalene. But unlike these sinners, Philologus's desire to repent does not summon a prosopopoetic figure of Mercy or Grace. Nor, as in the case of the reprobate Worldly Man, does it summon the damnation figure of Satan. Instead, no one comes: Woodes protracts the waiting between desire and will through the entirety of the remaining stage action. We learn about the result of his spiritual struggle only after Philologus leaves the stage (lines 2411–24).

Where did all the prosopopoeia go? Up until act 5, scene 2, the play was thick with personifications fighting over Philologus's soul: Hypocrisy, Tyranny, Avarice, Sensual Suggestion, Spirit, Conscience, and Horror. But in his despair scene the protagonist is alone with four friends, only two of whom have speaking parts. The single personification who might be said to remain is Conscience, the figure who has driven the psychological despair plot and who now resides in Philologus's mind rather than on Woodes's stage: "My Conscience, which for thousands stand, as guilty me condemn" (line 2197); "Of Judas and Barehu, these must my Conscience slay" (line 2310); "God hath condemned my Conscience to perpetual grief and fear" (line 2321). In these lines Philologus's conscience, in a way characteristic of Protestant thought, both passes judgment against the sinner and suffers judgment on behalf of the sinner. Conscience makes Philologus know the good and feel his culpability for doing the bad. But, unlike the other personifications that have intruded their presence, Conscience does not prompt Philologus to will anything. He can only make him wait for the power to will.

Conflict of Conscience does two things unprecedented in the Tudor interlude: (1) it declines, as I have mentioned, to dramatize the outcome of the protagonist's struggle—repentance or damnation—onstage, relegating this crucial information to a chorus figure named Nuntius, and (2) it offers two endings, one in which (according to Nuntius) Philologus "by deep despair hath hanged himself with cord" (line 2412) and another in which Philologus "is now converted unto God, with many bitter tears" (line 2413) (again according to Nuntius, in a revised issue of the play published in the same year as the original issue). So in the first issue, Philologus is a reprobate; in the second, he's elect. Woodes's phrasing conforms perfectly to the asymmetry thesis: the protagonist commits suicide in the active voice and receives grace in the passive voice. Further, Woodes follows the Protestant assumption that, once grace arrives, the sinner actively wills his repentance: "his errors all he did renounce, his blasphemies he abhorred" (line 2415, second issue). Yet although the details of this outcome conform to orthodox Protestant thought, these events take up very little of the play. Since *Conflict of Conscience* pushes the repentance/damnation offstage, Woodes could change the ending merely by revising a few lines.[87]

In altering so little text in the second issue, Woodes does more than save labor; he also demonstrates how closely the pre-grace experiences of the reprobate and the elect resemble one another.

Woodes did not, as he could have done, tinker with a few lines of dialogue in the second issue's despair scene to make it more optimistic. This psychological experience of waiting, of staying in the conditional, remains the same. This is the experience, I would suggest, that Woodes was most anxious for his audience to view. The *outcome* of this experience is out of the sinner's hands; he cannot will toward one end or another. But he can take an attitude about what his will is to be. Woodes thus leaves Philologus possessed by Conscience in the final dramatic scene in order to teach his audience how to wait.

Philologus certainly does not offer a perfect example of waiting: he presumptuously assumes he knows what God has planned for him (damnation), and he considers suicide at one point (line 2338). We might feel that he needs more *patience*, the virtue that Stoics and Christians alike agreed was one of the chief resources of the pious man. But the Protestant interludes are not, finally, plays about patience; they are plays about the daemonic ambiguity of Conscience, and Conscience provokes conflict and anxiety. Waiting is not the same as patience. Philologus's achievement is that he has just enough patience to keep waiting anxiously, refraining from blaming God or from killing himself. The result of this waiting is not up to us, but our attitude toward it is. The despairing sinner can imagine the desire to repent mastering the desire to sin and can imagine identifying with that desire as it carries him into action. The sinner can embrace the terms of the conditional: if God forgave me, I would repent. To assert more than this conditional agency is blasphemy. But to assert less is also blasphemy, a refusal of God's requirement that sinners and saints alike see the desirability of repentance, even if they can't will it when they want it.

"Desperatio." Giotto di Bondone, wall
painting from Scrovegni Chapel, Padua
(1306). Photo: DEA/A. Dagli Orti,
De Agostini Collection, Getty Images.

Chapter Four

DESPAIR IN MARLOWE AND SPENSER

The personification of Despair is a latecomer among the ranks of Christian vices. Prudentius does not include the sin in his *Psychomachia*, and the iconographic depiction of Despair as a figure killing himself does not become common until the thirteenth century.[1] The quality of contradiction suggested by this image—an abstraction that seeks to destroy itself—may help explain the late development of this prosopopoeia. It is odd to personify despair. Personifications are generally wholehearted; they exemplify the "vehement passions," as Philip Fisher has called them, those affections such as wrath, fear, and grief that for their duration possess the whole person.[2] The personification of Wrath is entirely wrathful, and Fear entirely fearful. Even Doubt is totally committed to her dubiety. Yet despair, although one of the vehement passions, is not wholehearted but features a fundamental inconsistency of attitude around questions of culpability, punishment, desert, and aversion.

When in despair, you believe that you have sinned and that you will be punished (the certainty of punishment distinguishes religious despair from melancholy). Furthermore, you believe that you deserve punishment, but you nonetheless dread divine retribution and wish to escape it. There is no way to reconcile these two impressions: you can neither deny the justice of divine punishment nor relinquish your aversion to this punishment. (If you are unmoved by the prospect of divine retribution, then you are not despairing but instead stoically resigned.) That is to say, despair is more demanding than guilt. As a guilty person, you might very well conclude both that you deserve punishment and that you would prefer to avoid punishment. But with ordinary guilt, focusing on desert tends to make one's aversion to punishment recede into the background, whereas focusing on aversion tends to make the conviction of desert recede. Despair is not like that: in despair, you are fully and equally committed to desert and aversion. In despair, you cannot square what makes sense in a divine economy with what makes sense in a creaturely economy. Despair thus precipitates, or perhaps discloses, a misrelation between how you relate to God and how you relate to yourself. This is not just a conflict of perspectives but the cancellation of any single standpoint by which one might have a perspective.

I borrow the term *misrelation* from Søren Kierkegaard, whose account of despair in *The Sickness unto Death* turns on the idea of a collapsed perspective. To describe it very briefly, Kierkegaard argues that despair arises out of the difficult condition of maintaining a simultaneous relation to God and to the world. God's "release" of the human creature from his hand, as Kierkegaard describes the event of our creation, causes the self to emerge as a composite stretched between time and eternity, between the limited and boundless, creating the possibility of the self's misrelation to either of the two poles.[3] In this misrelation, the infinite despairs over the finite, and the finite despairs over the infinite.[4]

Kierkegaard's account is admittedly rather esoteric, and not all its details are relevant to a sixteenth-century context—for example, Kierkegaard does not emphasize the idea of punishment. But throughout his exposition he defines despair in terms of mutually exclusive psychological states, in a way that recalls early modern accounts of spiritual hopelessness. For example, he remarks on the puzzling degree to which sinking deeper into despair involves a simultaneously increased consciousness of being in despair. This means that the more intensely one denies the possibility of divine forgiveness, the more lucidly one sees the deadly peril of this denial. The very combination that defines despair, Kierkegaard concedes, also appears to make the psychological condition of despair impossible. He confesses that he is unsure "to what extent perfect clarity about oneself as being in despair can be combined with being in despair, that is, whether this clarity of knowledge and of self-knowledge might not simply wrench a person out of despair, make him so afraid of himself that he would stop being in despair."[5] The despairing sinner cannot get a handle on his situation: despair entails a perspective that might end despair, but being in despair is precisely the inability to keep hold of this perspective. Translating this problematic into sixteenth-century terms, we might say that the despairing sinner, simultaneously approving of and shunning divine justice, cannot manage to get a perspective on what he really wants. As Richard Hooker described despair in his 1585 sermon on the prophet Habakkuk, "Men . . . are through the extremity of grief many times in judgment so confounded, that they find not themselves in themselves."[6]

That said, one must also acknowledge that Tudor literary writers usually avoided the inconvenience of despair's inconsistent perspective by making clear that the personification of Despair is not in despair. In the moral interludes, for example, Despair comes to the sinful protagonist in order to drive him or her into spiritual hopelessness. Despair himself, however, is oblivious to his own damnation, nor does he fear divine retribution. As we saw in the previous chapter, the personifications named Despair in Skelton's *Magnificence* and Wapull's *The Tide Tarryeth No Man* seem to almost enjoy their work. They're not trembling with dread; it is the protagonist who trembles. The Tudor figure of Despair, who advocates slaughter for others but not for himself, appears to escape the Kierkegaardian double bind that I describe above.

We can gain a clearer understanding of this effect by recalling that personifications tend to function along a continuum between enactment and transmission. As *enactment*, a personification displays the qualities of a given concept or passion; it is an exemplum by which we understand the concept or passion. As *transmission*, a personification imbues another character with the qualities of a given concept or passion; it is a medium by which energies in the external landscape pass into an agent. As enactment, a personification is possessed by daemonic energy. As transmission, a personification is the daemon that possesses another character.

Most personifications offer a mix of enactment and transmission. Wrath always appears angry but is also likely to enrage those around him; the same is true with Fear, Joy, Sloth, et cetera. We can find an extreme case of enactment in Edmund Spenser's Disdain, who reflects the scorn Sir Guyon has already expressed and whose self-expression creates a kind of self-implosion: "Disdayne he called was, and did disdayne / To be so cald."[7] Conversely, we find an extreme case of transmission in many personifications of Despair. As noted before, in sixteenth-century English plays by John Skelton, Richard Wever, Nathaniel Woodes, Lewis Wager, William Wager, and George Wapull the Despair figure appears either as a villain who gleefully goes about his work of spreading hopelessness or as God's scourge who sternly informs the guilty of their damnation. He inflicts upon his victims the painful misrelation between what they think they deserve and what they want to avoid. Yet Despair himself is untouched by this misrelation.

These highly transmissive personifications reflect what we might call the "majority report" on despair offered by Protestant theology and homiletic writing. In the majority report, despair is a clearly defined episode, sandwiched between a life of sin and the act of repentance (or suicide). The majority report delineates despair by coordinating it with a set of opposites and complements. As twin sins, despair and pride constitute the deficient and excessive versions of human self-esteem.[8] Despair itself suffers from a manic-depressive disposition, prompted by frantic impatience on the one hand and a torpid acedia on the other.[9] Furthermore, commentators relied on Paul's distinction between "godly sorrow" and "worldly sorrow" (2 Cor. 7:10) to oppose the salutary despair of one's own power over against the sinful despair of God's mercy.[10] (On the basis of this distinction, Calvin denied that the elect truly despair; only the reprobate sink that low.)[11] In the majority report, despair is not the ambiguous misrelation I described earlier but a sinful affliction susceptible to a variety of traditional remedies: pray for relief, try to exercise patience, don't remain solitary, avoid brooding over the question of your election. The personifications that inflict but do not suffer despair are figures for the devil, who deceptively urges men to dwell on the law that damns them and not on the grace that might save them.

This quick glance at the prosopopoetic tradition of despair allows us to appreciate the originality of Christopher Marlowe's and Edmund Spenser's depictions of this figure: their Despair characters are in despair. Marlowe's Mephistopheles, the play's daemonic stand-in for the traditional personification of Despair, responds to Faustus's question of how a devil can leave hell with a remarkable admission:

> Why, this is hell, nor am I out of it.
> Think'st thou that I, who saw the face of God,
> And tasted the eternal joys of heaven,
> Am not tormented with ten thousand hells
> In being deprived of everlasting bliss?[12]

In the latter part of the play Mephistopheles, like his cousins in the moral interludes, will seek to drive Faustus deeper and deeper into despair. Yet in these lines we see that the fiend enacts his own self-cancelling perspective: he believes that God is good and that the absence of this goodness yields torment and deprivation, but he simultaneously seeks to oppose God's goodness. Likewise, Spenser's Despair is a "cursed man . . . / Musing full sadly in his sullein mind," who, after seeing his intended victim escape from his cave, reveals that he suffers from the very condition he tried to inflict on Redcross Knight:

> He chose an halter from among the rest,
> And with it hung himselfe, unbid, unblest.
> But death he could not worke himselfe thereby;
> For thousand times he so himselfe had drest,
> Yet nathelesse it could not doe him die,
> Till he should die his last, that is eternally.
>
> (1.9.54)

Here the misrelation is conceptual rather than dramatic: recognizing the justice of divine punishment, Spenser's villain presumes to carry out his sentence; yet his inability to do so suggests the despairing sinner's aversion to the punishment he endorses. To claim that these depictions are innovative does not amount to denying that Marlowe and Spenser draw aspects of their despairing Despair figures from existing theological and iconographic traditions.[13] It is simply to note that late Tudor readers and audiences would recognize these two despairing figures as members of a literary tradition of personification in which Despair was not ordinarily in despair.

Why both Marlowe and Spenser, in the late 1580s, wrote texts that revise this bit of literary tradition as they do is hard to answer definitively. To start, we should observe that their protagonists, Faustus and Redcross, experience spiritual hopelessness rather differently than do their interlude predecessors. These two characters, in their despair, appear to look forward to the exquisite hopelessness of Shakespeare's Macbeth, Milton's Satan, and the speaker of Donne's holy sonnets. Yet it will not do to understand these two characters only retrospectively; we must also understand how and to what effect they alter the literary tradition that preceded them. To put it briefly, the interlude protagonists suffer despair as an episode that precedes repentance; once they repent (or commit suicide), they're done with despair. By contrast, as I will show in the pages that follow, Faustus and Redcross suffer despair as an ongoing condition of having a relationship to God. Marlowe and Spenser, then, give us Despair figures in despair to suggest that these villains do not merely afflict their victims but also resemble them. By enacting rather than simply transmitting despair, these personifications of despair imply that no one escapes the consequences of being a fallen creature of God.

Marlowe and Spenser, I want to suggest, are responding to the "minority report" on despair circulating in Protestant Europe. This report always lives under the shadow of its larger cousin, but it conveys the sense in which some Protestants saw the experience of despair as peculiarly suited to the Reformed faith. Luther famously asserted the simultaneous sinfulness and necessity of despair: "I myself was offended more than once, and brought to the very depth and abyss of despair, so that I wished I had never been created a man, before I realized how salutary that despair was, and how near to grace."[14] Such an attitude helps to make sense of Robert Burton's otherwise surprising claim, despite his insistence elsewhere on the spiritual danger of the Roman faith, that Catholics are *unable* to despair as Protestants do: "I see no reason at all why a papist at any time should despair, or be troubled for his sins; for let him be never so dissolute a caitiff, so notorious a villain, so monstrous a sinner, out of that treasury of indulgences and merits of which the Pope is dispensator he may have free pardon and plenary remission of all his sins."[15] Despair emerges here for a moment as a sign of Protestant authenticity, the freedom from idolatrous distractions and the commitment to rigorous self-scrutiny. The minority report implies that despair, although a terrible sin, provides one of the means by which we genuinely come to know God.

Even the distinction between "godly sorrow" and "worldly sorrow" did not reliably isolate despair from the experience of the elect. For example, William Perkins speaks of "holy desperation, which is when a man is wholly out of all hope ever to attain salvation by any strength or goodness of his own," yet he includes King David, perhaps the reformers' favorite Old Testament example of contrite devotionality, among those who "despair of God's mercy for a time . . . a dangerous sin."[16] In this account, despair certainly remains culpable, but it is no longer sanitized from the experience of the elect: even God's most prominent saints despaired of his mercy. Equally important, Perkin's phrasing ("for a time") suggests that the distinction between godly and reprobate despair involves a question of duration, not quality. One's despair may be a discrete episode or a permanent condition, but in either case despair is despair. Susannah Brietz Monta and Lisi Oliver have recently suggested that in Reformed thought the nature of despair depends on its timing: ideally, you suffer despair just long enough to appreciate the extent of your sins, thus making yourself ready for repentance. Unfortunately, this timing can go awry, and the spiritual hopelessness that should conclude after a brief duration ends up extending into an existential condition.[17]

Thus, although the minority report is not the exclusive property of the Reformation, it does have a special relationship with Protestant theology. Despair potentially occurs when we turn our attention from God's published will—repent and you will be saved—to his hidden will, by which he has arbitrarily selected some few for salvation and left the rest to their deserved damnation. For Luther and Calvin, this hidden will is the one that counts and the one about which we can do nothing.[18] Unintentionally adding to the anxiety, they further insist that God's published will, which should ideally give solace, has to be understood in terms that square with his hidden will. Thus scripture rightly says that if we repent we will be saved, but we cannot will ourselves to repent—that ability comes from God, of a piece with the predestination that will save or damn us. The one thing we might do to end our despair remains out of our control. In a scenario I have called the Protestant asymmetry thesis, we are free to will our sin but not our contrition.

This is the volitional version of the problem of despair. There is also an epistemological version, which was very important in Reformation England and has received extensive treatment from religious historians and literary scholars. In this version, despair results from the unfortunate conjunction of two conditions: (1) once grace arrives, elect people feel certain of its arrival, and (2) the cognitive-affective evidence that might yield this certainty is found equally in the reprobate. A strongly felt faith may turn out to be a false faith. The believer thus tries to reach a level of assurance that his available psychological equipment will not permit. Continental divines like Theodore Beza and Tudor puritans like William Perkins unintentionally exacerbated this dilemma by urging their readers to constantly search themselves for signs of this elusive assurance. Despair emerges as a problem of knowledge, since "the result of insisting on assurance was to create a scandal for believers by making a duty out of an impossibility," as one commentator has put it.[19]

The volitional and epistemological versions clearly overlap. The bounds of what we think we know influence our sense of what we think we can will and do. But it seems to me that the epistemological version, in so dominating the scholarly conversation in the last several decades, has produced a skewed picture of what actually happens in early modern literary texts about despair, including the Tudor interludes, *Doctor Faustus*, and *The Faerie Queene*. In these fictions, the sinful protagonists do not spend much time asking themselves about their election. Instead, they struggle to move out of their despair into sincere contrition—that is, they try to achieve an act of will. It is the problem of will posed by the asymmetry thesis that occupies these literary texts, so I focus on the volitional dimension of despair in the pages that follow.

Chapter 3 examined how the Protestant interludes used the personification of Conscience to explore the manner in which a sinner might come to *want* to repent yet still have to wait for the will to repent to come to her. This chapter examines how Marlowe and Spenser use the personification of Despair to explore the manner in which what seems like a will to repent ends up collapsing back into a mere desire to repent. Despair confounds willing and wanting because spiritual hopelessness is not simply an episode that one leaves behind. Marlowe dramatizes this quality of despair as a condition rather than an episode by depicting Faustus's will as either excessively externalized or excessively internalized, preventing him from ever getting a perspective on his desire to repent. Spenser, for his part, illustrates despair as a condition whose meaning is never quite determined by acts of will like suicide or repentance. To see this clearly will require that we recognize the Kierkegaardian distinction between worldly and religious despair operating within Redcross Knight's demonic tempter.

The Author of This Fact: Spenser's Suicidal Despaire

Spenser appears to have drawn some of the details of his personification of despair (1.9.35–54) from the "Tragedye of Cordila," which John Higgins included in the 1574 edition of the *Mirror for Magistrates*. In Higgins's version of the story, the British queen Cordelia is betrayed by her nephews and thrown into prison. As she languishes in the dark, a ghostly female figure, "of color pale, a deadly hue," appears before her, calling herself Despair.[20] She urges Cordelia to dwell on her past worldly losses and her present misery, insisting that the former queen has no hope of rising again. Death is better than a life of suffering. Cordelia then takes a knife from Despair, but hesitates as she weighs her options: "So still I lay in study with myself at bate and strife."[21] Despair redoubles her efforts, eventually persuading Cordelia to ask for her own death; the villainess obliges by stabbing her.

Spenser's depressive Despaire, with his "hollow eyne" and "raw-bone cheeks" (1.9.35), seems to recall the "color pale" and "deadly hue" of Higgins's Despair. Cordelia's tormentor has images on her clothing that depict "a thousand kinds of thrall"; likewise, Redcross Knight's assailant shows the hero the "thousand feends" (1.9.49) that torment sinners in hell. Higgins's Despair offers her victim a set of weapons, saying, "Do choose of these thou seest from woes to pass," and Spenser's villain similarly shows Redcross various means of death: "And bad him choose, what death he would desire" (1.9.50). Much as Cordelia is frozen in uncertainty as she holds the knife, so Spenser's knight hesitates as he holds his knife: "And troubled bloud through his pale face was seene / To come, and goe with tiding from the heart" (1.9.51). In writing his despair episode, Spenser, of course, drew on a general prosopopoetic tradition of Despair figures who counsel suicide, and perhaps on other specific texts, such as John Skelton's *Magnificence* and Wolfram von Eschenbach's *Parzival*.[22] But the verbal and situational resemblance with Higgins is nonetheless remarkable.[23]

Whatever qualities Spenser found in the "Tragedye of Cordila" that inclined him to draw from it, however, he must also have noticed that the British queen's despair is rather different from the despair he foists on his knight of Holiness. Cordelia does not feel guilty about anything. She describes herself as the victim of "guiltless smarts," and her ghost advises prisoners in straits like hers to nonetheless refrain from suicide "if they be guiltless."[24] Cordelia has despaired over worldly loss, but she is not in religious despair. God's wrath never occurs to her because she does not think that she has done anything wrong. Cordelia makes an arguably rational calculation, that her future earthly sufferings will be worse than the brief pain of suicide. Unfortunately, the pagan British queen leaves out a crucial Christian factor, which her ghost urges the reader to remember: suicides, upon killing themselves, "send / Their souls to hell."[25] In the case of worldly despair over earthly loss, suicide makes a kind of sense, provided one forgets that the earthly torments one escapes will be replaced by the eternal torments of hell.

Yet in the case of religious despair, such as that of Redcross Knight, it seems impossible to forget about the eternal torments of hell: the despairing sinner thinks of nothing else. In committing suicide, however, that sinner willingly and knowingly hastens his encounter with these torments. A deep inconsistency thus troubles the iconographic and literary tradition that links religious despair and suicide. Medieval and Renaissance Christian theologians, for their part, rarely associate the two sins in any direct manner. Of the many motives that Augustine lists for the sin of suicide, despair is not among them.[26] Gregory the Great appears to expect no contradiction when he claims that the despairing reprobate shuns death for fear of the judgment that will follow it.[27] The best Robert Burton can figure is that the sinner's despair creates such mental confusion that he can no longer think clearly.[28]

The link between despair and suicide thus emerges not from theology but from literature and iconography. It does not become common until the late Middle Ages, but soon after we start to see the extremely popular emblematics that represent the vice of despair as a man hanging or stabbing himself. In poetry and drama, such as *The Golden Legend* and the moral interludes of the late fifteenth and sixteenth centuries, the personification of Despair visits struggling sinners and encourages them to commit suicide. Why did iconography and poetry embrace a connection between despair and suicide that theologians found rather unlikely? More specifically, why is this connection generally expressed in personification, or at least in prosopopoetic emblems?

As I have argued, personification as a fictional character tends to communicate its significance by translating being into doing.

The Seven Deadly Sins, for example, are dispositions or passions that lead to characteristic actions. Pride tends toward rebellion or oppression, and Envy toward detraction. Wrath results in violence, Gluttony in eating and drinking, and Sloth in sleeping. Avarice engages in hoarding, and Lust in fornication (with a willing partner) or rape (with an unwilling one). This is to say, personification helps us understand a concept not only by its appearance but also by its behavior. If there is a characteristic action resulting from despair, it must be suicide. Indeed, it is unclear what characteristic action would accompany despair other than the taking of one's life. Suicide is the decisive act that expresses the depth of one's hopelessness, whatever the illogic of trading earthly ills for infernal ones. To go from despair to suicide is to go from passion to will. And moving from passion to will is how personification works.

When Spenser has Redcross almost commit suicide (1.9.52), he is following the prosopopoetic logic of revealing the nature of despair in an act of will. Higgins's Cordelia is the model, not because she believes she deserves divine punishment, but because her desire to avoid future worldly unhappiness leads naturally to her suicide. Basing Redcross Knight's religious despair on a literary model of worldly despair perhaps helps Spenser downplay the illogic of having his hero precipitate the infernal punishment he clearly dreads. And the attempted suicide makes the sinfulness of despair unmistakable.

That this is a specifically prosopopoetic sensibility is suggested by the way that Spenser, after he sends the rescued knight offstage, has Despaire take his place in a single, concluding stanza. We are within our rights, it seems to me, to understand this stanza as a commentary on what has taken place in the episode:

> He chose an halter from among the rest,
> And with it hung himselfe, unbid, unblest.
> But death he could not worke himselfe thereby;
> For thousand times he so himselfe had drest,
> Yet nathelesse it could not doe him die,
> Till he should die his last, that is eternally.
>
> (1.9.54)

The despairing human sinner is replaced by Despair itself, who translates the passion of despair to the act of suicide in order to reveal the sin that the knight has escaped. In trying unsuccessfully to hang himself, as he has many times in the past, Despaire becomes a figure of suicide, frozen in place, suspended unchanging between the present and Judgment Day. In effect, he becomes the pictorial emblem of despair, an example of the iconographic tradition that explains despair in terms of suicide. The stanza thus lays bare the self-defeating nature of despair and condemns the villain who prompts it. Despaire is punished in a manner that Jeff Dolven has identified as fundamental to allegorical emblems of justice: "The guilt of the criminal is transparent in the consequences of the crime. The medium of emblem itself fixes the blame, and accusation and punishment are condensed into a single symbolic tableau."[29]

Yet a serious problem stalls this reading. Despaire does not die, which is to say, he does not commit suicide. Emblems of despair are necessarily frozen in place, but they don't *fail* to commit suicide. Their iconographic significance assumes that the suicide does result in death, somewhere outside the frame of the image. Spenser arranges his narrative to disappoint this assumption. In this respect, his emblem reveals that suicide is not the act of will corresponding to the passion of despair. Instead, it suggests that despair entails a death wish that the sinner cannot realize in the course of his despair. Suicide itself is beside the point. "On the contrary," as Kierkegaard observes, "the torment of despair is precisely this inability to die."[30]

Indeed, decoupling despair from suicide points to what Kierkegaard means when he says that despair is existential: we despair over ourselves, not over the loss of earthly things. In this respect, his interpretation brings what I have called worldly despair back under the aegis of religious despair. For example, the man who pins all his hopes on becoming Caesar, and fails, does not despair over his failure to become Caesar. Rather, Kierkegaard insists, he despairs over being a person who is not Caesar. He wants to be rid of himself, but that is precisely what a creature of God cannot do.[31] Killing oneself is a mere runner-up to being rid of oneself, and suicide, as an act of will, does not reveal the true nature of despair, which turns out to be a consequence of being a creature of God.[32]

Again, Kierkegaard's account leaves out the sinner's fear of punishment, which is crucial to Spenser and the tradition in which he writes. But once this is acknowledged, the Danish philosopher's account of despair—that we truly despair over a version of ourselves that we cannot get rid of—prompts us to pay more attention than usual to the extent to which Spenser distinguishes spiritual hopelessness from the act of self-slaughter. Spenser's Malbecco, for example, transforms into a personification of jealousy in terms that recall the terrors of religious despair. The cuckold throws himself off a cliff, "desperate" and "fore-damned" (3.10.56), but fails to perish: "Yet can he never die, but dying lives, / And doth himselfe with sorrow new sustaine, / That death and life attonce unto him gives" (3.10.60). This is likewise how the narrator nominates Redcross himself as he receives treatment in the House of Holiness: "the man who would not live" (1.10.27). These examples tend toward the conclusion that, in the stanza in which Despaire tries to hang himself, Spenser proposes a radical reinterpretation of the traditional Despair emblem. The figure frozen in mid-act signifies not suicide but rather the failure to rid oneself of despair through suicide.

Appreciating the extent to which Spenser decouples suicide (an irrational act of will) and despair (the sinful condition of being a fallen creature of God), we can take a fresh look at the bifurcated tradition of criticism on the Despaire episode. One strand of this tradition has focused on the rhetorical shortcomings of Despaire's arguments.[33] Critics in this camp note, for example, how the tempter quotes biblical passages about divine justice but none about divine mercy. He claims at some points that the sinner deserves death as a punishment and at others that the sinner should seek death as a relief from pain. He contradictorily ascribes Redcross's sufferings to inevitable fate and to random chance. He characterizes suicide as merely a brief pain without mentioning that it is a mortal sin. And so on. The rhetorical strand of criticism sees Despaire as a demonic tempter whose falsehoods, although potent, can be exposed.

Another, smaller strand of criticism focuses on the predestinarian aspect of the Despaire episode. Without denying that the tempter is a villain, these critics note that Despaire responds to the peculiar double bind in which Reformation theology placed the Christian sinner. In a groundbreaking article of more than thirty years ago, Harold Skulsky explicated the manner in which the despair episode reveals the impossibility of a Protestant sinner achieving the level of "assurance" required of the elect according to Reformation theology.[34] More recently, Daniel Moss has demonstrated the ways in which readerly retorts to Despaire's arguments end up providing the villain with more material for his arguments. Only the assertion of grace would decisively defeat Despaire, and grace is the one thing that the reader cannot supply.[35] Critics in the predestinarian camp (to describe it in shorthand) tend to be skeptical that seeing through Despaire's false rhetoric neutralizes his threat, which remains immanent within the structure of Protestant faith.[36]

Although my sympathies are with the predestinarian view of the episode, there is no denying that Spenser goes out of his way to give Despaire an extended rhetorical monologue rich in sophisms that seem to ask for debunking. The conflict between these critical views fades, however, when we approach the episode understanding that Despaire is actually making two arguments to Redcross, a ridiculous one in favor of suicide and an excellent one in favor of despair. The villain's arguments for the first are conspicuously poor. The claim that "death is the end of woes" (1.9.47) has already been falsified by Despaire's reminder that earthly sins call forth judgment at "the day of wrath" (1.9.46). If that were not enough, the tempter further weakens his argument by showing his victim the place that awaits sinners after they die:

> He shew'd him painted in a table plaine,
> The damned ghosts, that doe in torments waile,
> And thousand feends that doe them endlesse paine,
> With fire and brimstone, which for ever shall remaine.
>
> (1.9.49)

So much for the "ease" that death supposedly affords the suffering pilgrim, as Despaire has tried to argue. It is hard to understand at first glance how the knight of holiness falls for a logic that so clearly advertises its own falsehood. In any case, Redcross arguably deserves Una's sharp censure: "Fie, fie, faint harted knight" (1.9.52). The knight need only assert a modest courage, it seems, to pause and outreason this case for suicide, whatever his confusion. The narrator makes this clear when at the final stanza he calls Despaire's temptation a "subtill sleight" (1.9.54). The rhetorical critics are right: Spenser invites us to see through Despaire's false argument for suicide, which, taken as a whole, does not hold together.

The argument seems stronger than it is, however, because Spenser interweaves it with Despaire's arguments for spiritual hopelessness. Unfortunately, the case for despair is excellent, and it is unclear how we might expect Redcross to make an effective response to it. The demon urges Redcross to weigh his sins "in true balance" (1.9.45), reminding him that God regards our deserts with "an equall eye" (1.9.47)—as Una herself has said earlier (1.8.27). Under these rubrics, the knight has every reason to fear the "righteous sentence of th'Almighties law" (1.9.50). One can object that Despaire cherry-picks his biblical verses to emphasize sin and erase mercy—for example, that he echoes the claim of 1 John 1:8 that all humans are sinful but leaves out the following verse mentioning divine forgiveness. But this objection is stymied by the fact that official statements of Reformed doctrine, such as the Elizabethan Thirty-Nine Articles, sometimes did the same in order to confirm the doctrine of human depravity.[37] The intention is different, but the theology is the same.

One can also object that Redcross ought to trust that God will save him instead of presumptuously assuming his own damnation. But this is not a counterargument; it is a leap of faith, and Redcross cannot choose to have faith in his salvation. He responds according to the knowledge available to him, "well *knowing* true *all* that he did reherse" (1.9.48, my emphasis). All that the demon says about the knight's moral insufficiency is true. Spenser does not write "And fondly thinking true the wicked lie," or something like that. Redcross recognizes the accuracy of what his conscience reports. His rescue by Grace makes this truth irrelevant but does not contradict it. That Una calls him chosen suggests both that he was always safe and also that, prior to the calling, he was never in a position to assert his own election. Redcross arguably deserves her sympathetic appeal, one of the most moving acts of comfort in Renaissance literature: "Come, come away, fraile, feeble, fleshly wight" (1.9.53).[38] These words don't reflect the glittering assurance of election; instead, they imply the ongoing, wearying ordeal of being a sinful creature of God.

To be sure, Spenser interweaves the distinct arguments for suicide and despair because he does not wish simply to jettison the long-standing prosopopoetic link between them. The heuristic value of suicide is that, as a deliberate act of will, it highlights the sinfulness of despair. It makes despair legible to outside observers, in the way that personifications characteristically make concepts legible by acting them out. Yet the limitation of suicide is that, as a deliberate act of will, it fails to capture despair as an ongoing condition that acts of will cannot manage. In this respect, suicide operates as a feint to distract us from the true nature of Redcross's malady. To the degree they do not appreciate the distinction between suicide and despair, predestinarian readings of the episode risk falling for this feint. Skulsky tries to finesse the incommensurate strands of Despaire's rhetoric by reducing suicide to a figure of spiritual hopelessness: "Thus it must be understood . . . that suicide is a synecdoche for the deliberate rejection of hope. . . . What Despair has been recommending all along is not literal suicide but, far more generally, the abandonment of [Redcross's] former dedication."[39] Moss writes, "Were the poet to deny Redcrosse Una's intervention, the hero would simply be damned by his creator to suicide — would become an allegory for the reprobate man in the absence of grace."[40]

The unintended consequence of these views is that they imply that escaping from suicide amounts to escaping from despair. This is a widespread critical assumption, underwriting even those readings that attend to the fine-grained varieties of sadness within Spenser's representation of religious despair.[41] Yet we have good reasons for doubting that Una rescues her knight from despair when she rescues him from self-slaughter. To start, the knight fails to repent after Una intervenes by taking away his knife. This bucks the tradition of the just-averted suicide topos, in which you end your despair either by repenting or by killing yourself. The rescued sinners of the interludes, including Magnificence, Mankind, Wastefulness, Juventus, and Xantippe, all repent when their Mercy figure intervenes. Even Doctor Faustus, after the Old Man interrupts Mephistopheles giving the conjurer a dagger, says he will "ponder on my sins."[42] Redcross Knight has no response: he does not repent, he does not ponder on his sins, he does not say anything.[43] He simply leaves the stage: "So up he rose, and thence amounted streight" (1.9.54). Remarkably, Spenser denies his knight the act of will that the vast preponderance of Reformation thought and literary tradition would lead us to expect. Escaping from suicide does not amount to escaping from despair.

Nonetheless, it is easy to understand why readers have assumed an equation between the two things. Spenser seems almost to tempt us to assume it by conjuring a personification of despair in the first place. Suicide, after all, is what personifications of despair are all about. But even here Spenser makes his particular personification unusual. Almost without exception, Despair figures employ suicide in one of two ways: they kill themselves, as in the iconography of the despairing sinner wielding noose or knife; or they prompt *other* people to kill themselves, as in the moral interludes by John Skelton, Richard Wever, Nathaniel Woodes, Lewis Wager, and others. In the first convention, the personification of despair is in despair, whereas in the second convention a nondespairing personification seeks to drive others into despair. In Spenser's figure of Despaire, the poet has cross-pollinated these two conventions within a single personification. Spenser's Despaire is both the demonic tempter of the interludes and the suicidal sinner of the iconography.

The manner in which this personification both transmits and enacts religious despair partly short-circuits the agency typically implied in literary prosopopoeia. With Spenser's figure, we can neither entirely divorce suicide from despair nor identify the two things. If we think of despair as transmitted to Redcross Knight from the outside, as it were, entering him as he becomes aware of his sins, then we will likely understand it as an episode that an act of will resolves one way or another. But if we think of the personification's attempted suicide as an enactment of the despair that the knight has long unconsciously suffered—perhaps from the beginning of the adventure when we meet him "too solemne sad" (1.1.2)—then we are likely to think of it as an ongoing condition. In canto 9, religious despair encourages us to anticipate the act of suicide without quite letting that act define the state of despair.

Nor does the act of repentance definitively end this state in the House of Holiness. Although Patience brings Redcross to Una with a "cured conscience" (1.10.29) after the knight has undergone the ministrations of Penaunce, Remorse, and Repentance, he never has his hero distinctly voice his contrition. All Redcross does is scream in agony. This is not to claim that the knight is not saved. The poet has already called him "Saint George": no doubt remains (for us) about his election. We are concerned, rather, with Spenser's depiction of the psychological experience of a sinner waiting for salvation. Without hearing the knight utter his repentance, it is hard to say what act of volition accompanies a "cured conscience," particularly since with this same conscience Redcross calls for death during the dragon fight (1.11.28). This is, in fact, a narrative version of what Marlowe will render as Faustus's dramatic assertion: "I do repent, and yet I do despair."

Indeed, Redcross's painful process of moral self-awareness in Caelia's house does not so much reverse as recapitulate, in different terms, his experience with Despaire. Of course, the House of Holiness is a place of spiritual healing: it represents the antithesis, for example, of Lucifera's House of Pride. Yet despair, although a blood relative of pride, shares a secret kinship with contrition. This kinship derives in part from the fact that repentance, like suicide, is an act of will that defines the meaning of one's despair. Despair always contains within itself both repentance and suicide as potential acts that make despair calculable, defining it as an episode that must end in one of two ways. Yet Spenser refuses to allow either act to exhaust the meaning of spiritual hopelessness, presenting despair as the incalculable condition of being a creature of God.

Spenser does not, then, use prosopopoeia to translate the passion of despair into a distinct act of will. Instead, he has his Despair personifications brutally expose calculable episodes of worldly despair (i.e., despair over earthly losses) as mere symptoms of the incalculable condition of religious despair. Malbecco, for example, starts out as the laughable butt of Helinore's adulterous maneuvers, a greedy worldling for whom the abduction of his wife amounts to the same category of loss as the abduction of his gold. But his transformation into the personification Gelousy reveals a more profound affliction, one that marks him as a "fore-damned spright" whose agony "doth transfixe the soul with deathes eternal dart" (3.9.56, 59). Likewise, Despaire reveals that Terwin, who we thought suffered from the melancholy of a rejected lover, in fact bore the weight of his sinful condition, a "guilty mind deserving death" (1.9.38).[44] Even Trevisan, who appeared merely to labor under the sympathy for his friend's unhappiness, turns out, under Despaire's scrutiny, to suffer from the same "bitter byting grief" (1.9.29) that afflicts Terwin. As these characters' worldly despair is reinterpreted as religious despair, the act of suicide no longer reliably signifies the meaning of their condition: Terwin kills himself, but Trevisan doesn't, and Malbecco tries and fails. Yet they all suffer from the same spiritual malady.

Spenser's representation of his hero's encounter with Despaire in a single episode invites us to misunderstand despair as an affliction that an act of will, or the conclusion of a canto, might end. Redcross shares in this misunderstanding. Critics commonly note that when the knight initially confronts Despaire with a demand for blood justice, he has himself paved the way for the villain's later arguments about divine judgment. It is less commonly noticed that the desire for blood justice does not at first motivate the knight to seek out Despaire. He feels this "firie zeale" only upon seeing the "piteous spectacle" of Terwin's bleeding corpse (1.9.37). By contrast, he initially wants to confront Despaire in order to experience his power: "Certes (said he) hence shall I never rest, / Till I that treacherours art have heard and *tride*" (1.9.32, my emphasis). This is less overweening pride and more a fantasy of self-restoration: Redcross resolves to transform the condition he already suffers into a defined encounter from which he might depart victorious. In vowing to *try* Despaire's art, as an assault that a personification might transmit onto him, the knight dissembles to himself the nature of his own despair.

This dissemblance becomes most pointed in the manner that Redcross describes Despaire's responsibility for Terwin's death: "Thou damned wight, / The author of this fact we here behold" (1.9.37). The knight quickly assumes that the act of suicide—the consequence of which he sees right in front of him, right "here"—captures the meaning of Terwin's condition. He wants to identify the appropriate object of his wrath, but his statement is far more complicated than he suspects. Who is the *author of this fact*? There are at least three answers:

1. Despaire is the author of this fact, as Redcross rightly alleges. He is the villain who, by means of rhetorical arts, wrongly persuades Terwin to commit suicide. Like all Despair figures, Spenser's man of hell represents the work of Satan, who goes about the world encouraging men and women to sin. Also, like all personifications of this sort, Despaire gives concrete agency to a phenomenon that we would otherwise experience as a state of mind or as diffuse energy in the world. Redcross has earlier asked Trevisan, "How may a man (said he) with idle speech / Be wonne, to spoyle the Castle of his health?" (1.9.31). The knight's question points to the fundamental nature of personification, which translates being into doing and passion into action. To call Despaire the author of Terwin's death aligns despair most closely with the act of self-murder.

2. Terwin is the author of this fact, as Redcross fails to appreciate. Sinners have wills of their own, and no one forces them to violate the law. Despair responds to the knight's accusation by claiming, "None else to death this man despayring drive, / But his owne guiltie mind deserving death" (1.9.38). If the villain seeks to exculpate himself here, he also says nothing but the truth. Despaire could not do his work if the object of his attention were not already conscious of his guilt. Terwin chooses to kill himself, much as Redcross, who suffers from the same consciousness of guilt, will resolve to kill himself before Una

snatches the dagger away. To call Terwin the author of his own death suggests that Despaire merely brings to the surface what has remained hidden within the knight.

3. God is the author of this fact, as Redcross dare not acknowledge lest he come face to face with his own despair. God authorizes the justice (but not the sin) of Terwin's death. At a point in the encounter where it is hard to tell whether Despaire or Redcross speaks, Spenser asks, "Is not his deed, what ever thing is donne / In heaven and earth?" (1.9.42). This question suggests the necessary misrelation between a Maker who gathers all means and ends to himself and a creature who seeks to authorize actions that he can never fully own. In the case of Terwin, Redcross, and Despaire—despite the differences in their actions—the name of this misrelation is despair. To call God the author of Terwin's death prevents the act of suicide, or any act of will, from exhausting the meaning of despair.

Despaire, Terwin, and God. Or, as Calvin would put it, Satan the tempter, man the sinner, and God the justicer.[45] Religious despair is the condition in which the relation among these three sources of action—demon, human, and deity—remains profoundly ambiguous. You cannot end your despair by committing suicide, as the villain Despaire illustrates, and you cannot end your despair by not committing suicide, as Redcross Knight illustrates. This is what it feels like: damned if you do, and damned if you don't. Divine grace would cut this Gordian knot, but grace is precisely the thing you cannot summon through an act of will. Following this line of argument to its conclusion means that holiness is not the virtue that triumphs over one's despair; instead, it is the virtue of managing, or at least living with, one's despair. It requires maintaining the uncomfortable obscurity about the precise origin of the suicidal act of will.

This observation provides a means for us to transition to the problem of despair in Christopher Marlowe. Thomas Beard, in his well-known animadversions against the playwright, trades in a similarly indistinct sense of agency when he describes Marlowe's stabbing death in a London street fight, suggesting that God "compelled [Marlowe's] own hand which had written those blasphemies to be the instruments to punish him."[46] Did Marlowe kill himself accidently, or was it a partly conscious act of self-murder, or did God kill Marlowe? Suicide cannot define despair because the act is caught up in an ambiguity about origin, and it is hard to be sure *who* exactly is thrusting that dagger into the sinner's heart. Marlowe, in his greatest play, understands this ambiguity to involve the sinner's inability to formulate a consistent perspective on his own will to repent or despair. To explain this effect properly requires a thoroughgoing reassessment of the role of prosopopoeia in *Doctor Faustus*.

Who Pulls Me Down? Faustus in Despair

Why is there so little traditional personification in *Doctor Faustus*? The drama owes obvious and deep debts to the morality play and the Tudor interlude, both of which feature prosopopoeia as their chief literary device. Yet the interlude stage vices such as Hypocrisy, Greediness, and Pride have been replaced with devils from hell, most notably Mephistopheles. The tug-of-war for the sinner's soul, traditionally given to characters like Mercy and Despair, or Spirit and Sensual Suggestion, here occurs between a good angel and a bad angel. As Douglas Cole has observed, Marlowe's angels are a striking departure from the morality tradition: before *Doctor Faustus*, angels do not appear in post-1500 English drama.[47] A procession of the Seven Deadly Sins does occupy the bulk of act 2, scene 3, but this is a tame and orderly group compared to the cunning vices of the interludes. Lacking disguises, they openly announce their villainous natures one by one, easy targets for Faustus's ridicule. Why does Marlowe set his story in what obviously resembles a moral interlude while seemingly stripping it of the very feature that constituted the heart of the interlude tradition?

Marlowe critics have tended to offer versions of two primary answers. First, Marlowe's chief source for the story, the so-called *English Faust Book*, includes no personifications. Instead, this chapbook, translated from a German original, relates the historical case of Johan Faustus's contract with the devil, his despair, and his eventual damnation.[48] In leaving out personifications, Marlowe was being faithful to his original.[49] Second, Marlowe's play participates in a larger inclination in Renaissance drama to experiment with psychological realism. In this shift, the external allegorical machinery of interlude personification yields to the internal drama in the soul of the conflicted protagonist. This view sees the real action of the play occurring in Faustus's head, through his soliloquies, while the devils and the good and bad angels serve as mostly tangential correlatives of Faustus's consciousness.[50]

Neither of these answers is entirely satisfactory. For the first, Marlowe is quite willing to revise the details of the *English Faust Book* when it suits him. The chapbook story lacks any angels, for example, whereas Marlowe makes these prosopopoetic figures rather important to his play. Furthermore, the Old Man in the chapbook is an elderly neighbor whom Faustus visits in the hope of gaining spiritual advice. Yet in the play he has a distinct prosopopoetic quality, suddenly appearing onstage, with no explanation given of his relationship to Faustus, warning him of his sin, and preventing him from committing suicide.[51] The Old Man resembles a personification of Admonition or Mercy more than he does the kindly gentleman of the *English Faust Book*.

For the second answer, that Marlowe is writing psychological realism, we should note the degree to which Faustus's fluctuating moods depend crucially on his contact with the devils, who sometimes behave very much like the personifications of the interlude stage. Indeed, although Marlowe draws Mephistopheles from the *English Faust Book*, he in many ways has the devil interact with Faustus as if he were an interlude vice, urging the sinner not to dwell on questions of salvation, distracting him with comic pratfalls, and offering him a dagger to commit suicide. When, in his final speech, Mephistopheles gleefully reveals to Faustus, "'Twas I that, when thou wert i' the way to heaven, / Dammed up thy passage" (B:5.2.96–97), he exposes his kinship with the stage tradition of personified vices, such as Lewis Wager's Infidelity, who cheerfully informs the despairing Mary Magdalene, "Well Mary, I have condemned thee unto hell fire."[52]

Doctor Faustus, then, does not so much leave out prosopopoeia as give us prosopopoeia with a difference. The devils and angels are not-quite-personifications who nonetheless carry out traditional prosopopoetic functions. We can appreciate the nature and effects of this difference by dwelling on the play's single instance of traditional personification, the procession of the Seven Deadly Sins in act 2, scene 3. Lucifer himself conjures these figures in an attempt to distract the guilty Faustus from thinking about repentance. One by one the Sins give a brief account of themselves to Faustus, who usually responds with a derisive quip. At the end Faustus dismisses them back to hell, commenting, "Oh, this feeds my soul!" (A:2.3.166).[53] Faustus consumes these figures rather than registering their influence on him. This gesture provides a crucial insight into how Marlowe revises the role of personification allegory in his play.

In chapter 1 we discussed the link between literary prosopopoeia and the premodern quality of selfhood that I called "transactional." This self enjoyed, and suffered, a constant intercourse with the external world. Transactionality deemphasizes the boundaries separating inside from outside, making the difference between "me" and "not me" a less pressing issue than it would become in the modern era. Timothy Reiss employs the term *passibility* to name this premodern fuzziness of boundaries, arguing that the autonomous agent detached from his environment is a fairly recent invention.[54] Charles Taylor describes a "porous self" in regular contact with the forces and presences of the outside world, a situation in which "the line between personal agency and impersonal force was not at all clearly drawn."[55]

Personification was *the* literary trope of agency for this transactional model of self. In their dealings with interlude protagonists, for example, personifications illustrate the manner in which human volition is a transaction between mind and landscape, a pressure imposed from the outside that might suddenly shift to express an inclination inside the agent. For example, when Despair and Faithful struggle over Wastefulness's soul in Wapull's *The Tide Tarryeth No Man* (1576), they are not simply taking over his will. Despair arrives only after Wastefulness begins to feel the gravity of his sin, and Faithful arrives only after it has occurred to the sinner that he might repent.[56] The protagonist is not simply the puppet of the personifications, but neither is he immune to them: his will has a transactional relation to the external energies of the landscape. In this respect, the transmissive dimension of prosopopoeia corresponds to the flexible understanding of volition in the medieval and Renaissance period, according to which we control our passions with our will but must also take care to control our will. My will belongs to me but does not always coincide with me.

That Faustus consumes rather than interacts with the personifications in act 2, scene 3 suggests he renounces the transactional model of will. He seeks instead a deep mastery over his volition, one that refuses commerce with outside influences. He wants the scope of his desire to determine the grandeur of its object, deploying a power that extends "as far as doth the mind of man" (A:1.1.63) in such a way that it becomes hard to tell where mind leaves off and world begins. His project is the project of his own will. Faustus can scarcely stand to acknowledge that the persuasions of Valdes and Cornelius have influenced his decision to study magic: "Yet not your words only, but mine own fantasy, / That will receive no object for my head / But ruminates on necromantic skill" (A:1.1.105–7). That the object "ruminates" suggests that Faustus's fantasy has produced it rather than received it from the external landscape. External things that would ordinarily influence his mind turn out to be products of that mind. In act 2, scene 3, then, Lucifer has shrewdly given Faustus what he wants, personifications that are the mere object of his will rather than its vehicle.

The conjurer's attempt to cleanse himself of outside influence and secure a deep autonomy is not, however, the cause of his despair. It is instead a symptom of this despair. In the typical moral interlude, the evil characters initially tempt the protagonist to indulge in some kind of worldly pleasure, and only in the latter half of the plot does despair set in. Pride comes before a fall. There is pride in *Doctor Faustus*, but it can barely stay ahead of the plunge. When Cornelius asks Faustus, "What shall we three want?" and he responds, "Nothing, Cornelius" (A:1.1.150–51), Marlowe initiates a slippage between desire and lack that will dog Faustus throughout the play.[57] We see this slippage at work in his initial conversation with Mephistopheles as they negotiate their contract. Faustus instructs the devil to inform his lord Lucifer that "seeing Faustus hath incurred eternal death / By desperate thoughts against Jove's deity, / Say, he surrenders up to him his soul" (A:1.3.90–92). The conjurer imagines his punishment as the motive, rather than consequence, of his sin.

Having the protagonist give away his bargaining chip before the bargaining starts is scarcely logical and suggests that the contract itself is merely another symptom of Faustus's despair.[58] Faustus, we might say, tries to replace a transactional model of will with a contractual model, whereby his present resolve to gain power ideally extends unalterably into the future. Yet the contract merely serves as a lure to distract Faustus, and the audience, from the despair that motivates it. After all, the contract ends up confirming nothing about Faustus's will: when Faustus threatens to turn to God, Mephistopheles angrily makes him sign a new contract in blood, "with unfeigned heart" (A:5.1.74). But if a second signature is needed to confirm the sincerity of the original signature, then confirming the sincerity of the second must require a third signature, and so on to a Derridean regress. A contractual model of will does not end up successfully replacing the transactional model.

Indeed, feeding on personification instead of transacting with it ends up signaling less mastery than Faustus might hope. The prosopopoetic figures who appear to actually influence Faustus's will in the play remain curiously outside his grasp: on the one hand, devils who are almost entirely external to Faustus, and, on the other hand, angels who appear almost entirely internal by merit of the fact that he never acknowledges their objective existence. This state of affairs leaves Faustus "over-solitary" (A:5.2.7), as the Third Scholar puts it: he never really dwells with the otherworldly characters. This distance isolates his mind from them but also reduces his ability to manage their presence in his world.

This isolation from the forces and energies of the external world also speaks to the curious presence of second- and third-person self-address in Faustus's dialogue, occurring at a far greater rate than probably in any other London play of this era. Faustus constantly speaks of what "Faustus" will or should do, or he urges "Faustus" to pursue a given course of action. Critics have offered a variety of explanations for this verbal tic: it represents a deliberate effort at self-disassociation, or a reflection of the conjurer's skeptical frame of mind, or a gesture at dialogic thinking in order to avoid confronting the prospect of damnation.[59]

Yet a primary implication of Faustus's acts of self-address is that he has no one else to talk to. The personifications of the interludes are denied to him, or he has denied them—it is probably impossible to say which definitely. Of course, when the interlude protagonists speak to Good Hope, Shame, Hypocrisy, Flesh, Piety, Infidelity, and Repentance on stage, they are also speaking to themselves. Conscience is the prosopopoetic paradigm of speaking to oneself by speaking to another—it obliges the sinner to view his interior from an exterior perspective. Yet in despair Faustus has no such perspective; he has only himself. He may intend his constant appeals to "Faustus" as a form of self-creation, conjuring himself into existence, replacing the daemonic presences that travel between self and nonself with an autonomous interior that is all him. But it does not work: these appeals to himself reverberate hollowly, sapping his resolve rather than comforting him. He eagerly talks to Faustus, but Faustus will not talk back.

Marlowe imagines despair, then, to involve a misguided desire for impassibility and autonomy that ends up isolating the sinner from human community and the forces of the natural landscape. This isolation is a repeated theme of despairing sinners in Renaissance literature, from Macbeth's anxious complaint that he is "cabin'd, cribb'd, confin'd, bound in / To saucy doubts and fears" (3.4.23–24) to the deluded optimism of Milton's Satan that "the mind is its own place" (1.254). In Faustus's case, despair prompts him to secure his internal will from external influence but ends up denying him a perspective by which he might say what is inside and what is outside. He is at once oblivious to and completely vulnerable to outside influence.

For example, consider Faustus's reaction to the first appearance of the angels onstage. After a short speech by the conjurer that voices his fears of damnation but also his resolve to contract with Lucifer, the angels intervene:

EVIL ANGEL. Go forward, Faustus, in that famous art.
GOOD ANGEL. Sweet Faustus, leave that execrable art.
FAUSTUS. Contrition, prayer, repentance—what of these?
GOOD ANGEL. O, they are means to bring thee unto heaven!
EVIL ANGEL. Rather illusions, fruits of lunacy,
That make men foolish that do use them most.
GOOD ANGEL. Sweet Faustus, think of heaven and heavenly
    things.
EVIL ANGEL. No, Faustus; think of honour and of wealth.
[Exeunt ANGELS.]
FAUSTUS. Wealth?
Why, the signiory of Embden shall be mine.
When Mephistopheles shall stand by me,
What power can hurt me? Faustus, thou art safe:
Cast no more doubts.

(B:2.1.14–22)

When Faustus utters, "Wealth?" after the angels depart, we are presumably to understand that he is making up his mind to sell his soul. Yet it is hard to determine the role the angels play in this decision. Are they figurative externalizations of the thoughts that Faustus debates in his mind—in which case they have no influence? Or are they daemonic spirits who impose on Faustus's will—in which case they potentially have irresistible influence? With traditional personification, which occurs somewhere on a sliding scale between daemon and figure, the answer is usually both/and. Yet Marlowe, by preventing Faustus from acknowledging and addressing the angels, prompts us to answer either/or.

I say it is either/or because the episode allows for no transaction: *either* Faustus wills on his own, and the angels, unbeknownst to him, reflect his will for the audience to see; *or* the angels, unseen by Faustus, pull his strings to make him go back and forth as they wish. This ambiguity explains why Marlowe criticism has found the issue of influence in this scene so important and why critics are so divided on the issue. For Wilber Sanders, the angels confirm the fact of Faustus's agency: "It is the act of choice in slow motion, a dramatization of his strained attention to the faint voices of unconscious judgment."[60] For John Stachniewski, the angels, instead of objectifying choices open to Faustus, "invade his mind and take over his will."[61] I think we must acknowledge that these views are mutually exclusive and that Marlowe has deliberately not given us the tools to say which one is right. By sealing himself off from external influences, Faustus seems to make his will simultaneously too removed from the world's influence and too susceptible to this influence.

This self-defeating isolation from the world helps explain the otherwise puzzling hold the devils have over Faustus. Several times in the play they prevent him from repenting by threatening him with physical harm. This method of dissuasion, however much Marlowe derives it from the *English Faust Book*, is quite unusual compared to that found in the religious drama preceding *Doctor Faustus*. The personified vices of the interludes do not use physical force on their victims. They discourage repentance by advocating the pleasures and advantages of sin. Their verbal assaults, unlike physical violence, assume that the external suggestions they offer have a corresponding existence inside the sinful protagonist—*precisely because these personifications operate within him and outside of him simultaneously.* Not so Marlowe's devils. Their proposed method of getting inside Faustus is to physically rip him apart. As Mephistopheles warns, "Revolt, or I'll piecemeal tear your flesh!" (A:5.1.69). The play interweaves this demonic threat of dismemberment with the comic scenes in which Faustus loses his head and legs. The very nature of Faustus's magical powers appears to correspond to a constant potential for bodily dissolution. Denying the daemonic traffic of traditional prosopopoeia does not yield integrity for Faustus. Pushing external influences radically to the outside simply makes him more vulnerable to penetration by them.

A similar isolation of self from landscape occurs in the episode that many critics have argued represents the point of no return for Faustus: his indulgence in demoniality with the shade of Helen (A:5.1.94–110).[62] Bodily intercourse with demons was understood to be a mortal sin, and shortly after this episode the Old Man, the devils, and the good angel all offer comments implying that Faustus cannot gain salvation.[63] Yet none of their comments specifically mention demoniality, and Faustus's encounter with Helen, although certainly erotic, is not particularly sexual. In the *English Faust Book*, Faustus lives with Helen and even has a child with her.[64] Marlowe's Helen, by contrast, lacks this day-by-day domestic quality and in her brief appearance resembles a personification of Beauty, or Eros, or Lust. The B-text stage directions enhance this effect by having her enter the scene "between two cupids" (B:5.1.93sd).

If we think of the encounter as prosopopoetic, then we can appreciate the extent to which it replays the earlier scene in which Lucifer summons the Seven Deadly Sins. A devil again provides Faustus with an object for his will—"to glut the longing of my heart's desire" (A:5.1.83)—much in the way the conjurer earlier claimed that the procession of personifications fed his soul. Faustus goes on to use Helen as the fuel for a fantasy about playing the Greek hero Paris. But this apparition, like the angels, is not quite a personification: her name is Helen, not Eros, and she says nothing during the entirety of her encounter with Faustus. And in that encounter, unlike his earlier encounter with the Seven Deadly Sins, Faustus does not feed on Helen, but she on him: "Her lips suck forth my soul. See where it flies!" (A:5.1.94). His request in the next line that she return his soul is met with silence. She is an altered prosopopoeia that has no transaction with him, a figure either wholly outside Faustus as the recipient of his desire or so deeply inside him that he cannot tell the difference between losing his soul and giving it away.

Faustus's effort in the early scenes to secure his will against his despair has rendered him, in the later scenes, unable to modulate his response to external influences that might help gain a middle ground between sin and contrition. He's too sealed off to get a grip on his dilemma: his despair is either radically inside him or radically outside. Faustus lacks what the protagonists in the Protestant interludes enjoy: a transactional relationship with the landscape vis-à-vis personified passions, virtues, and vices. These sinners, just like Faustus, labor under a vaguely predestinarian theology, unable to repent without God's grace but fully culpable for their failure to repent. In this regard, the absence of traditional prosopopoeia in *Doctor Faustus* is a primary reason, I would suggest, that the debate about free will and fatality has dominated critical discussions about the play over the last six decades. By contrast, in the interludes the unceasing activity of personification makes it obvious that the will to repent or despair comes both from external forces and from the internal disposition of the sinner that summons these forces.

Faustus's despair is more terrifying than that of his interlude predecessors because he lacks their lucid understanding of their condition. However sinful the presumption of claiming to know what God has in store for them, the interlude protagonists see the stakes of their situation. Recall, for example, Philologus's expression of hopelessness in Nathaniel Woodes's *Conflict of Conscience*: "I would fain attain / The mercy and the love of God, but he doth me disdain."[65] Philologus knows that he should repent and that God has not yet given him the power to do so. The personification of Conscience has obliged him to reflect on his sin, precipitating his despair but also allowing him to imagine a hypothetical act of contrition: "I would fain attain. . . . " In effect, he utters a second-order volition about what he would like his will to be. Sensual Suggestion and Spirit have both, along with Conscience, sought to influence Philologus, and he has responded variously to their efforts. He cannot simply master their effect on him, but he is aware of it and can form preferences about it.

Faustus in his despair entirely lacks the sense of the perspective given by the transactional model of volition. Indeed, despair in *Doctor Faustus* is itself the condition that denies the sinner a perspective on his situation. It was despair, after all, that inclined Faustus to isolate his will from outside influences. Sealed off from the external landscape, he swings between the extremes of contrition and resignation:

> Ay, and Faustus will turn to God again.
> To God? he loves thee not.
>
> (A:2.1.9–10)

> Accursed Faustus, where is mercy now?
> I do repent; and yet I do despair.
>
> (A:5.1.63–64)

> The devil will come, and Faustus must be damned.
> Oh, I'll leap up to my God! Who pulls me down?
>
> (A:5.2.76–77)

This oscillation between optimism and pessimism is riveting, but it prevents us from understanding the rules by which the play's universe operates. The question "Who pulls me down?" has no clear answer. Something outside or inside? The devil or Faustus himself? The transactional apparatus of personification, which would incline us to affirm both possibilities, is not available in *Doctor Faustus*.

"I do repent; and yet I do despair." Faustus is always committed to one extreme or the other; he has no perspective by which he might understand his relation to these extremes. Robert Ornstein protests, "Though Marlow superbly portrays his hero on the heights of aspiration and in the depths of despair, he does not trace the path which leads Faustus from one spiritual extreme to the other."[66] If we take away the tone of complaint, this kind of observation yields shrewd insight into a character who seems to be missing a cognitive dimension that might mediate between hope and despair. In the terms of Harry Frankfurt's account of agency, which we discussed in the previous chapter, Faustus lacks any second-order volition about his will, remaining a bundle of conflicting first-order desires. In terms of Reformation psychology, Faustus lacks the perspective of conscience, which obliges the sinner to reflect on his sinful desires. In this respect, it is worth noting that the word *conscience* appears not at all in the A-text of *Doctor Faustus* and only once in the B-text (5.2.13), where Mephistopheles gleefully notes its torturing effects on Faustus. This is a striking departure from both the interludes and English Reformation homiletics.

The absence of conscience suggests that the "majority report" on despair, which treats despair as an episode between sin and repentance, will offer limited help in understanding Faustus's situation. Instead, we must turn to the less common comments about despair of the sort I considered earlier. This minority report paints the line between despair and repentance less starkly than usual, as if despair protracted into contrition. For example, we find an on-point commentary on Faustus's above dialogue, I would suggest, in William Perkins's remarks about the despair of Francis Spira (the subject of Nathaniel Woodes's play), the Italian lawyer who infamously recanted his Calvinist convictions and, as a consequence, fell into a prolonged and suicidal despair: "Yet they are much overseen that write of him as of a damned creature. For first, who can tell whether he despaired finally or not? Secondly in the very midst of his desperation, he complained of the hardness of his heart, which made him that he could not pray. No doubt then he felt his hardness of heart, and the feeling of corruption in the heart is by some contrary grace, so that he was not quite bereft of all goodness, though he neither felt it then nor showed it to the beholder."[67] Remarkably, Perkins insists that the scenario of despair, seen from the outside, remains finally unreadable. The very experience that signals reprobation—hardness of heart—simultaneously signals the moral consciousness brought on by grace. In this account, despair spills out of its boundaries and touches on sincere contrition. Something like this happens in Faustus's expression of agony. "I do repent; and yet I do despair": this is a Kierkegaardian misrelation, in which the effort to repent seems to deepen the despair, and the feeling of despair gives rise to an effort to repent.[68]

This is part of the reason that Faustus does not seem more wicked as his despair grows more dominant. Unlike Shakespeare's Macbeth, whose moral sensitivity hardens into sadistic desperation after he kills Duncan, Faustus comes to know God, in a sense,

through his despair. He tries several times to submit himself to
Christ:

Ah, Christ, my savior,
Seek to save distressed Faustus' soul!
                    (A:2.3.82–83)

See, see, where Christ's blood streams in the firmament!
One drop would save my soul, half a drop. Ah, my Christ!
                    (A:5.2.78–79)

Attempting to relinquish his former refusal of outside influence,
Faustus calls on his redeemer for help. He seems ready to renounce
his former sins. But do these exclamations count as willing or merely
wanting repentance? They certainly sound like the expression of
contrition, but in context they are immediately followed by statements suggesting that he has no hope for salvation. Can one repent
while remaining in despair? Distinguished critics continue to dis-
agree about whether or not Faustus, in effect, repents in these lines.[69]
Although the ambiguity of this question is remarkable, even more
remarkable is the fact that there is a question at all. The moral interludes and Reformation homiletics unfailingly posed a strict threshold between the "before" and the "after" of repentance: in despair
you may want the power to repent, but only God can allow you
actually to will it. Yet in the lines above, wanting and willing repentance seem to blur into each other.

Again, Marlowe signals the collapse of perspective brought on
by despair by replacing the transactional activity of traditional personification with devils and angels who remain either too external
or too internal for him to engage. This prosopopoetic adjustment
plays a crucial role on the single occasion where Faustus utters a
first-person conditional about repentance—that is, where he seems
to have a perspective on what he would like his will to be.[70] Surrounded by his fellow scholars, he confesses that he has contracted
with the devil and then wails, "Ah, my God, I *would* weep, but the
devil draws in my tears. Gush forth blood instead of tears. Yea, life

and soul! O, he stays my tongue! I *would* lift up my hands, but
see, they hold them, they hold them!" (A:5.2.30–34).[71] Sanders saw
this scene with the scholars as the emotional heart of the play, suggesting that these lines reveal "humility and a new maturity . . .
something real and immediate and unselfconscious."[72] This effect,
I suggest, derives partly from the intimacy between abject despair
and sincere remorse in these lines. Faustus has never wanted more
genuinely to reach God than in these lines that report he cannot
reach him.

But how exactly does Faustus understand his inability to reach
God here? It is remarkably perplexing. Marlowe presumably intends for us to understand tears and uplifted hands as the bodily
confirmations of an internal state of contrition. Possibly, then, when
Faustus claims that the devils obstruct these somatic signs, he refers
to their wicked influence in his heart and mind. Faustus projects his
internal misery out onto external figures, as a kind of prosopopoetic
fiction. In this reading, his reference to the devil drawing in his tears
is a metaphor for his internal sinfulness that prevents genuine contrition. He would like to repent, but the despair within him makes
him unready to do so.

Yet he seems ready. "Ah, my God" sounds like a prayer, as when
he elsewhere appeals to Christ. But Faustus goes on to say that he
cannot weep, speak, or lift his hands. His prayer informs God that
he cannot pray, again confounding willing and wanting. If he is
ready to repent, filled with genuine contrition, then he is claiming
that the devils are there with him, on the stage, preventing his inclination to repent from finding realization in willed action. By crying
out, "See, they hold them, they hold them," Faustus seems to ask
his interlocutors to behold the devils physically obstructing him. At
least, this is what the scholars appear to assume when they respond
in puzzlement, "Who, Faustus?" (A:5.2.35). The devils, it is true,
have threatened Faustus with physical violence throughout the play,
and they have the power to make themselves invisible. But thus far
they have never been invisible to us.

Are the devils really there, in the external landscape, magically
preventing a contrite heart from willing its repentance? Or are the

devils simply a metaphor for the unspeakably deep despair that Faustus feels within him? The scene both prompts us to ask these questions and foils our attempt to arrive at a confident answer. Marlowe has denied Faustus the transactional energy of traditional personification, and the altered prosopopoeia that attend him serve to point out his misrelation to the world. He is either too isolated from the influences of the landscape or too susceptible to them. Despair denies him the middle ground by which he might mediate these extremes, even as it imposes on him a painful intimacy with God. Faustus cannot fix the location of the devils in relation to himself any more than he can get a coherent perspective on his despair: as a condition of his life it is with him *here*, but he suffers it as an external affliction that he cannot escape (it is *there*). Or, as Mephistopheles puts it, "Why, *this* is hell, nor am I out of *it*."

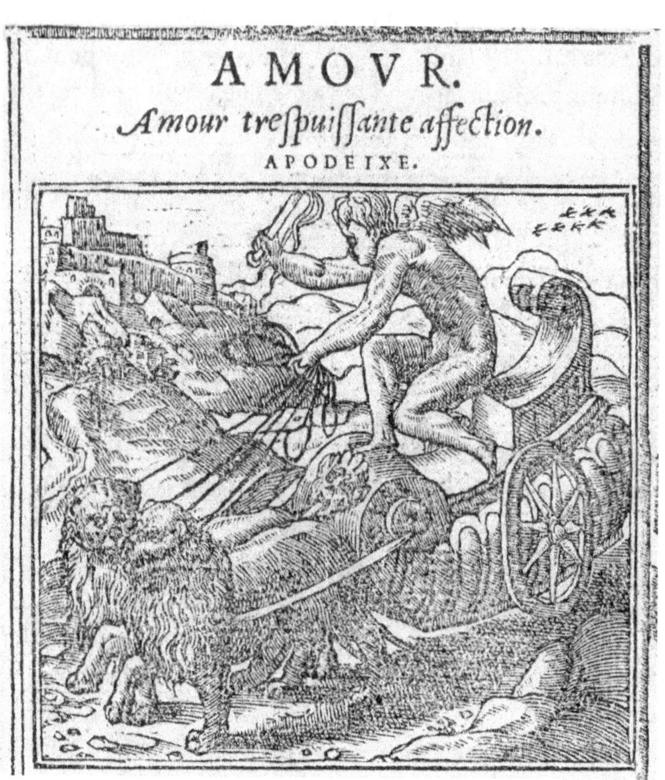

"Love, the Most Powerful Passion." Andrea Alciato, *Emblemes* (Paris, 1549), 128. Reproduced with permission of the Folger Shakespeare Library.

LOVE AND SPENSER'S CUPID

It is almost possible to sketch a history of the personifications of Conscience and Despair prior to their appearance in Tudor literature. There is no hope of such a sketch in the case of Love. By the time Hesiod depicts Eros in the eighth century BCE, love already slides among the overlapping categories of human passion, deity, daemon, and personification. Moreover, in subsequent Greek and Roman portrayals it is sometimes notoriously difficult to discern whether the poet understands the character named Love as an actual god or as a poetic figure. Even in later Christian poetry, where the one god has chased away the many, we cannot always be certain if a given appearance of Cupid belongs to a fictional pagan pantheon (Jove, Apollo, Diana, etc.) or a prosopopoetic projection of human passions (Joy, Doubt, Jealousy, Wrath, etc.). In the history of Love there are too many personifications, and too often we can't even be sure that they are personifications.

There is no point pretending, it seems to me, that the tradition of personifying Love involves less messiness than it does. What I propose to do instead in this chapter is confine myself to a particular strand of messy love discourse—Platonism—and briefly follow that strand through to its prosopopoetic culmination in Renaissance literature, Spenser's *The Faerie Queene*. This chapter's argument, then, will hinge on the claim that the poem's personification of love derives less from the poetic accounts of Cupid in Moschus's *Idylls*, Apuleius's *Metamorphosis*, or Petrarch's *Trionfi*, and more from a tradition of philosophical commentary that imagined the figure of Cupid to accommodate love's cruelty with its goodness.

Interpreting the personification of Love through a Platonic lens is a choice with consequences, of course. Bruce Smith may be right that the Platonic dialogues represent an early effort to domesticate desire within the house of logos: "All attempts to reconcile *eros* and words, in queer theory no less than in Renaissance Neoplatonism, follow from Plato's attempt in the *Symposium* to ally *eros* with ideas."[1] Yet by the same token, as David Halperin has remarked, the *Symposium* and the *Phaedrus* represent the first formal analysis of erotic desire in the West.[2] And the terms of Plato's analysis include prosopopoeia.

At the heart of his account of love in the *Symposium*, Plato inserts what appears to be a personification allegory, spoken by the prophetess Diotima. During Aphrodite's birthday party, Need (Penia) shows up at the door begging for food and shelter. Once inside, she notices Resource (Poros), the son of Craft (Mētis), in the garden of Zeus, sleeping off his liberal consumption of strong nectar. Thinking that getting pregnant by someone like Resource might lessen her neediness, Need lies with Resource and eventually gives birth to Love (Eros), who becomes a pursuer of beauty because he was born on Aphrodite's birthday.[3] In subsequent retellings, the details are sometimes rearranged: Natale Conti has an inebriated though conscious Resource petition Need for a sexual liaison, and Spenser, in his *Hymn in Honour of Love*, tries to combine Love's parentage from these two figures with his Venerian parentage.[4] But the basic plot persists through the Renaissance and after.

Taking this miniallegory as a starting point in our discussion of Love personification immediately plunges us into the ambiguity between prosopopoeic figure and daemonic agent that has concerned the argument of this book. Modern commentators, noting that Plato doesn't bother to mention Need and Resource again in the *Symposium*, often assume that he intends them as fictional projections that illustrate his larger argument about the nature of love.[5] But Plato's premodern expositors often assumed, by contrast, that Plato was literally calling Love a daemon. After all, Plato has Diotima herself report that Love is neither man nor god but instead one of the intermediate spirits, "the envoys and interpreters that ply between heaven and earth, flying upward with our worship and our prayers, and descending with the heavenly answers and commandments" (*Symposium* 202e). Moreover, Plato talks about daemons in other dialogues, so he presumably accepted their existence as inhabitants of the realm between heaven and earth.[6]

The uncertainty of Love's status in this story—a fiction of human passion or a divine spirit—prompted responses from many of Plato's followers. Plotinus found the problem gripping enough that he began his essay on love by wondering whether it was an emotion, a god, or a daemon. He concluded that love belongs to all three categories.[7] Yet elsewhere there was vigorous resistance to the idea that Eros might enjoy actual godhead. Seneca, Alain d'Isle, Dante, and others warned that poetic depictions of Love as a god falsely provided cover for bawds seeking to excuse their lust as divine coercion.[8] For them, Cupid was a personification posing as a deity. Nonetheless, Plato's Renaissance followers affirmed the Plotinian interpretation by which love was both a human feeling and the divine force that imposed that feeling. Marsilio Ficino, Leone Hebreo, Louis Le Roy, Baldesar Castiglione, and Natale Conti all insisted that love was a daemonic agent, although they differed about whether a single daemon encompassed all love or whether Love came in two versions, a good daemon and a bad one.[9] At the same time, these Platonic writers acknowledged that Diotima's story allegorized aspects of Plato's philosophy of love.[10] They likewise conceded (and usually approved of) the fact that poets presented Cupid as a personification of a human passion, even as they insisted that Plato had called love a daemon.[11]

The Platonic tradition that Spenser inherits in *The Faerie Queene* thus willingly tolerated an ambiguity between Love as a personification and Love as a literal daemon.[12] This ambiguity allowed the Platonists to assert love's divinity while insisting that love poetry sometimes veiled philosophical truths that could be understood in Platonic terms. Spenser, for his part, uses the ambiguity to suggest an analogy between love daemons and love personifications: as daemons interact with human beings, so personifications interact with fictional characters. In both cases, as we will see, Love *possesses* agents and turns them into lovers. Yet the ambiguity also allows Spenser to hedge the terms of this analogy. Since the Platonic tradition, broadly construed, allows one to understand daemons as fictional figures, Spenser avoids the baldly literal (and potentially blasphemous) claim that love is a god. But since this tradition also reads Cupid as a daemonic force, Spenser intimates that his Love personifications are more than fictional projections of his heroes' passions. "Well did Antiquitie a God thee deeme," says Spenser to the sacred fire that has possessed Britomart. The poet does not himself claim godhead for love. But the poet nonetheless thinks this is a good claim to make.

Recognizing Spenser's cautious approval of Love deified will help qualify interpretations that exaggerate the poem's hostility to Cupid personifications, in the name of either anti-Petrarchan aesthetics or Protestant iconophobia.[13] Jane Kingsley-Smith has offered the most recent example of the latter, arguing that, upon the shift from Catholicism to Protestantism in English society, "the religion of love now exists in an antithetical relationship to the 'true' faith rather than serving as an affectionate parody and this has a profound effect on the interpretation of Cupid."[14] Without a doubt, readers of *The Faerie Queene* encounter images of beauty intended to deceive and entice. Yet despite the risks attending the sexual imagination, Spenser's poem assumes no fundamental opposition between Eros and virtue. On the contrary, virtue needs erotic love for its prompt and fuel. Spenser's Cupid never simply conforms to Philip Sidney's charge of idolatry: "It is most true, what we call Cupid's dart, / An image is, which for ourselves we carve; / And, fools, adore in temple of our heart." Cupid's dart amounts to more than a fantasy in *The Faerie Queene*, in the sense that Spenser thinks love is a divine force that inspires us to pursue beauty.

Conversely, recognizing that Spenser places his Cupid within a tradition of prosopopoetic figures will help us avoid exaggerating Love's divine benevolence in the poem, as Thomas Hyde does in his otherwise exemplary study of Cupid in Renaissance literature. According to Hyde, "Cupid is a god in *The Faerie Queene* because he is omnipotent and benevolent," and we can have confidence in this benign godhead because the poem has translated prosopopoeia into divine presence: "a fictional world where, without the trappings of Neoplatonic cosmology, the distinction between gods and personifications has little meaning."[15] Yet, on the contrary, Spenser relies on the Platonic ambiguity between (not conflation of) personification and deity to suggest that Cupid represents an aspect of human will. The love god is not just a literal feature of an external, pantheistic landscape. Rather, Cupid figures the passion inside Spenser's heroes that seems, at times, to make *them* behave like personifications— that is, like agents driven by a single-minded pursuit of an object.

So as a daemonic personification Cupid both inspires and obsesses our will. Inspiration and obsession are, in *The Faerie Queene*, forms of possession. Like Plato, Spenser imagines that love comes upon lovers as a madness that deprives them of reason. This may sound, upon a first hearing, as if Love abrogates the human will. Indeed, of all the examples of personification considered in this book, Love comes closest to volitional constraint and compulsion. But ultimately this is a false conclusion: one agent's obsession may be another agent's inspiration. Spenser has read in Plato that Eros overwhelms the soul in order to remind it of what it really wants. Plato says that, for the enfleshed soul, this recollection remains imperfect and comes at the cost of the agent's self-mastery and freedom of choice. Spenser recognizes these costs but takes them to mean that only by taking over human agents, and depriving them of their liberty, can Love imbue them with a sense of moral purpose unavailable until the moment of possession. He most immediately signals this dual function of love with his depiction of Cupid.

The Winged God Himself

One of the basic challenges of coming to grips with Spenser's Cupid is how divided the figure appears to be. Cupid seems so dichotomous that critics have often concluded that Spenser presents us with two separate characters, a true Cupid and a false Cupid. I plan to resist this conclusion, but it is worth reviewing those aspects of *The Faerie Queene* that have produced the impression of two Cupids. Spenser certainly did not hold a consistent, single vision of the love god through his poetic career. In the *Hymns*, Cupid is a daemon of cosmological proportions; in the *Amoretti*, a capricious love-god; in the Anacreonic stanzas, Venus's self-pitying brat; in *Colin Clout's Come Home Again*, the severe deity of true love revered by shepherds but profaned by Petrarchan lovers at court. But although Cupid changes from text to text, at least the figure displays consistency within each individual text.

Not so in *The Faerie Queene*. On the one hand, Cupid is fantastically cruel and tyrannical. At least fourteen times in the poem Spenser uses "cruel" to describe the god himself, his bow and arrows, or his actions. His cruelty consists in the malice with which he assaults his victims and the pleasure with which he views their suffering. In Busirane's house, Cupid removes his blindfold so that he can watch Amoret's agony, "which seene, he much rejoiced in his cruell mind."[16] Elsewhere, the poet plaintively asks the god what glory he finds "in feeble Ladies tyranning so sore" (4.7.1), helpless victims incapable of defending themselves. Cupid's tyranny also upsets existing hierarchies, bringing kings, kaisers, and the gods themselves down to miserable thralldom. As a tyrant, then, Cupid is lawless, and his victims rightly call him "the disturber of all civill life, / The enimy of peace, and author of all strife" (3.6.14).

On the other hand, in contrast to his cruelty and tyranny, Cupid is a little boy, playful and "wanton," as Spenser calls him on five occasions. These references usually occur in contexts when Cupid has set aside his bow to enjoy peace and pleasure. In the restorative Garden of Adonis, Cupid, "laying his sad darts / Aside, with faire *Adonis* playes his wanton parts" (3.6.49). The word *wanton* has a range of meanings in *The Faerie Queene*, but a primary one involves generative sexuality. The fecund Garden of Adonis is itself called wanton, and the life-bestowing angel who rescues Guyon is compared to Cupid consorting with the Graces in "wanton play" (2.8.6). In this respect, Spenser seems to associate Cupid with life itself. Appearing in personified form at the trial of Mutability, "Life was like a faire young lusty boy, / Such as they faine Dan Cupid to have been" (7.7.46). True, the word here is not *wanton*, but *lusty* seems to come awfully close.

So Cupid practices sadistic cruelty but also wantons in playful harmony. No wonder critics have tried to distinguish between the true and false Cupid. In his later work, C. S. Lewis made this distinction the centerpiece of his interpretation of Spenserian married love. He went so far as to suggest that the sadistic master of ceremonies in Busirane's house was not really Cupid at all but instead "the show of an actor representing him."[17] More recent critics, seeking a subtler version of Lewis's thesis, have posited good and bad versions of Cupid that signify opposing aspects of love: ideal and real, celestial and earthly, natural and artificial, peaceful and martial, use and abuse, and so on.[18] Even Thomas Hyde, who among Spenser critics argues most strongly for a single, benevolent Cupid throughout the poem, can't stomach the tormentor of Amoret: "Cantos eleven and twelve present a temple to that god and the rite appropriate to his worship, but now Busirane is responsible for them. . . . [Britomart's] opponent is not Cupid, but an abuse of Cupid."[19]

I want to argue that even these subtler divisions risk misunderstanding what Spenser wishes to signify with the figure of Cupid. But I will also concede that Cupid is a difficult character to account for, if *character* is the right word. Even on a basic plot level he is puzzling. In the Garden of Adonis, where Amoret spends her childhood, Cupid plays with the other inhabitants as a friendly companion. In Busirane's House, Cupid oversees Amoret's torture. Why would this god, if he is one and the same throughout the story, want to hurt his old playmate?

One way to address this question is to note that Cupid is not only a daemonic agent in the poem; he is also a personification of love, and love is not, for example, like fear. When Fear appears at the mouth of Mammon's cave (2.7.22) and then appears again in the mask of Cupid (3.12.12), we do not bother to ask whether the same personification or a different one has walked on stage. Whatever its intensity as a passion, fear is fear. But love encompasses a range of disparate qualities. In the Garden of Adonis, Cupid participates in an allegory in which the Soul, finding Love after many trials, yields Pleasure. In Busirane's house, he participates in a quite dissimilar allegory that anatomizes the passion of Love as a psychological process involving Fancy, Desire, Doubt, Suspicion, Fury, and so on. Although love is positive in the first allegory and negative in the second, they both count as versions of Eros. Cupid is not like Fear, who signifies a single note. But neither is he like Una or Duessa, a figure on one side of a dyad of opposites. Cupid doesn't have an opposite.

None of this is to deny that love, at its worst, becomes truly terrifying in *The Faerie Queene*. The "deadly dart" that transfixes Malbecco's despairing heart started out as Cupid's arrow, and the final figure in Cupid's masque is "Death with infamie" (3.12.25). The link between the arrows of Cupid and Death was a commonplace in the sixteenth century, and, as we saw in the previous chapter, Despair and Love are prosopopoetic cousins in Spenser's poem.[20] Spenser's view of this kinship is echoed decades later, in a somewhat ironized form, by Andrew Marvell's "Definition of Love":

> My Love is of a birth so rare
> As 'tis for object, strange and high;
> It was begotten by Despair,
> Upon Impossibility.
>
> Magnanimous Despair alone
> Could show me so divine a thing,
> Where feeble hope could ne'er have flown,
> But vainly flapped its tinsel wing.[21]

Likewise, Spenser thinks that despair is an entirely likely, and in some cases even magnanimous, origin or terminus of erotic desire. He doesn't endorse the agony of love, but neither does he think that agony is not really love.

By not literally dividing Cupid into true and false versions, we keep hold of the fact that this personification signifies various qualities encompassed by a single force—Eros. I will have more to say about the unity of Spenser's conception of erotic love shortly, but for the moment I offer a set of examples that, in my view, discourages us from dividing Cupid into two personages or into authentic and phony versions. Whenever Spenser presents us with the peace-loving wanton Cupid, he takes pains to mention that the god has laid aside the bow and arrows that ordinarily accompany him. For example:

> Like as *Cupido* on *Idæan* hill,
> When having laid his cruell bow away,
> And mortall arrowes, wherewith he doth fill
> The world with murdrous spoiles and bloudie pray,
> With his faire mother he him dights to play,
> And with his goodly sisters, *Graces* three;
> The Goddesse pleased with his wanton play.
>
> (2.8.6)

> And eke emongst them litle *Cupid* playd
> His wanton sports, being returned late
> From his fierce warres, and having from him layd
> His cruell bow, wherewith he thousands hath dismayd.
>
> (2.9.34)

> Who when he hath with spoiles and cruelty
> Ransackt the world, and in the wofull harts
> Of many wretches set his triumphes hye,
> Thither resorts, and laying his sad darts
> Aside, with faire *Adonis* playes his wanton parts.
>
> (3.6.49)

William Junker has recently argued that the figure of the disarmed Cupid signals Spenser's commitment to the value of erotic joy, and I agree with this interpretation.[22] Yet let us also note how carefully Spenser couples the disarmed Cupid with the armed one. Remarkably, these passages that detail the love god's peace-loving gentleness give almost equal space—sometimes more—to Cupid's sadistic cruelty.[23] Spenser repeatedly reminds us that the playfully amorous Cupid is also a cruel Cupid. The overall impression is that these qualities of erotic love imply each other: mortals cannot enjoy the one without suffering the other. Spenser has little interest, then, in the strain of Renaissance Platonism that identifies two or more distinct kinds of love daemons.

Nonetheless, to read Cupid as comprising both the painful urgency of love and its playful wantonness *is* to read Cupid Platonically, as we will see. I am preferring this kind of reading to a psychoanalytic one, which might take Cupid's characterological inconsistencies as symptomatic of sexual deflection. For example, David Lee Miller sees the contrast between the warlike and peaceful Cupid as indicating a sublimation of the raw violence of Eros to the civil protocols of courtly culture. Miller finds this especially apparent in Cupid's friendly appearance in the wooers' lounge in Alma's Castle (2.9.34), where "this modest courtship has already enacted the sublimation of eros inasmuch as it involves the strategic displacement of sexuality from the anatomical center of the body to 'the midst' of the chest cavity."[24] If we are talking strictly about sexuality, then this is a brilliant observation. But if we keep in mind Debora Shuger's observation that in premodern thinking "sexual desire is an inflection of erotic longing, not its origin or essence," then we are in a position to argue that applying the notion of displacement to Cupid generally implies that Spenser thinks love is really about the genitals (and the appetitive soul), not the heart (and the passionate soul).[25] Yet Spenser is more Platonist than Freudian in this matter: love is a passion that includes the sexual appetite. The former is not only a compensatory disguise of the latter. Eros always potentially includes both elements.

Thus far I've argued that Spenser presents Cupid as a single character signifying disparate aspects of love. But another strand of criticism has responded to Cupid's contradictions, not by dividing him into two personages, but rather by arguing that he represents the diverse *responses* of mortal agents to the passion of love: villains respond basely, heroes respond nobly; the inexperienced, naively; the practiced, cynically.[26] There is clearly merit in this view: the poet himself says almost as much in the middle of the legend of chastity (3.5.1). The literary tradition of Cupid's triumph and capture, which we will discuss later, would have encouraged Spenser to take this view. In the *Trionfi*, Petrarch says that Venus's son "is held a god /

By slow and blunted and deluded minds," while Barnabe Googe's *Cupido Conquered* reports that the blind god primarily plagues "the simple sort" and "seely souls."[27] Even more fundamentally, *The Faerie Queene* is a personification allegory. Personifications of the psychological persuasion represent the various passions teeming within a fiction's characters. To the degree that Cupid is a personification of Eros, he does this also. The lust-kindling Cupid in Malecasta's house reflects the "sensuall desires" (3.1.39) the revelers already feel, whereas the playful Cupid in Alma's house reflects the "modest" (2.9.34) dispositions of the lovers who flirt there. This is exactly as we should expect: Cupid personifies love diversely in diverse lovers.

Yet this view, left unqualified, misleadingly underestimates Cupid's external daemonic presence. For these critics, Cupid is *merely* a personification, so the cruelty and falseness associated with him represents simply the misunderstandings of erotic neophytes such as Amoret, Timias, Britomart, and Arthur. The most extreme, and elegant, version of this view comes from A. Leigh Deneef, who argues that Cupid's nature depends on "the point of view, the visual scope of the perceiving eye"; erotic miseries thus stem from "the lover's own distorted perspective."[28] Love doesn't itself tyrannize a virtuous heart; rather, the lover does that to himself. For Deneef, we must avoid confusing the personification of Love with the living reality of love, lest we fall into the error made by the poem's reductively literalist characters: "When characters like Malbecco or Marinell enclose themselves in classifiable roles, they become emblems; they lose or relinquish their humanity through an act of misperception and misreading. Correct action seems instead to involve a process of activating the emblematic, unfreezing it, broadening the perspective. . . . Only by unlocking the poetic emblem from its status as emblem can the reader learn the human lesson. To forget the fiction is fiction is to run, like Malbecco, the correlative risk of forgetting we are men."[29] Deneef sees a grim lesson here. To narrowly understand love as a tyrant is to misunderstand a poetic figure as an agent who has power over you. And to confuse an agent with a figure is to confuse life with death. As so often in modern literary criticism, personification is bad for you.

To deny Cupid any daemonic agency, reading him only as a self-consciously figurative figure, risks fundamentally misunderstanding Spenser's notion of erotic desire. Such a view falsely sanitizes love of its painful qualities, failing to see that these qualities make it possible for Eros (ideally) to produce purposeful virtue in Spenser's heroes. In the fiction, Cupid really does assault the characters, does tyrannize them, and does take over their will. In short, Love possesses them. Yet some of the heroes are eventually able to own this possession as a source of strength, will, and, above all, purpose. This means that erotic feeling does not involve "broadening the perspective," as Deneef puts it. Instead, as we will see, it makes the heroes *more narrow*, more single-minded, more like personifications of the virtues they champion.

Spenser's Cupid makes us witness both the pleasure and the pain of Eros. In the House of Holiness, Charissa presumably has good reason to hate "Cupids wanton snare" (1.10.30). At the beginning of the poem, Spenser asks for a peaceful respite from Cupid, who "with thy cruel dart / At that good knight so cunningly didst rove, / That glorious fire it kindled in his hart" (1.pr.3). The virtuous love and heroic ambition that drive Arthur have their origin in Cupid's cunning cruelty. And when Spenser, describing Cupid's ambush of Britomart as she gazes into Merlin's magic glass, calls the god a "false Archer" (3.2.26), *false* does not merely signal Britomart's limited perspective. It also acknowledges that there is something false about the way Cupid possesses people, depriving them of their reason and autonomy. Yet, in a case like Britomart's Cupid does this for her own good—or, at least, for *a* good. The philosophical template of this salutary tyranny is divine *mania*, which Spenser read about in Plato and in the Platonists.

PLATO'S DIVINE MADNESS

Nearly everyone knows better, but people still sometimes imply that "Platonic love" involves an antisexual form of spiritual calm characterized by mild desires. Even Michel Foucault, in his influential account of Platonic Eros in *The Use of Pleasure*, emphasizes the role of self-mastery and is almost entirely silent about the prominence of ecstasy in Plato's dialogues of love.[30] Likewise, discussions of Platonic love in Spenser's poetry often emphasize a process of abstraction in which the initial shock of love is smoothed away by a vision of the good.[31] Yet this is not the only story of the dialogues, and it is not the story that Plato's Renaissance followers cared about the most. In popular dialogues such as the *Phaedrus* and the *Symposium*, violent rapture persists as a model of virtuous action and knowledge.[32]

Two commentators in particular have been alert to this fact, and we will do well to have their words before us as we undertake a brief review of the dialogues. The German Catholic philosopher Josef Pieper, despite an inclination to Christianize Plato, identifies erotic madness as the foundation of Plato's sexual ethics: "If we consider all the aspects of *mania* which Plato mentions, we shall have to say that he uses the word to mean, primarily, a being-beside-oneself, a loss of command over oneself, surrender of autarchic independence and self-control; a state in which we are not active, but passive. . . . When [*mania*] happens, it does so in such a manner that *sophrosyne* and all that goes with that is forcibly annulled, however much the dignity of the human person depends on it."[33] Similarly, Alexander Nehamas has recently urged us not to confuse spirituality with coldness in Platonic love: "And although these 'higher' beauties [the Forms] are abstract and seemingly impersonal, they never cease to provoke action and inspire desire and longing. . . . Tellingly, the philosopher wants from the Form just what men who know no better want of beautiful boys: intercourse (*sunousia*)—without a second thought, Plato applies to the highest point of this philosophic ascent the very same word he uses for its lowest. In that way, he reminds us that beauty cannot be sundered from understanding or desire."[34] In both these accounts, rapture is not merely a beginning that the Platonic scheme leaves behind; rather, it represents a self-alienation that permanently changes the moral agent. Keeping this interpretation in mind as we review relevant passages from Plato and his Renaissance redactors will prepare us to avoid certain misunderstandings about love and free choice in Spenser.

Erotic rapture in Plato is sudden, compulsive, and violent. It involves a temporary and salubrious evacuation of reason brought on by an encounter with beauty. In the *Phaedrus*, Plato's Socrates explains that sages of old understood that "the greatest blessings come by way of madness [*mania*], indeed of madness that is heaven-sent" (*Phaedrus* 244a). Of the four primary kinds of *mania*—prophetic, mystic, poetic, and erotic—Socrates reserves his highest admiration for erotic madness. He makes it clear that the voluntary faculties of reason have nothing to do with the initial experience of beauty. The soul, having fallen from its vision of the pure being and entered a body on earth, encounters a beautiful person: "But when one who is fresh from the mystery, and saw much of the vision, beholds a godlike face or bodily form that truly expresses beauty, first he shudders [*ephrize*] and then there overtakes [*hupēlthen*] him the awe which the vision inspired, and then reverence as at the sight of a god, and but for fear of being deemed a very madman he would offer sacrifice to his beloved, as to a holy image of deity. Next, with the passing of the shudder, a strange sweating and fever seizes [*lambanei*] him" (251a–c).[35] The language of arrest and seizure underscores that love is something that *happens to* a virtuous soul. Lovers don't exercise control over whether to have this experience or not, and there is no hint of the habituated temperance over *eros* that Plato recommends in other dialogues.[36]

Plato contemptuously dismisses the possibility of free calculation in love by exposing Lysias's speech (which Phaedrus initially reads to Socrates) as a false model. In this misleading interpretation, nonlovers surpass lovers because they are "free agents under no constraint" and so can "regulate their services by the scale of their means, with an eye to their own personal interests" (*Phaedrus* 231a). The nonlover says to himself, "I am the master of myself, rather than the victim of love" (233c). Freedom is just another name for parsimony, and such ungenerous comportment provides no path to virtue, so far as Plato is concerned. The *Symposium* likewise underscores the falseness of free agency in erotic attachment. Pausanius cautions that lovers must accept servitude as the condition of erotic virtue, the lover "lawfully enslaving himself to the youth he loves, in return for his compliance, the latter lawfully devoting his services to the friend who is helping him to become wise and good" (184d–e).

True lovers are just free enough to give up their freedom, entering a relationship of mutual thralldom.

Plato's preference in these passages for rapturous lovers over calculating ones recalls David M. Halperin's account of the distinction between erotic desire and irony in the Platonic dialogues: "In moments of intense, overwhelming sensation, we have little awareness of context and no attention to spare for more than one set of meanings. In such states, we become literalists: we can experience only one kind of thing."[37] Rapture collapses the gap between experience and expression upon which irony thrives and which might allow the agent a "perspective" on the situation confronting him. Part of Plato's point is that erotic desire has no perspective. Halperin does identify a deeper irony in the Platonic account of love, namely, the gap between what we think we want (a lover's body or person) and what our desire really wants (transcendent beauty or being). "Love's ironics . . . come down to a single paradox: the object of desire is not what you think it is."[38] Yet this irony provides no mastery for lovers; rather, it hurls them deeper into the abyss of misrecognition. I suggest that this helplessness, which rapture both exemplifies and signifies, constitutes a Platonic version of erotic *sincerity*. It is an odd kind of sincerity, to be sure, since it consists not so much in coinciding with yourself as in relinquishing (or losing) a self that might fail to coincide. If you really are the master of yourself at the first moment of encounter, as Lysias recommends, then you are not really a lover.

This is not to deny that erotic *mania* presents a danger in Platonism: rapture is both a promise of authentic virtue and a risk of degradation, an ambiguity that emerges as the hallmark of Spenserian eroticism. Not all agents can manage their soul's response with equal success. Plato details his notion of the tripartite soul—rational (in the head), passionate (in the heart), and appetitive (in the lower abdomen)—in the *Republic* (435b–444e) and the *Timaeus* (69d–72d). In the *Phaedrus*, he famously figures this model of the soul as a chariot, with a driver in control of two horses, one noble and passionate, the other wanton and vainglorious (246a–b). This is precisely where erotic rapture can go wrong: if the rational charioteer fails to control the appetitive horse, the initial experience of rapture degenerates into mere lust (*Phaedrus* 253c–254e). If rational control wins out and the lovers resist sexual consummation, a philosophical calm does indeed soften the initial feeling of rapture: "Their days on earth will be blessed with happiness and concord. . . . They have won self-mastery and inward peace" (256a–b). Yet it is important not to exaggerate this calm in Plato's thought, since even sexual lovers gain bliss:

> Such a pair as this also are dear friends, but not so dear as that other pair, one to another. . . . When death comes they quit the body wingless indeed, but eager to be winged, and therefore they carry off no mean reward for their lovers' madness [*mania erotikē*], for it is ordained that all such as have taken the first steps on the celestial highway shall no more return to the dark pathways beneath the earth, but shall walk together in a life of shining bliss, and be furnished in due time with like plumage the one to the other, because of their love. (256c–e)

The point to grasp here is not only the obvious idea that sexual passion, though subordinate to purely spiritual love, remains a legitimate form of affection in Plato but that erotic *mania* persists as a model of spiritual reward.

We should pause to dwell on this idea, since it is often overlooked in discussions of Renaissance Platonism. The oft-cited "ladder of love" does not *only* abstract from passionate rapture to spiritual calm; on the contrary, rapture reappears on the upper steps. As the prophetess Diotima teaches Socrates in the *Symposium*, "Whoever has been initiated so far in the mysteries of Love and has viewed all these aspects of the beautiful in due succession, is at last drawing near the final revelation. And now, Socrates, there suddenly bursts upon [*ezaiphnēs katopsetai*] him that wondrous vision which is the very soul of the beauty he has toiled so long for" (210e–211a).[39] This is the same kind of language that attended the lover's initial, rapturous vision of physical beauty. It guarantees the authenticity of the attainment of true beauty.

Later commentators did not miss the language of rapture, constraint, and sincerity in the dialogues or fail to observe the prominence of these themes in Plato's thought. Plotinus, the crucial second-century disseminator of Platonic ideas, echoes the vocabulary of seizure in his essay on beauty, insisting that spiritual loveliness ravishes souls even more violently than physical loveliness: "They must be delighted and overwhelmed [*ekplēxin labein*] and excited much more than by those beauties we spoke of before . . . [experiencing] wonder and a shock of delight [*ekplēxin hēdian*] and longing and passion."[40] Here beauty has the force of an overwhelming blow. Likewise, in his essay on love Plotinus confirms that Eros is a daemonic force by noting how often, in ordinary speech, we say things such as "love for this particular person possesses him," indicating, in Plotinus's view, our intuition that love seizes us from the outside.[41]

The Platonic and Plotinian account of love as divine madness arrived at the Renaissance, if not as a commonplace, then at least an eagerly repeated theme among humanist writers of all stripes. Even Castiglione, who more than other commentators focuses on the ladder-of-love abstraction from the physical body to spiritual contemplation, does not scruple to celebrate love's violent rapture.[42] The same is true for Plato's most important Renaissance editor, Marsilio Ficino, who repeatedly notes in his commentaries the centrality of Platonic *mania*, which he usually translates as *furor* or *alienatio*: "Whoever experiences any kind of spiritual possession is indeed overflowing on account of the vehemence of the divine impulse and the fullness of its power: he raves, exults, and exceeds the bounds of human behavior. Not unjustly, therefore, this possession or rapture is called madness and alienation [*Itaque occupatio hec sive raptus furor quidam et alienatio non iniuria nominatur*]."[43] Ficino maintains Plato's sense of violent erotic possession (*occupatio*, *raptus*), and even more than Plato underscores the encounter with otherness (*alienatio*) that such possession entails. Erotic rapture temporarily sets you outside yourself, and to complain that such alienation compromises self-control or reason misses the point: "Anyone who condemns intemperate love on the grounds that it is a frenzy, that is, an alienation of the intelligence, errs. For the love that alienates a soul, which has been seized by a god and raised above man, is also a frenzy, though a frenzy we should venerate since it comes from a god."[44]

We find an even more remarkable coordination of the themes of rapture, constraint, and sincerity in work of Leone Hebreo, author of one of the most popular (and learned) Renaissance treatises about love. *Dialoghi d'amore* (1535) presents its ideas through a conversation between two figures named Philo and Sophia, setting Platonic Eros within a heterosexual template. Although at one point he has Philo distinguish between the god Cupid (carnal desire) and the god of Love (virtuous desire), Leone maintains a focus on the overwhelming effects of all erotic feeling.[45] Love, although born of reason, eschews its parent once it is out in the world and refuses to stay within rational bounds.[46] Leone repeatedly underscores the misery that often attends lovers, especially when their love is not reciprocated, as in the case of Philo's devotion for Sophia.

Indeed, the lover's suffering and lack of self-control guarantees, in Leone's view, that lover's sincerity. Philo outrightly rejects Sophia's suggestion that lovers exaggerate their suffering in order to secure sympathy from the women they want: "How could you imagine that a lover's tongue might remain free to invent fabulous passions, while he finds himself plunged in such affliction and utter confusion, that his reason is dismayed, his memory preoccupied, his imagination distraught, and his sense overcome by endless grief?"[47] Leone's lover suffers a state that resembles the lack of ironic perspective and calculated self-interest we found in Plato's account of erotic madness. The lover can't help but express his real feelings because he has no distance from them by which he might construct a false front. This is why Leone, for all his qualms about Cupid's carnality, insists that "the true Cupid . . . symbolizes amorous passion and *whole-hearted desire*."[48]

Leone draws this implication about sincerity right from his source. The *Symposium* reveals a pronounced scorn for lovers who prefer self-protection over authentic intensity. Plato makes this point by contrasting Orpheus with Alcestis:

Thus heaven itself has a peculiar regard for ardor and resolution in the cause of love. And yet the gods sent Orpheus away from Hades empty-handed, and showed him the mere shadow of the woman he had come to seek. Eurydice herself they would not let him take, because he seemed, like the mere minstrel that he was, to be a lukewarm lover, lacking courage to die as Alcestis dies for love, and choosing rather to scheme his way, living, into Hades. And it was for this that the gods doomed him, and doomed him justly, to meet his death at the hands of women. (179d)

Plato's Orpheus refuses to give himself over to the risk of love, scheming and calculating how most safely to achieve his goal. He *chooses*, in the weak sense of the term, and gains only the shadow of his beloved, unlike Alcestis, who uncalculatingly surrenders herself to death with the result that she gains both life and love. If the history of Western erotic discourse since Plato has often aligned rapture and death, it has done so because both phenomena attest so persuasively to a lover's sincerity.[49]

Spenser and the Sincerity of Rapture

The Platonic tradition of Eros helps explain, I think, why Spenser's Cupid practices such cruelty while also modeling the peaceful satisfaction lovers sometimes enjoy. This Cupid launches the erotic assault that the Platonists call *mania, ekplēxis, raptus*, and *furor*, and in so doing he enjoins on the knights a deep sense of ethical purpose.[50] In claiming this, I have no wish to deny that other traditions, such as Petrarchan lyric and medieval romance, inform Spenser's representation of the arrest of beauty. The *coup de foudre* was a literary commonplace in Spenser's time.[51] Yet Spenser derives a combination of several elements from Platonic rapture that he would not have found elsewhere, at least not with the same set of interlocking significances. With his prosopopoetic Cupid, Spenser translates the Platonic account into a poetic conviction that Love is a daemonic force, something that comes upon the lovers from the outside and refashions them on the inside.[52]

Rapture supplies Spenser with a means to potentially distinguish disingenuous from genuine love within a fictional world that works against the genuine. *The Faerie Queene* functions according to a protocol of hermeneutic ambiguity, such that a hero's progress nearly always coincides with a narrative movement from simple to complex patterns of meaning that make it difficult to discern what actually counts as progress. In a process that Harry Berger has called "revisionary play," what initially seem like victories over, say, Error or Malecasta end up in retrospect seeming like misunderstandings or simplifications of the challenge confronting the hero.[53] Spenser's heroes are not deceivers, but they live in a world in which an assertion of virtue remains incomplete in itself, potentially qualified by other contexts and episodes that call it into question. In a poetic landscape such as this, rapture stands out because it is unmistakable as rapture. Certainly, its *consequences* following the moment of seizure are uncertain, but rapture itself never functions as a calculated deception or ambiguity. The false Florimell, under the mechanical guidance of a built-in sprite, perfectly replicates the behavior of a virtuous woman in love (3.8.7–8, 10, 14), and it is precisely this *distance* between truth and expression that precludes the possibility of *mania* for her. You can fake almost anything in *The Faerie Queene*, but you can't fake rapture.

In the poem's typical scheme, the rapture of beauty temporarily dispossesses the lovers it assaults of their reason and voluntary control. In doing so, it creates the occasion for either virtuous feeling or crass sexual impulse. In the case of virtuous feeling, the rapture divides the lover's life into a distinct before and after, between a prior drifting freedom and a subsequent sense of ethical purpose. This sense of purpose, although requiring the exertion of moral will, presents itself not as a set of choices to be made but rather as a series of shocks that, echoing the original experience of rapture, inspire the lovers (sometimes painfully) to pursue their moral goals. Like Platonic love, Spenserian rapture is teleological, and, as William Oram has argued, characters in *The Faerie Queene* appear to function according to a model whereby the heroes unevenly but progressively approximate a telos that lies in wait for them.[54] Another way to put this is that rapture initiates a process by which the heroes more and more closely (if never absolutely) resemble a personification of the virtue they represent.

Most often, erotic seizure represents the start of a conversion from sexual or social immaturity to a mature care for others. Arthur, Marinell, Arthegall, and Britomart leave behind their youthful traits (what we might identify as sadism, priggishness, savagery, and naïveté, respectively) not through a process of reason or choice but through the *mania* of love. Seeing or hearing their beloveds for the first time, Arthur is "ravished with delight" (1.9.14.6), Arthegall suffers "secret fear" and "trembling horrour" (4.6.21 and 22), Marinell's "stubborn heart, that never felt misfare / Was toucht with soft remorse and pitty rare" (4.12.12), and Britomart feels "sudden joy, and secret feare withal" (4.6.29). The assault of love victimizes all of these characters, cruelly denying them their self-control for a time, but in so doing it imbues them with a sustained (if fallible) sense of virtue. Arthur shifts from a riotous youth to a knight of grace, Arthegall from a savage knight to a knight of justice, Marinell from proud indifference to solicitude, Britomart from girlish innocence to martial womanhood.[55] This "conversion" to ethical purposiveness does not simply leave the moment of erotic ravishment in the past. Rapture continues to seize the characters in reiterations of the original assault of beauty, as when Arthur, recounting his first vision of Gloriana to Redcross and Una, suddenly becomes pale and faint (1.9.16), or when Britomart, watching the reunited Amoret and Scudamour embrace, is briefly overcome with passion for her own love (3.12.46).

Love, then, operates though possession: it seizes and shocks, and keeps shocking. This is why Spenser finds the cruelty of Cupid indispensible, if also lamentable. But as love possesses, it also daemonically imparts energy and purpose to the agent. The grandest and most generous invocations of the love god in the poem emphasize the inspirational, regenerative effects of Eros. Think of the angel who protects Guyon after his faint, whom the narrator compares to "Cupido on Idaean hill" (2.8.6), clearly glancing at the Platonic association between angels and daemons. This messenger not only protects the knight of temperance but promises that renewed life will be instilled in the lifeless body: "But dread of death and dolor doe away; / For life ere long shall to her home retire, / And he that breathlesse seems, shal corage bold respire" (2.8.7). "Corage" means life, of course, but combined with "bold" it also promises life energy, force, will. We ought to have this Cupid-like angel in mind near the beginning of book 3, when the narrator, addressing love as that "most sacred fire," observes,

> Well did Antiquitie a God thee deeme,
> That over mortall minds hast so great might,
> To order them, as best to thee doth seeme,
> And all their actions to direct aright;
> The fatall purpose of divine foresight,
> Thou doest effect in destined descents,
> Through deepe impression of thy secret might,
> And stirredst up th'Heroes high intents,
> Which the late world admyres for wondrous moniments.
>
> (3.3.2)

This stanza provides a good example of how erotic obsession can be translated into inspiration. Here the god of love, aligned with providential power, does not simply compel or constrain but also motivates: "stirredst up th'Heroes high intents." Daemonic love does not set the heroes free, but it inspires their intentions, encouraging them to will. It can "direct aright" the actions of men.

Of course, the lovers must rely on their moral character to modulate the initial experience of erotic rapture, and therein lies the simultaneous risk and promise of love that Spenser adapts from Plato. The sight of Gloriana leaves Arthur "ravished with delight" (1.9.14), and the sight of Belphoebe likewise enraptures Braggadocchio, though he, "with her wondrous beauty ravisht quight, / Gan burne in filthy lust" (2.3.42). Neither character chooses to feel ravishment, and neither exactly chooses to respond virtuously or basely: rapture activates what is already in them. The heroes do not deliberate and then decide how to respond to ravishment but rather let erotic instinct guide them, as Arthegall does despite his urgent passion for Britomart:

> Yet durst he not make love so suddenly,
> Ne thinke th'affection of her hart to draw
> From one to other so quite contrary:
> Besides her modest countenance he saw
> So goodly grave, and full of princely aw,
> That it his ranging fancie did refraine,
> And looser thoughts to lawfull bounds withdraw;
> Whereby the passion grew more fierce and faine,
> Like to a stubborne steede whom strong hand would restraine.
>
> (4.6.33)

Strikingly, Arthegall's effort at temperance makes his desire both more lawful and more dangerously intense. Spenser's metaphor of the "stubborne steede" may owe something to Plato's description, in the *Phaedrus* (254b–e), of the increasingly violent efforts of the soul's appetitive horse to resist the governing bridle of the rational charioteer. As Plato notes, some lovers succeed in this restraint, and some do not. Because a model of erotic seizure so fully dispossesses the lover of voluntary response, the initial modulation of desire becomes a tricky affair: in the moments following his rapture, Arthegall comes perilously close to Braggadocchio. As in Plato, rapture supplies the initial, overwhelming energy that the lover's ethical character tries to channel in an appropriate direction, but the sheer risk of erotic *mania* is never far from Spenser's mind.

One of the finest recent scholarly accounts of this risk in Spenser comes from Melissa E. Sanchez, who traces the role of Petrarchan love discourse in early modern political theory. Renaissance writers depicted political subjects and Petrarchan lovers alike as willfully confusing their own internal desires with the external coercive figures of the tyrant and the mistress or suitor. They tacitly cooperate with the enslavement of which they complain.[56] Although Sanchez focuses on suffering rather than rapture in *The Faerie Queene*, she sees a similar emphasis on the demonstration of sincerity, since Amoret's "ability to withstand Busirane's violence proves the sincerity of her choice" of Scudamour.[57] Erotic suffering likewise blurs the difference between inner desire and outside pressure, in such a way that love appears "as an invasive force, at once the most involuntary and incoercible of emotions."[58] This is the daemonic price of erotic sincerity, the absence of a clear line between the voluntary and the compelled.

Indeed, as the foregoing discussion already suggests, Platonic rapture in Spenser acquires its intensity from a denial of choice, in the sense of Plato's dismissal of a lover's "free agency," or what Spenser censures as "liberty." When Mirabella was "Ladie of her libertie" she "Did boast her beautie had such soveraine might, / That with the onely twinckle of her eye, / She could or save, or spill, whom she would hight" (6.7.31). Likewise, Prince Arthur confesses that his time of "libertie" (1.9.10, 12) was characterized by the "looser life" (12) of adolescent sadism, when he "joyed to stirre up strife, / In midst of their mournfull Tragedy, / Ay wont to laugh, when them I heard to cry, / And blow the fire, which them to ashes brent" (10). Cupid the love daemon can practice incredible tyranny in this poem, as we have seen, but in cases such as Mirabella and Arthur only tyranny will restrain the casual cruelty of free agents.

Looking at rapture through the lens of Platonic Eros thus suggests a salutary dimension of Cupidic tyranny, which focuses and reforms otherwise indifferent and undirected agents. Yet Sanchez's political perspective reminds us that tyranny can destroy the self instead of motivating it. In her view of the poem, "It is disturbingly difficult to locate the precise line between rape and ravishment, tyranny and kingship."[59] Now, I would argue that Spenser does posit a difference between rapture and rape, and the difference has to do with the will. Rapture violently makes you want something, whereas rape violently makes you engage in something you don't want.[60] It would be hard to deny the aversion that Una and Florimell display when threatened with physical force by Sansloy and the fisherman (1.3.43–44; 3.8.25–27). Yet there are also ambiguous cases: when

Lust abducts Amoret (4.7.4–8), exactly *whose* desire is personified, that of a male aggressor or Amoret's own? Although I do not think that such an example requires us to doubt the wholeheartedness of Una's and Florimell's aversion, rapture does temporarily confound the voluntary with coercion. We can still speak of "consent" (or, better, "assent") in Spenserian eroticism, but only as an acquiescence to an external pressure, not as a considered decision to love or not. Spenser thinks that his lovers ideally ought to have the freedom to do what they want, but they cannot will what they want.

Even in the case of the poem's most dynastically important couple, Spenser emphasizes the protocols of constraint and limited assent. Arthegall, when he is smitten by the sight of Britomart, desists from leaping on her because he knows that such an act would violate her will, even though she already loves him. But Spenser describes the knight's subsequent courtship as an assault in which he "did lay / Continuall siege unto her gentle hart," until "at the length unto a bay he brought her" (4.6.40 and 41). The language of siege and hunt is a metaphor for romantic persuasion, of course, but Spenser's formulation of Britomart's acceptance of the knight's love reveals the limited purview of volition in desire: "she *yielded* her consent / To be his love, and take him for her Lord" (41, my emphasis). As a lover, Britomart is servant to her lord, just as Arthegall becomes "a Ladies thrall" (4.6.28). Pausanius's mutual thralldom (*Symposium* 184d–e) is as free as love gets in *The Faerie Queene*.

If this model strikes us as somewhat unstable, it is because rapture can always go wrong. A lover such as Arthegall, newly ravished by the sight of the wicked Radigund, may consent to be "her thrall," "willfully" abandoning his moral responsibilities (5.5.17). This kind of possibility confirms Joseph Loewenstein's claim that in Spenser's work "the *arresting* power of beauty constitutes both a narrative and poetic problem."[61] Yet such is the way of daemonic desire. Spenser realizes that there is no final rebuttal of Lysias's cynical observation, in the *Phaedrus*, that the intensity of your lover's devotion presages how thoroughly he will forget you when he falls in love with someone else (231c). The poet offers no sense that an ethics of free will might assuage this problem of arrest, certainly not

in the form of A. Kent Hieatt's suggestion that the poem promotes
a "room of one's own for decisions" about love.[62] In Spenser's version of Platonic rapture, the room is not simply one's own, and one
doesn't make decisions in it.

The occasional comments about erotic freedom in *The Faerie
Queene* are easily misunderstood. Britomart, for example, censures
Malecasta's knights' attempt to force Redcross to change his love by
telling them, "Ne may love be compeld by maistery; / For soone as
maistery comes, sweet love anone / Taketh his nimble winges, and
soone away is gone" (3.1.25). Likewise, Arthur chides the knights
for continuing to battle over possession of Florimell, since "of their
loves choise [ladies] might freedom clame" (4.9.37). Crucially, both
of these assertions speak to contexts in which knights try to determine a woman's love by battle. Spenser does indeed find this kind
of mastery illegitimate, precisely because it seeks to override the imperatives of authentic rapture. Lovers surely *should* have the freedom to refuse any external compulsion to abandon the beloved
whose beauty has already enthralled them. But neither of the above
formulations argues for the freedom to fall in love or not.

We in fact hear the advocation for free decision making about
love only from characters such as Duessa, who taunts Scudamour
with Amoret's supposed infidelity by informing him that "love is
free, and led with selfe delight, / Ne will enforced be with maister-
dome or might" (4.1.46). This is a version of the "free agency" that
Plato despises in the *Phaedrus*, and we should distinguish it from
the more limited freedom of assent and faithfulness espoused by
Britomart and Arthur. Duessa's formulation in fact represents a
casual indifference to any single beloved, describing the freedom of
the false Florimell, who looks at every knight "as though she wished
to have pleasd them all" (4.5.26), or the freedom of Paridell's easy
welcome to the wound of love:

> But nothing new to him was that same paine,
> Ne paine at all; for he so oft had tryde
> The powre thereof, and lov'd so oft in vaine,
> That thing of course he counted, love to entertaine.
>
> (3.9.29)

This kind of love, to recall Halperin, is ironically detached from itself; it has escaped mastery at the cost of authentic intensity. Or, in the parlance of Leone Hebreo, it allows seducers to fabricate passions they don't feel because, unraptured, they are *free* to do so. Yet feigning passion does not, in Spenser, end up amounting to purposeful action. Such lovers simply drift because love pushes them in no particular direction.[63]

It is perhaps easy enough to show this insincerity in villains like Duessa, Paridell, and the false Florimell. But what about ostensibly virtuous lovers, namely Scudamour and Calidore, who have no distinct moment of erotic rapture? Such cases do indeed represent exceptions to the protocols of daemonic possession—but they are meaningful exceptions. The lack of rapture saddles both knights with suspiciously ambiguous motivations. Throughout the poem Scudamour appears alternately overaggressive and undermotivated. He seizes Amoret from the Temple of Venus against her will, but also, at the crucial moment, has to *choose* whether or not to pursue his courtship (4.10.53), as if he were still deciding how much he loves her. Does he pursue Amoret because of the "deadly wound" (6.10.1) of love that Cupid gave him? Or does he pursue her for the sake of "the fame of this renowmed prise" (6.10.4)? Scudamour is "Cupids man" (4.10.54), but as much as anything the knight's adventures reveal that Cupid's power is not something a lover can simply choose to wield.[64]

Similar questions arise about Calidore's love. The poet tells us that the knight of courtesy, upon seeing Pastorella, is indeed "surprisd in subtile bands / Of the blynd boy" (6.9.11), yet Calidore remains surprisingly in command of himself:

> But after he had fed, yet did he stay,
> And sate there still, untill the flying day
> Was farre forth spent, discoursing diversly
> Of sundry things, as fell, to worke delay;
> And evermore his speech he did apply
> To th'heards, but meant them to the damsels fantasy.
> (6.9.12)

No erotic rapture here. Calidore maintains a distance between what he feels and what he shows so as to fashion a *strategy* for pursuing his courtship. We have every reason to believe that his intentions toward Pastorella are not simply carnal, but in this double speaking Calidore faintly recalls Paridell's more sinister flirtation with Helenore. The double speaking also presages Calidore's interaction with Meliboe (6.9.16–34), where readers have been unable to shake the suspicion that the knight's sudden appreciation for the contemplative life covers a more self-interested desire to remain near the object of his affections. It likewise presages the manner in which Spenser makes it hard to distinguish Calidore's apparent generosity to Coridon (6.9.39–45) from his self-interested effort to secure Pastorella for himself. Not only does Calidore refrain from wearing his heart on his sleeve, but his lack of rapture seems tied to his inconsistent sense of purpose. Uniquely among Spenser's heroes, love for a virtuous person dilutes, rather than promotes, Calidore's commitment to his quest.

I don't wish to suggest that the unraptured Scudamour and Calidore are really villains in disguise. Spenser invites us to sympathize with the suffering they endure in love. We might venture to say that, in the second half of *The Faerie Queene*, these characters represent experiments in different kinds of virtuous love. Perhaps, in the case of Calidore, the virtue of courtesy requires that erotic desire be represented in a politic manner, much as the legend of temperance in book 2 requires a heroism uninspired by love. But nonetheless Scudamour's and Calidore's capacity to choose or to calculate comes at the cost of sincerity: we cannot have complete confidence that they are not faking it. They don't appear to have the same drive and sense of sustained purpose as the other heroes. They are like Plato's Orpheus: they haven't given themselves up to love.

Cupid in Triumph

The House of Busirane episode offers a good place to test the foregoing ideas. Not only does Cupid come forth at the height of his sadistic power, but his victim Amoret—bound, bleeding, with her heart torn out—seems to make a strong case against the claim that Eros inspires and focuses the will. If Cupid's daemonic assault produces a prosopopoetic single-mindedness in his heroes, as I have maintained, then the Busirane episode would seem to associate this single-mindedness with stasis and compulsion, after all. Britomart's rescue of Amoret, in this view, would involve refusing personification and seeing through Cupid's illusionary poetics—or, if you prefer, Busirane's illusionary poetics, which allegedly employ a phony version of the true god of love.[65] Yet although Britomart and Amoret offer contrasting examples of agency and helplessness, they also have much in common: both women, both waiting for marital consummation, both wounded by Cupid. In this final section of the chapter, I argue that the two characters have been possessed equally by the daemonic spirit of love and that despite appearances both undergo a prosopopoetic narrowing. The difference lies in the mode of this narrowing: one woman's inspiration is another woman's self-dispossession. With this contrast Spenser illustrates the promise and risk of Eros.

Spenser goes out of his way to show the degree to which Amoret's interaction with the personifications around her tracks her loss of agency. A captive in Cupid's sadistic parade, Amoret hovers between the living and the nonliving: "She dolefull Lady, like a dreary Spright, / Cald by strong charmes out of eternal night, / Had Deathes owne ymage figurd in her face" (3.11.19). If we recall that Spenser began this canto with a reference to Malbecco's fate (11.1), we will notice a significant echo in these lines: much as jealousy consumed Malbecco until he is "like an *aery* Spright" (3.10.57), so does Cupid's daemonic compulsion make Amoret "like a *dreary* Spright." Personification is imposed on her, a *prosōpon* of terrifying stasis: "Deathes owne ymage figurd in her *face*." Whatever their ethical differences, both Malbecco and Amoret experience daemonic possession as a violent self-dispossession.

Indeed, part of Amoret's problem is that the prosopopoetic scenario has transformed her into one of the consequences of a psychological process that she otherwise might have originated.

Traditionally, as Thomas Roche noted some time ago, it is the courtly lady who inspires in the male admirer the experiences personified by Cupid's allegorical masque: Fancy, Desire, Doubt, Danger, Fear, Hope, and so forth (3.12.7–18).[66] Amoret is in fact held by two personifications, Despite and Cruelty, who would otherwise represent the agency of a woman to refuse love. These figures should be helping Amoret say no, but instead they work to coerce a yes out of her. Even the literal fact of Amoret's rapture by love remains mediated by prosopopoetic representation. Earlier in book 3 Spenser tells us that she "cast" her love to Scudamour above all other suitors (3.6.53), and later in book 4 Scudamour tells a rather different story in which he abducts Amoret from the Temple of Venus (4.10). So when does Eros actually possess her? We see this moment only metaphorically, in the image of the "deadly dart" that pierces her heart, which her tormentors display on a silver basin (3.12.21). This striking image has inspired a variety of interpretations about its referent, including literalized Petrarchan love discourse, Amoret's self-defeating love for Scudamour, and Busirane's artificial deformation of erotic desire. All these reading have a claim, but let us not forget the obvious referent: the arrow belongs to Cupid, the same archer who "that arrow shot / So slyly" at Britomart herself (3.3.26). The arrow represents the effect of personifying love as an agent, with the result of turning Amoret into a spectacular victim.

In Busirane's house, then, daemonic love has taken over Amoret's whole person, abrogating her will, demoting her from agent to consequence. In this regard, we can appreciate the aptness of the "be bold" and "be not too bold" messages as glosses on Amoret's plight. These messages come from the folk tale about Bluebeard (or, in other iterations, Mr. Fox), the homicidal husband who warns his new bride not to look in the closet containing the corpses of his past wives, admonishing her, "Be bold, be bold, be not too bold, lest that thy heart's blood should run cold."[67] I suspect that Spenser found this folk tale an apt analogue to Amoret's situation because of the threat of daemonic stasis: Busirane's sadistic love turns the blood cold, freezes the will, imposes an immobilizing prosopopoeia.

Of course, the messages also address Britomart, so they potentially draw her, like Amoret, into an immobilizing erotic relationship with Busirane.[68] Yet Britomart appears to maintain her agency in the face of this relationship: Spenser repeatedly designates her as "bold" (3.9.50; 3.12.2; 3.12.29), distinguishing her bold will from the too bold will of Scudamour (the overeager lover), which degenerates into mere willfulness, and the insufficiently bold will of Amoret, which remains too vulnerable to the daemonic agents that afflict her. How does Britomart get her boldness just right? Significantly, she receives her "bold" designation in Busirane's castle only after she confronts the statue of Cupid, who holds bow and arrow in his cruel hand as he stands over the wounded dragon:

> That wondrous sight faire Britomart amazd,
> Ne seeing could her wonder satisfie,
> But evermore and more upon it gazd,
> The whiles the passing brightnes her fraile sences dazd.
>
> (3.11.49)

Spenser presents Cupid as a stone statue at this point to signal the threat of daemonic compulsion: desire can turn you into stone, much as Bluebeard can freeze your blood, and much as Amoret now wears her prosopopoetic death mask.

Yet it appears that Britomart's acquisition of bold agency involves risking rather than shunning these dangers. To liberate Amoret, she cannot reject the prosopopoetic statue, in the way she rejects "beauties chace" (3.1.19) at the beginning of her adventure. Instead, in this encounter she momentarily experiences again the effects of divine mania, the erotic rapture that Cupid inflicted on her when she saw Arthegall's image in Merlin's mirror. Her agency derives not from avoiding but from embracing daemonic possession. Rapture does not dispossess Britomart and turn her into something else, as it does Amoret and Malbecco. Instead, it inspires her with boldness and a sustained sense of purpose: "She was no whit thereby discouraged, / From prosecuting of her first intent, / But forward with bold steps into the next roome went" (3.11.50). Britomart does not here enjoy increased psychological complexity or a broadened perspective; rather, she become more fixed in purpose, more like a personification acting out its inner daemon.

If this is a plausible reading of the prosopopoetic stakes of the episode, then what about the personification of love? After Cupid's triumphal procession he and his fellow masquers disappear into the inner room, vanishing from the scene, and Spenser then tells us that "Bold Britomart" was "Neither of idle shewes, nor of false charmes aghast" (3.12.29). Do not these details suggest that the power of Cupid is an illusion that true lovers must see through? We can find some help in answering this question by appealing to the tradition of Cupidic triumph and capture that partly informs Spenser's portrayal of the love god in this episode, particularly Petrarch's *Trionfi* and Googe's *Cupido Captured*, which I briefly mentioned earlier. Like Spenser, both Petrarch and Googe imagine Cupid in opposition to a figure of chastity, Laura in the *Tronfi*, Diana in *Cupido*. Both poets supply their avatars of chastity with personified minions—Honor, Modesty, Prudence, Continence, Labor, and Abstinence, among others, whom Petrarch calls *"alme"*—and Googe additionally puts his Cupid in the company of Idleness, Excess, Gluttony, and Fancy.[69] Also like Spenser, they portray Cupid as an enslaving tyrant leading a procession in triumph: Petrarch describes him as a "cruel youth / With bow in hand and arrows at his side," who has overcome "mortals beyond count: / Some of them were but captive, some were slain," while Googe's Cupid travels in a chariot and "for triumph leads / A thousand wounded hearts / That gush abroad hot streams of blood / new pieced with his darts."[70] Spenser appears to follow his predecessors regarding his Cupid's cruelty, his place among personifications, and his antagonism to a Chastity figure.

The crucial difference, however, lies in the outcome of the battle and the fate of the love god. In Petrarch and Googe, the forces of chastity capture Cupid and deprive him of his power. The "Triumph of Chastity" has him bound in chains and his weapons despoiled: "For they had broken all the shafts of Love / And torn away the quiver from his side, / And they had plucked the feathers from his wings."[71] Googe's Cupid, his army defeated, calls to his mother for help and tries to run away.[72] Once captured by Diana's general Hippolytus, Cupid abjectly begs for mercy "with trembling voice."[73] These Cupids are not only defeated by Chastity but also humiliated.

Furthermore, the two poets conceive of Love and Chastity as occupying fundamentally different spaces. Laura leads her defeated Cupid from the valley of love to "the fane of Chastity," while Diana's minions prevent Cupid from entering the sacred space of her "gorgeous castle."[74] Now, this is not to say that either Petrarch or Googe thinks that chastity simply does away with erotic desire. Laura's victory in the *Trionfi* is followed by her defeat by Death, who is defeated by Fame, followed by Time, and then Eternity, in a process that simultaneously involves progression and revision.[75] Googe's narrator was himself wounded by Cupid before the story began. After the love god is captured, he wakes up from his dream and then passes a sleepless night, "tormented thus / with fond lamenting sprite,"[76] suggesting that the point of Diana's victory has not quite taken hold in his own desire-wounded heart. Neither of these poets believes that the problem of desire simply vanishes when opposed by chastity.

Yet we can acknowledge these complexities and still affirm the vast difference between the fate of Cupid in the *Trionfi* and *Cupido* and his fate in book 3 of *The Faerie Queene*. Cupid is not defeated, captured, or despoiled by Britomart, who (unlike Laura and Diana) has already been wounded by the love god. Britomart captures only Busirane, who inflects Cupidic desire toward its most sadistic and destructive ends, as Spenser's Merlin inflects it toward dynastic ends. But such ends are both within the purview of Spenserian rapture. The shows and charms of Cupid's masque are indeed "idle" and "false" in that they take Eros to yield only suffering and joylessness, much as the god who originally pierced Britomart with an arrow was a "false archer" (3.2.26), and much as the seductive guises in the second room are characteristic of "false love" (3.12.51). Britomart's relation to Cupid is complicated because chastity is complicated. Insofar as chastity is distinguished from virginity, Cupid attends chaste desire. But insofar as chastity is distinguished from promiscuity, Cupid does indeed threaten chastity. Britomart cannot simply succumb to Eros, but neither can she simply reject it. According to the Platonic scheme, the Cupid driving the procession is, for all its tyranny, a version of the noble image of Cupid the ancient god in canto 3.

When Britomart liberates Amoret, then, she frees her from Busirane's prosopopoetic death mask, but not from rapture in general. At the end of the 1590 version of the episode, Spenser tells us that Amoret's body, "late the prison of sad paine," has now become "the sweet lodge of love and deare delight" (3.12.45). Here we have the fulfillment of the poet's hope, expressed at the beginning of the episode (3.11.1–2), to shift from jealousy to love. Yet this shift is not from compulsion to liberty, but rather to a new kind of daemonic possession, when Amoret and Scudamour embrace:

> But she faire Lady overcommen quight
> Of huge affection, did in pleasure melt,
> And in sweete ravishment pourd out her spright:
> No word they spake, nor earthly thing they felt,
> But like two senceles stocks in long embracement dwelt.
>
> (3.12.45)

It is tempting to read this passage as an ironic qualification of Britomart's rescue of Amoret. "Senceles stocks" reminds us of the constraining versions of personification elsewhere in the poem, and the "ravishment" of Amoret's "pourd out . . . spright" here uncomfortably recalls what Busirane tried to do when he presented Amoret "bleeding forth her fainting spright" (3.12.20).[77] Yet again the risk of such associations is the way of daemonic love. Once we give up the erroneous expectation that Spenser will associate love with freedom or choice, we can understand the alienation of "sweete ravishment" and "long embracement" as love's potential for virtue. Spenser elsewhere conceives of virtuous love in this manner: at the betrothal ceremony of Redcross and Una, the angel's voice—like a Platonic daemon—leaves the listener "ravished with rare impression in his sprite" (1.12.39).

No doubt, daemonic ravishment *does* pose a risk, and Britomart must be cautious in the way she identifies with the reunited couple, who in their embrace resemble "that faire Hermaphrodite" (3.12.46). Lauren Silberman has noted what is most distinctive about this classical reference: Spenser cites not Hermaphroditus but rather an (absent) *statue* of Hermaphroditus, "of white marble wrought" (3.12.46).[78] We have before us, then, a second daemonic statue. Spenser here pointedly replays Britomart's earlier encounter with Cupid's tyrannical image. She again confronts and responds to a potentially petrifying version of love, and again she maintains a distance ("*halfe*-envying their blesse") without rejecting the vision, "much empassiond in her gentle sprite" (12.46). To the degree that this vision inspires her to continue the search for her own love, it also reveals the degree to which Britomart, through an exertion of virtuous will, has reclaimed love from Busirane's sadistic and moribund representations. The reunited lovers, likened to a statue, still bear the trace of the tyrannous Cupid but do not simply recapitulate its tyranny. This is as much as Britomart can do for them, and Spenser suggests that, whatever her will's limitation, it amounts to a great deal.

The personification of love does sometimes yield compulsion, reducing what is lively and multifaceted to a single obsession. But not always: one character's compulsion can be another character's inspiration. Freedom is not the only condition of ethical action; for Spenser, it is not even a primary one. Love tyrannizes in order to enjoin a sustained sense of moral purpose over against a tendency to drift, ambiguate, and wander. In Britomart's case, this amounts to saying that she is not simply free from the allegory of love but that she has the potential to will it to ends other than the destructive ones preferred by Busirane. Britomart succeeds not because she manages to overcome her allegorical status and move toward authentic personhood but, on the contrary, because she is able to intensify her daemonic nature and become what she is: *chastity*, which for Spenser is always a bold engagement with desire.

"Sin." Detail from Caesar Ripa, *Iconologia, or Moral Emblems* (1603; repr., London, 1709), 59. Reproduced with permission of the Folger Shakespeare Library.

Chapter Six

SIN AND MILTON'S ANGEL

Sin is a central topic in Christian theology and moral psychology, but the personification of Sin appears more rarely in literary texts than we might expect. This is probably because the sheer broadness of the concept of sin limits its utility as prosopopoeia. Moral allegory tends to personify *kinds* of sin by which poets explore nuances of fallen behavior. Prudentius gives us Libido, Ira, Superbia, and Luxuria in the *Psychomachia*, but no character named Vitium. When Sin proper appears in a text or image, it is sometimes contrasted with the personification of Virtue, a contrast that intimates some of the general metaphysical qualities of evil, such as ignorance, deficiency, and weakness. In such cases, Sin's prosopopoetic function is fairly clear.

But in other cases the personification of Sin bears a more onerous burden, a burden that makes Sin a compelling example for this study about prosopopoeia and will. When Sin appears in a genealogy of personifications, rather than as one item in a dyad, it poses an awkward question: Who is the father, or mother, of Sin? If sinfulness begets various kinds of vices, what begat Sin? Commentators naturally turned to the Bible to address this question. The claim in 1 Timothy that "the love of money is the root of all evil" (KJV 6:10) formed the basis of any number of personification fictions about sin. Yet explaining the causal relation between money and evil was not necessarily easy. For example, Thomas Lupton's 1578 play,

All for Money, imagines a prosopopoetic genealogy in which Money vomits up Pleasure, who vomits up Sin, who vomits up Damnation.[1] Simple enough: taking pleasure in money is a sin, and leads to damnation. But the genealogy becomes confused when Lupton has Satan come on stage to ask his "friend" Sin to help him populate his kingdom, since the devil is "without company in Hell."[2] Sin surprisingly refuses to help, and Satan orders his own sons, Pride and Gluttony, to coerce Sin to obey, even though these Satan-spawns call Sin their "Lord and Master" and concede Sin's angry rebuke that "I am thy chief head and thou art of me a member."[3]

In other words, detailing Sin's prosopopoetic genealogy can quickly run into complications. Why in Lupton's play is Sin only a friend to Satan and not a relative? Do Pride and Gluttony derive from Satan, as his sons, or from Sin, their chief? Are they older or younger than Sin? A similar question of seniority arises in the epistle of James, which, denying that our wicked inclinations come from God, appeals to the genealogical impetus of personification to give an account of Sin's origin: "Then when lust hath conceived, it bringeth forth sin, and sin, when it is finished, bringeth forth death" (James 1:15). At first glance, this is clear enough: temptation seduces us into committing evil, which prevents our salvation. Yet sin's conceptual broadness keeps reasserting the question of origin: if lust is a *kind* of sin, then lust is giving birth to the general condition that must precede it.

James's statement forms the scriptural basis of John Milton's well-known allegorical account, in book 2 of *Paradise Lost*, of Sin emerging out of Satan's head as he conspires against heaven's king. Seeing her, Satan is smitten with lust and impregnates her with a child named Death, who himself eventually rapes his mother. Milton derives Sin's cephalic birth from the myth of Zeus and Athena, but he gets her snaky form from a variety of literary sources. Spenser's serpentine female in book 1 of *The Faerie Queene* is named Errour, the first opponent whom the Redcross Knight encounters, and if she is not Sin itself, she is a close approximation. Phineas Fletcher provides no less than two snaky Sin personifications, in *The Purple Island* and *The Locusts*. Although less directly based on James's genealogy than the Sin in *Paradise Lost*, these other Sins share with the Miltonic one a preoccupation with harmful birth and generation. After Spenser's Errour has been decapitated, her numerous young feed upon her corpse until, swollen with blood, they themselves burst apart. Fletcher's Sin and Harmartia, once born, both dream of murdering their mother Eve. Milton's Sin, impregnated by her son Death, gives birth to hell hounds that rip her loins apart.[4]

Although the Genesis serpent may seem the obvious common source for these serpentine Sins, the association between snakes and self-destructive birth comes from natural history. Herodotus in his *Histories* reports that female vipers, immediately after impregnation, viciously bite off the head of their male partner, who enjoys postmortem vengeance in that the baby serpents chew their way out from their mother's womb, killing her as they emerge.[5] This story was affirmed by dozens of commentators, including natural historians like Pliny, theologians like St. Basil, and poets like du Bartas.[6] These writers tend to emphasize the providential nature of this serpentine self-destruction, treating it as nature's example of divine justice. Here we have what seems like a perfect illustration of James's genealogy of evil: lust, followed by sin, followed by death. No doubt Spenser, Fletcher, and Milton, in producing Sin personifications modeled on the tradition deriving from Herodotus's serpent, found the moral convenient to their purposes: sin ends up harming itself, or ends up harming the one that brings it into the world.

There are, however, different ways of using personification to demonstrate this moral, some of which put pressure on the genealogical question of origin and some of which do not. Spenser's depiction of Errour, for example, scarcely even seems to broach the issue of where sin comes from. The episode instead focuses on the self-defeating quality of evil, and perhaps on Redcross Knight's involvement with that quality. And we know as little about what act of will the knight performed to merit this involvement as we do about Errour's parents. Redcross has not deliberately chosen to do anything evil; rather, he has wandered into error (via the Wandering Woods) and must suffer the consequences for the rest of the legend of Holiness. For Spenser, the ultimate origin of evil is not an act of free will. Instead, he locates this origin in figures of metaphysical absence, such as his personification of Night (*Faerie Queene* 1.5), who has ruled her dark underworld, it seems, from the beginning of time.

Milton does not think about evil in this manner, and in whatever ways we should believe that Spenser is Milton's original, this is not one of them. Milton holds that sin is a product of a distinct act of will and that the will's freedom guarantees an agent's moral responsibility. For him, only a careful consideration of what the rebel angel literally did in heaven (the first sin) will shed light on the nature of sin. Yet this chapter will argue that Milton recognizes that a literal account of the first sin can go only so far before it runs into trouble. As a result, Milton hedges his bets by introducing a personification allegory in order to intimate the radical freedom he has in mind for moral agents. By way of an introduction to the perplexities of Milton's poem, then, I would like to consider for a moment another prosopopoetic writer who dwells on the genesis of sin.

Prudentius turns to the story of the viper's matricidal brood in order to personify Sin, not in the *Psychomachia*, but in his *Hamartigenia*, a treatise on the origin of evil. The viper, Prudentius writes, "becomes a mother by her own death" and so offers the perfect analogy for how evil is born in human beings:[7] "Just so does our soul conceive. In the same way it imbibes the baneful fluid poured into it from the serpent's mouth, mating with the son of Belial . . . in the same way it burns with the gall of desire and is filled with sins by its union with a spouse that is doomed to perish. . . . Again, cruel wounds tear the soul too in a thousand labor-pains, as she gives birth to her unnatural progeny, to wit a multitude of sins, children that have fed on their mother's corpse" (608–20). Unlike Spenser, Prudentius provides the serpent's sin-children with a father, Satan, by which we might understand sin's origin. However, Prudentius also limits this genealogy's capacity to determine the presence of sin. Satan is in an obvious sense the father of evil, offering his seed to our soul. Yet that soul is already a willing participant, its lustful nature curiously preceding the birth of sin. (This is the same difficulty we encountered with James's genealogy.) And the sins themselves come into the world by murdering their own mother, "a family of orphans at their very birth" (606), as Prudentius puts it. This is not genealogy so much as antigenealogy, a refusal to explain sin as a natural consequence of sinful ancestors.

Indeed, despite its title, Prudentius's *Hamartigenia* is very cautious about using *genos* to explain the existence of sin in any definite way. This is because genealogy risks succumbing to what Prudentius ominously calls "that seductive argument" (637), which holds that the chain of causation—the sinful act comes from the sinful soul, which comes from the sinful devil—eventually leads up to the divine source that created the chain in the first place. God becomes the origin of evil. The seductive argument created no end of trouble for early Christian writers, who tried to combat it with a notion of moral freedom produced by the power of the human will. This power of will ideally breaks the genealogical chain that leads from sin to God. Prudentius calls it the "strength of liberty" (*vim libertatis*), a "power" (*potestas*) over the "unfettered judgment of the free will" (*laxae soluto / iure voluntatis*) (673, 675–77).

We discussed in chapter 2 some of the ways in which this argument about free will emerged in late antiquity and developed during the Middle Ages; later in this chapter we will consider its continuation in the seventeenth century. What I want to stress for the moment is that this doctrine of moral freedom, for Prudentius, amounts to the philosophical corollary of the prosopopoetic viper of sin. We produce sin out of our own capacities and power, willingly coupling with the Satan-serpent to satisfy our lust, destroying him, and then suffering destruction ourselves at the hands, or teeth, of our sinful children. The genealogical chain does not expand so much as implode here, and the allegory will not even allow us to blame the Satan-serpent as a prior causal source of our sin.[8] Evil does not produce our wicked choices; rather, we produce evil by freely willing it into existence. Indeed, one commentator has recently argued that Prudentius assumes that physical "evil" (floods, earthquakes, sickness) is entirely the consequence of moral evils freely chosen by human beings.[9]

When Prudentius discusses the rebel angel elsewhere in the treatise, he likewise denies the possibility that it acquired its evil nature from its divine source. Although created good, this angel becomes corrupt "of his own will, because tainted Envy marked him and pricked him with her sore stings" (186–87; *sponte sua, dum decolor illum / inficit invida stimulisque instigat amaris*). Capitalizing "Envy" here is tendentious, I realize, but this is the moment in the exposition when the cracks begin to appear. The angel chose corruption through the power of his own will, but he made this choice because *invidia* prompted him to do so. On the one hand, this is a turn of phrase, a poetic way of saying that the angel chose to feel envy. On the other hand, it addresses the perplexing question of *why* the angel felt envy in the first place. Surely not because of an evil tendency built into his nature. But then from where did this stinging envy come? I submit that the author of the *Psychomachia* would understand the rhetorical utility, in this case, of reading the feeling of envy as the prosopopoetic agent Envy.

Prudentius immediately tries to manage this confusion about origin, significantly, by employing the serpent personification that he elsewhere uses to discuss the birth of human sin. Once pricked by envy (or Envy), this angel undergoes an abrupt and rapid transition from sinless to sinful. He feels the "spark of hate," and this hatred "suddenly [*subitus*] kindled" hostility (188–89): "A beast hitherto without spot, for upright wisdom then kept his long, young body straight, he suddenly [*ecce*] begins with sinuous breast to gather himself in strange twinings, twisting his bright belly in intricate coils. His darting tongue, single before, has now the trick of diverse speech, and being divided in guile, utters three-forked words. From him is the original fountainhead of sin, from its beginning in him sprang the source of evil" (197–204). The buck stops with the rebel angel. Prudentius emphasizes the suddenness of the transition in order to avoid the impression of a causal chain leading from the angel's corruption up to the angel's creation. Nothing causes the angel's act of sin; his fall is a radical break between before and after. Yet this effort to manage the sudden presence of sin also raises familiar chicken-and-egg questions. Why did the angel come to personify sin? Because he chose to rebel. Why did he choose to rebel? Because he was devious and serpent-like. This amounts to asking:

Is the prosopopoetic serpent the cause or effect of sin? We could pose the same question about Prudentius's personification of human evil: Does the lust felt by the viper amount to sin, or does sin appear only when her matricidal brood emerges?

Whatever they owe to Prudentius, Spenser's and Fletcher's Sin personifications show little interest in balancing a reliance on causal origin with a commitment to moral freedom. Yet Milton, although no allegorist, is profoundly interested in this balancing act. This is why, of the many places in which one could begin a meditation about the personification of sin, this chapter has begun with Prudentius. *Paradise Lost*, seeking simultaneously to explain sin's origin and to affirm the freedom by which we choose sin, is the direct poetic heir of the *Hamartigenia* and the philosophical debate in which it participates. Like Prudentius, Milton recognizes that any coherent account of sin's origin in Christian cosmology must confront the archangel's puzzling choice to rebel in heaven. Indeed, it is fair to say that, in book 5 of *Paradise Lost*, the angel makes the most puzzling choice in the history of literature. Like Prudentius, Milton recognizes that the poet seeking to reconcile this choice with a doctrine of moral freedom will eventually find himself making use of the prosopopoetic pregnant serpent.

MILTON'S ANGEL

When does Milton's Satan first choose to rebel in heaven? We first meet him in hell, of course, when *Paradise Lost* opens, and it is not until Raphael's flashback in book 5 that Milton dramatizes the initial emergence of angelic rebellion. In this earliest chronological view of him in the poem (5.658), he is not yet called Satan, and having just witnessed the Father's exaltation of the Son, he is "fraught / With envy against the Son of God" (5.661–62). "Fraught with envy": this does not sound good. Prudentius's difficulty becomes Milton's. Does feeling envy count as rebellion; has he already fallen? At first glance, it seems unlikely that an unfallen angel would experience wicked feelings in heaven, where no provocations to evil exist. Making the angel[10] already fallen before we see him would allow Milton to avoid the awkward representation of a superintelligent creature inexplicably believing he could defeat God in battle.[11] If the angel has made his evil choice before Raphael's narrative begins, then we can read the episode as a celebration of the loyal angels, such as Abdiel, who can serve as heuristic models for Adam, Eve, and Milton's readers.

Milton would have been prudent to arrange his poem in this way. His contemporaries regularly expressed their bewilderment about why an angel, a divinely rational being, untouched by original sin, in the manifest presence of God in heaven, freely chose to rebel against his maker. The fall of Lucifer was even more mysterious than the fall of Adam and Eve, since Eve at least had the tempting serpent, and Adam had Eve.[12] Richard Baker's series of incredulous questions typifies Renaissance accounts of the war in heaven: "But how could Lucifer fall, that had such stays to hold him up? . . . But how could Lucifer fall, that was an Angel? . . . Lucifer, why wouldst thou fall, when thou mightst have stood?" Likewise, the angelic chorus in Hugo Grotius's *Adamus Exul* (1601) asks the fallen Lucifer, "Why would you, rushing to your own destruction, refuse to submit to the Creator of things; why, when so high a status had already befallen you, would you vainly aim for higher things?" Thomas Heywood, trying to imagine the circumstances of angelic rebellion, wonders of the angels why, "if they were / In Time before Time was, and with sincere / Faith and Obedience had so long abode, / They only *then* revolted from their God?"[13]

These expressions of puzzlement hint at the extent to which the question of *when* the angel chose to rebel is bound up with the question of *why* he rebelled. What event or sequence of events prompted his disobedience? Stella Revard has surveyed pre- and early modern theological and literary explanations, which point variously to the creation of humans, the promise of the Son's incarnation, or (Milton's preference) the exaltation of the Son.[14] Yet nearly all of these commentators recognize that further explanation is required, since these precipitating events did not prompt all the angels to rebel, only a third of them. What moral deficiency made

Lucifer susceptible? The most popular answer was pride. Heywood describes Lucifer "swelling . . . with pride and envy," and Baker wonders "how could such pride enter into the mind of Lucifer?"[15]—as if "pride" itself entered into Lucifer or that he himself was pride's embodiment. Milton's Raphael mentions envy in his account but also states that the rebel angel "could not bear / Through pride that sight" (*PL* 5.664–65) of the Son's exaltation, and the narrator notes at the opening of the poem that the rebel angel's "pride / Had cast him out from heaven" (1.36–37). Pride carries a considerable burden in these passages, serving as the motivating force behind Lucifer's otherwise puzzling choice.

Baker, Heywood, and Milton probably derive pride as an explanation of angelic sin directly or indirectly from a source coeval with the *Hamartigenia*, Augustine's *City of God*, which contains one of the earliest and most influential Christian responses to this perplexing issue. Yet the chapters devoted to Lucifer's fall supplied less of an "explanation" than has often been claimed, since Augustine himself clearly states that pride describes, but did not cause, the rebel angels' evil choice.[16] For him, as for Prudentius, the language of causation can never succeed in accounting for free will: "Nothing causes an evil will, since it is the evil will itself [*ipsa*] which causes the evil act."[17] Strictly speaking, volition "itself" has effects but never causes. Certainly, in his later polemic with the Pelagians Augustine would emphasize the deleterious influence of original sin and wicked habit on the otherwise free will, but these involuntary dispositions postdated, and were irrelevant to, Lucifer's choice to rebel in heaven.

For Augustine, then, pride cannot be a daemonic presence possessing Lucifer from the outside. To explain pride in this manner would oblige us to conclude, in Manichaean fashion, that "the Devil has evil as the essential principle of his being."[18] Free will thus prevents Lucifer from devolving from a responsible moral agent into what—in literary terms—we think of as a personification (such as Pride), which is indeed essentially evil and thus fails to meet Augustine's free-will criterion for moral responsibility. Anne Ferry, in her influential study of *Paradise Lost*, made much the same point about

Lucifer's agency five decades ago: "We cannot reduce the fallen Archangel as we are first made to see him to an abstraction—Pride or Wrath or Despair or even Evil—because we . . . must feel that his actions did in fact transform our own history."[19] The assumption here—an apt one—is that personifications cannot operate as historical agents, insofar as Renaissance readers understand historical personages as literal, not figurative. Personifications function as agents in fiction, but in history they can be understood only as signs. Yet although this view sanitizes the rebel angel of prosopopoetic essentialism, allowing him alternate possibilities of choice, the motivation for what he *does* choose (sin) remains elusive. Thus the options facing Milton seem undesirable: either to represent the angel's choice as free but incomprehensible or to explain it as a prosopopoetic expression of Pride, which nullifies moral responsibility. All of this militates, again, in favor of the view that Milton, a free-will advocate himself, has the rebel angel's moment of choice predate the earliest chronological moment of *Paradise Lost*. When did Lucifer fall? Don't ask, don't tell.

This arrangement makes such good sense that it is curious that so many elements in the episode specifically, and in the poem generally, contradict it. For one, Milton seems to go out of his way to have Raphael insist that the envious angel is called Satan *now*, at the time of Raphael's speaking to Adam, but *not* when he first felt envious in heaven (5.657–58). A fallen angel ought to have a fallen name, one would think. Then there is the unusual nature of Milton's heaven, which gives evil desires considerable range before they incur divine wrath. Angels thought bad thoughts well before the uprising, and perhaps even before the exaltation of the Son: Mammon coveted the gold pavement "even in heaven" (1.680), and Satan—according to Gabriel—secretly dreamed of supplanting God even as he hypocritically worshipped him (4.957–61). Milton describes these wicked habits of thought with language that makes them sound like ongoing activities in heaven. We could speculate that Milton wished to present a scenario in which lots of fallen angels inhabited heaven long before the rebellion, but this arrangement oddly severs the link between fallen behavior and God's response to such behavior. It seems less bizarre to assume that unfallen angels can experience unvirtuous feelings and remain unfallen, provided they do not act on them. The angel's initial envy, then, does not necessarily constitute evidence of his fallen nature.

There is also the related problem of the involuntary nature of feelings like envy. We can imagine accusing someone of willfully persisting in the feeling of envy after enough time has passed for her to get control over herself. But we are much less likely to describe the first sting of envious feeling as an act of deliberate will. This is why Prudentius describes *invidia* marking and pricking an initially passive-seeming angel. Milton creates a similar effect by characterizing his angel as "fraught" with envious feeling. Envy has come upon him and weighs him down; he has not chosen it. His moral agency will come into play—so we might expect—only when he chooses how to respond to this feeling of envy. It is worth recalling that Prudentius's angel slips into snake form only *after* Envy pricks him.

Certainly, in another poem we could overlook this matter and say that envious people get what they deserve, but we cannot say this in *Paradise Lost*. "Freely we serve," Raphael tells Adam, "Because we freely love as in our will / To love or not: in this we stand or fall" (5.538–40).[20] The sustained feeling of love, which in Spenser derives from an overwhelming rapture, in Milton results from an ongoing act of free will. This means that in Milton's heaven the angels do not serve out of habit or nature but rather actively choose to stand or fall.[21] The possibility of such ongoing insecurity in heaven nauseated Augustine, who insisted that after the expulsion of the rebel angels it would be "intolerable to suppose that the holy angels are now uncertain of their bliss, and that they themselves are left in ignorance about their future."[22] What Augustine finds intolerable Milton sees as the guarantee of angelic virtue. An involuntary inclination, in this view, cannot count as a choice, and sin (*anomia*, lawbreaking)[23] emerges only through choice. "Evil into the mind of god or man / May come and go, so unapproved, and leave / No spot or blame behind" (5.117–19), as Adam assures Eve. *Paradise Lost* is a poem in which the metrical caesura in the line describing Eve's hand

"Forth reaching to the fruit, // she plucked, she eat" (9.781) maintains the threshold between intention and choice—"all was lost" (9.784) only *after* Eve chose. The envious angel hasn't crossed this threshold yet.

If the angel is not yet Satan when we first see him, then the episode bears the burden of dramatizing his fall. To appreciate the narrative challenge that the commitment to free choice places on Milton, it is worth digressing for a moment to consider another seventeenth-century account of the war in heaven. We do not know if Milton had read the work of the Dutch dramatist Joost van den Vondel, but in any case Vondel's *Lucifer* (1654) offers an illuminating set of similarities and contrasts. Like Milton, Vondel has no interest in treating Lucifer as an allegory of Pride or Evil, making him instead a quite verisimilar character.[24] Yet, unlike Milton, Vondel provides several compelling reasons for angelic discontent: Adam and Eve get to have sex whereas the angels do not (14), it is rumored that "man threatens to displace us" (15), and Gabriel announces that humankind will be "preferred to Angels even" (16), with the angels taking on extra guard duty to protect the humans. By the time Lucifer complains, in act 2, that man "usurps our birthright for his own" (20), he is simply adding to previous angelic commentary. The other angels in fact actively try to persuade him to lead the insurrection, and his decision to rebel appears to derive in part from the exhortations of his fellows. These narrative details suggest the degree to which Vondel seeks to make angelic sin psychologically and literally intelligible, even if it means jettisoning the pretense of superintelligent angels who would intuitively understand the futility of opposing God.

Yet Vondel weaves into the fabric of narrative plausibility a series of dramatic choices made by Lucifer. The story line does not push the archangel off the cliff—he must jump off it himself, and the loyal angels remind him of this fact. In act 4, just prior to the battle, when the vacillating Lucifer laments, "No good being sorry now.... It is too late," Vondel is careful to have Raphael reply, "There is! I'll mediate; I warrant you that mercy shall be found" (55). Lucifer in fact actively *chooses* to rebel repeatedly in the play: at the end of act 2, when he resolves to "hoist my Throne to Heaven's highest place" (25); at the end of act 4, when, after prolonged and anguished indecision, he gives the order to attack: "I give it. . . . follow me!" (56); and even after the battle, in act 5, when the victorious Michael, standing over the supine Lucifer, offers one more chance to repent (62). Lucifer again chooses to fight on, and is finally cast into hell, his physical countenance changed from angelic to monstrous. Until this final moment, Lucifer's "choices" may seem curiously to lack definitive consequences,[25] but Vondel's apparent intention is to create an effect of dramatic and lengthy process. The archangel is confronted with a narrative circumstance, deliberates, and chooses a path, which leads him to a new circumstance, requiring deliberation, a new choice, and so on—each time coming closer to the point of no return. This narrative structure preserves the impression of Lucifer's free agency while making his evil decision psychologically comprehensible.

Returning to Milton, we might conclude that he likewise opts to describe the angel's transformation as a slow process, perhaps beginning with the feeling of envy and culminating at some later point, such as the start of the angelic war in book 6. Milton does provide hints throughout Raphael's narrative that the envious angel is gradually moving toward rebellion before he openly broaches the subject with his followers (5.772ff.). He "resolved / With all his legions to dislodge and leave / Unworshipped, unobeyed, the throne supreme" at lines 5.668–70, and a bit later God scornfully notes that "a foe / Is rising who intends t'erect his throne / Equal to ours throughout the spacious north" (5.724–26), with "foe" punning on the Hebrew meaning of Satan's name. Later, Raphael refers to the discontented angel as "Satan" twice before the end of book 5 (743 and 756); and he reminds the angel of his peril by saying that "pardon may be found in time besought" (848). Such moments in the episode create an (admittedly perilous) space of ethical suspension between intention and choice: the point of no return looms somewhere ahead, presumably getting closer and closer. John Leonard nicely captures this gradual sense of volition when he suggests that Milton handles the rebel angel's transformation from unfallen to fallen "smoothly and unobtrusively. We cannot see the change happen before our eyes, but we can, with Raphael, say that it has taken place."[26]

Yet comparison with Vondel also helps us see what Milton does not do: he provides no series of distinct choices that actively cooperate with the downhill narrative incline from Lucifer to Satan. Vondel's angel repeatedly makes choices that, if not individually definitive, nonetheless dramatize the exertion of a powerful will. In Milton's version, by contrast, we see no distinct moments in which the angel decides to rebel. Indeed, in this episode we have oddly little access to his interior thought, compared to the open and fascinating window into Satan's mental life that the poem provides elsewhere. Milton in fact makes it hard even to say what the angel's intentions are. Do his *resolution* (5.668) to march north and his ambiguous midnight communications to his lieutenant about "new counsels" (5.681) definitively indicate that he plans to rebel in the future? God does later ridicule the angel's *intention* to erect a rival throne (5.724–26), but Milton never lets the angel himself express this intention. Even when Raphael mentions that the rebel angel renames his palace as the "Mountain of Congregation" (5.766)—essentially a public declaration of war—Raphael curiously defers the precise moment of renaming: "not long after" (762) the host reaches the north. Likewise, Abdiel's later offer of "pardon" could mean either that the angel has not yet definitively chosen (since he could still take it back and gain forgiveness) or that he already has (since only criminals need pardons).[27] Even the angel's "haughty" (5.852) response to Abdiel's warning does not seem like deliberate choice but rather indicates a mind already made up, predetermined by the earlier series of events and inclinations. These ambiguous signals make it hard to say at any given moment in the episode whether the angel has already fallen or is still planning to do so in the future.

This absence of inner deliberation and distinct choice is surprising, since it risks giving the impression that the narrative sequence *determines* Milton's angel to rebel. The angel's initial involuntary envy, we might conclude, sets off a chain of mental and narrative events that lead almost irresistibly to sin. Again, some poems, such as *The Faerie Queene*, depend precisely on this ambiguity between intention and choice, but not *Paradise Lost*. Milton carefully separates out Eve and Adam's dramatic deliberation (9.744–79 and 896–916) from their subsequent choice to "freely taste" (9.988). Why is the narrative in heaven so different? One reason that Milton declines to give his angel a *series* of choices, as did Vondel, may be that for him a moral choice counts as such if it has definitive and clear consequences. Adam, Eve, Samson, and the Lady in *Comus* do not make multiple moral choices that follow a gradual process—they each make one choice, one that counts for everything.[28] This follows from the manner in which Milton refuses to see gradual degrees of error but rather, as Gordon Teskey has described, "forces the concept to either side of a distinction between evil and good."[29] We should perhaps therefore expect that the movement from Lucifer to Satan will involve, for Milton, crossing a definite threshold, rather than, as for Vondel, following a gradual degeneration. The problem with the "smoothly and unobtrusively" interpretation of the episode, despite its power to explain the angel's decision in terms of his envy, is that it diffuses the distinct moment of choice into an obscure narrative sequence.

If we return to Raphael's narrative flashback with this notion of a single, crucial choice in mind, can we locate a precise moment of decision? Not a decision to rebel, perhaps, but this raises a prior question: What counts as sin in heaven? Augustine, the Scholastics, and Calvin—despite important differences—all agree that Lucifer sought to end his dependence on his maker. If sin in heaven amounts to claiming autonomy from God, then we can locate it in the rebel angel's reply to Abdiel:

> We know no time when we were not as now;
> Know none before us, self-begot, self-raised
> By our own quickening power, when fatal course
> Had circled his full orb, the birth mature
> Of this our native Heaven, ethereal sons.
>
> (5.860–64)

The rebel angel asserts his self-creation, and saying it presumably counts as choosing it. Here we have, perhaps, the moment of sin, the threshold at which the angel-who-will-be-Satan becomes Satan.

As partial confirmation, we might note that immediately after this speech Abdiel stops debating with the angel, telling him that "I see thy fall / Determined" (5.878–79)—which we could plausibly read as "You have just determined your own fall."

Milton also emphasizes the perceived freedom of the angel's assertion by declining to include prior events or statements that appear to lead up to it. That is, we hear about the rebel angel's envy, pride, and sense of displacement, but nothing that specifically prepares us for his claim of autogenesis. When Abdiel argues that the Son created the angels (5.835–40) we no doubt expect the rebel angel to dispute this, but Milton has him take the *additional* step of asserting self-creation. Along these lines, Philip J. Gallagher sees the freedom of this sinful claim to lie precisely in its disconnection from temporal or narrative contexts. For him, no relation exists between the rebel angel's earlier cognitive activity and his eventual choice— or, at least, no relation that matters. Gallagher wants to justify Milton's representation by making the will radically free from prior cognition: "Volition does not *deliberate* in *time*; it *chooses* in a *moment*."[30] Choice, in this view, eschews impinging circumstance, and Gallagher will not even allow the angel's initial envy to be more than a "distant occasion" for his later execution of will.[31]

Such an account secures the Miltonic ethic of choice and identifies a precise threshold between unfallen and fallen. Yet the radically free and distinct nature of the angel's choice brings us back to an earlier question: *Why* does the angel choose to sin? Emphatic volitional freedom appears to come at the cost of narrative intelligibility. Outside of narrative, it may be possible to think of choices as freestanding, instantaneous events, in the way that Gallagher describes. But within narrative, events impinge on one another, encouraging us to understand an action in terms of those that precede it. To say, then, that in *Paradise Lost* the rebel angel's choice is an absolute threshold between unfallen and fallen, untouched by earlier circumstances, obliges us to impose an unsustainable neutrality on Raphael's narrative. It obliges us, among other things, to treat as curiously insignificant all the signals that earlier hinted at the angel's degenerating moral status—his identification as "Satan," God's pun on "foe," and so on—details that draw the moment of choice back into the entangling narrative process. Even the seemingly simultaneous options facing the angel—to deny or affirm his creaturely status—possess an almost irresistible temporal aspect, since an option's legibility must partly depend on its link to past events. The angel's initial envious disinclination to acknowledge the authority of the Son makes it possible for us to understand what is at stake when he chooses to assert his self-creation. To unyoke the involuntary envy from the later voluntary announcement risks turning deliberate choice into an inexplicable, arbitrary whim. One commentator, although in the process of defending the cogency of Miltonic free will, significantly calls the angel's choice "bizarre."[32]

To recap, we have at least three ways of interpreting Milton's presentation of the rebel angel in Raphael's narration: (1) he has already fallen before the episode begins; (2) he gradually becomes fallen over the course of the episode; (3) he suddenly chooses to fall during the argument with Abdiel. All three of these views avoid reducing moral agency to allegory, or a mere "principle of evil," as Augustine puts it. Yet each interpretation involves a significant drawback. The first risks erasing the distinction between fallen and unfallen in heaven; the second makes the transition from fallen to unfallen seem determined, not chosen; and the third makes the moment of free choice seem arbitrary rather than deliberate. To make sense of the angel's character in the episode we must choose one of these interpretations, yet the episode itself, it seems to me, provides no definitive evidence allowing us confidently to select one over the other two.

Sin in Narrative: Freedom and Intelligibility

Some readers may object at this point that I am making up problems in order to have something to solve. When the rebel angel's movement from unfallen to fallen appears gradual, I complain about determinism, and when it appears sudden, I complain about arbitrariness. Yet these complaints do not arise from any perceived deficiency

in Milton's art or theodicy, and I do not plan to solve any of the
problems I have mentioned.[33] Instead, I offer them as evidence of
the audacity of Milton's undertaking in book 5. Nearly every literary account of angelic rebellion before *Paradise Lost* made Lucifer's
sinful choice comprehensible either by turning him into an allegory
of Evil or by turning him into the equivalent of a human sinner,
fraught with moral frailties we can all recognize. Milton, by contrast, sought to keep his rebel angel both verisimilar and superhu-
man, boldly balancing an ethos of free agency with a narrative scenario (the bliss of heaven) that would appear to make evil choice
highly unlikely.

This is to say that Milton places all his cards on the table: he realizes that to make the final case for sin as freely chosen he needs
to cancel out external influence. Eve's tempting serpent, Samson's
pleading wife, Cain's preferred brother, Judas's thirty pieces of
silver—all such outside prompts explain wicked choice but also
threaten to limit its freedom. True, God does announce the new
authority of the Son (*PL* 5.603–8) and raise the possibility of dis-
sent (5.611–15), but Milton (unlike Vondel) offers no sense of why
an unfallen angelic being might possibly take this event as an occasion to feel discontent. Indeed, Milton suggests the oddness of
this response by mentioning the envy of only a single angel and no
others. In doing this, Milton refuses to deny the inherent strangeness of the Lucifer legend when it is juxtaposed with an ethic of
free will. This strangeness is, finally, one of the signature qualities
of Miltonic free will.

Why is free will strange, and why is it especially strange in narrative? Let us address the first question before the second, and let
us try to get some help from the philosophers. The place to start, in
this case, is the dispute between John Bramhall and Thomas Hobbes,
Milton's contemporaries, a dispute that began as a private argument
in the Parisian home of the Duke of Newcastle in 1645 and blos-
somed into a public pamphlet exchange between 1654 and 1658.
Hobbes and Bramhall enact the first "modern" debate about free
will in European letters. In their debate, the idea of free will is not
a means to explain the relation between human action and divine

providence; instead, divine providence serves as an example (among many others) to illuminate what it means to say that the human will is free or determined. Milton critics have considered this debate before, but I want to revisit it in the hope of isolating the dimension of the exchange that most closely affects Milton's narrative representation of the archangel's choice, namely, the question of whether the freedom of an action is compatible with its intelligibility.

Since Hobbes's argument for necessity is less intuitive than Bramhall's for freedom, let us try to avoid ascribing claims to him that he does not make. Hobbes does not argue, for example, that humans have no freedom. Rather, he argues that their freedom is compatible with determinism. In Hobbes's formulation, "a 'freeman' is he that in those things which by his strength and wit he is able to do is not hindered to do what he has a will to."[34] We lose our freedom only when something prevents us from doing what we want to do. Otherwise, we are free to do what we want, but not to will what we want. Our wants, preferences, and inclinations derive from a chain of causation that we cannot simply alter by will. I choose to buy the green car because I prefer green, but I didn't choose to prefer green.

Bramhall thinks this view of freedom is merely a dodge. Even absent external coercion, if natural determinism renders all human actions and choices necessary, then there is no true human freedom. To accede to Hobbes's thesis, he insists, negates human moral responsibility and ascribes the origin of evil to God, the first link in the determinist's chain.[35] This was Prudentius's concern, as we saw earlier. Yet Bramhall realizes, in a way that Prudentius does not, that denying acts of will any cause whatsoever risks making them random. Hence, he posits that an act of will (*volitio*) derives from the faculty of willing (*voluntas*). Willing thus "causes" an act of will, in a sense, but willing itself is an ongoing power within us, not an event itself caused by external sources.[36] Neither determinism nor random chance makes the will do what it does: *we*, vis-à-vis our power of willing, have control over our will, and this arrangement allows us to act as agents. Bramhall gives us, essentially, Prudentius's *vis libertatis* and *voluntas laxa*, but updated with the late medieval notion of the will as an independent faculty.

Hobbes, for his part, objects that Bramhall secures the freedom of the will at the cost of its intelligibility. To say that *voluntas* produces *volitio* leaves unexplained what causes *voluntas* to behave as it does. The problem of randomness appears simply to recur at the next level of explanation. Indeed, Hobbes thinks that we need the idea of causation to make sense of events and actions as "happenings" in the first place. If an event lacks a cause, then it lacks a beginning and must be understood as always happening, which amounts to never happening.[37] Causation provides shape and intelligibility to events, which otherwise devolve into random flux. But human action is not random, which means that it operates according to cause and effect, which means that it is subject to necessity.

Not so, responds Bramhall: Hobbes is confusing the idea of causation with the idea of necessity. The faculty of will avoids randomness by consulting reasons produced by the faculty of understanding. Yet although the will consults these reasons it is never determined by them: the will enjoys independence from the advising faculty of understanding. Like the late medieval theologians he follows, Bramhall promotes the will to the position of chief ruler of the soul, "the lady and mistress of human action," while the understanding serves merely as "her trusty counselor."[38] Again, the upshot of this arrangement, in Bramhall's view, is that no concatenation of cause and effect necessarily leads to an act of will: "The agent may determine itself otherwise, the event may come otherwise to pass, even until the last moment before production."[39] Even until the *last* moment: this is the drama of choice that animates Milton's Eve as her hand slowly reaches for the fruit.

Hobbes accepts none of this. Bramhall, he complains, argues by mere stipulation: reasons are somehow cause enough to secure the will against randomness but not cause enough to determine the will. Hobbes counters that insofar as causation is concerned there is no difference between the deliberations of the understanding and the promptings of appetite.[40] A cause is a cause. Likewise, it is merely a trick of language to posit distinctions among the agent, an autonomous faculty of will, and individual acts of will.[41] No matter at what level of remove Bramhall tries to locate human self-determination, the question of intelligibility will recur: "And if a man determine himself, the question will still remain: what determined him to determine himself in that manner?"[42]

What emerges in the debate between Bramhall and Hobbes is a question about what counts as a choice. Bramhall thinks that a choice without alternate possibilities amounts to mere animal motion. Hobbes thinks that a choice undetermined by causation amounts to a random hiccup. The descendants of Hobbes and Bramhall are known in modern philosophy as compatibilists and libertarians. Compatibilists assert refined versions of Hobbes's claim that freedom is compatible with determinism, and they likewise charge their libertarian opponents with asserting the freedom of the will at the cost of its intelligibility. Libertarian philosophers have sought to deny the link between determinism and intelligibility by appealing to neo-Kantian versions of agent causation, special theories of intentionality, and notions of indeterminate causation.[43] They also insist that determinism cancels out alternate possibilities, which negates moral responsibility.[44]

The modern debate about free will travels in directions far beyond the terms set out by Hobbes and Bramhall, but it is fair to say that the central problematic remains the tension between freedom and intelligibility. What I've discussed thus far suffices to make a start in responding to the question of why free will is strange, at least in terms of a philosophical tradition that was familiar to Milton. Now I want to turn to the question of why free will is especially strange in narrative. Setting aside the question, then, of whether the action of real human beings is determined or not, we can note that compatibilism has the advantage when we are considering narrative action. The inherently temporal nature of narrative obliges it to represent deliberation as one thought after another after another, creating the impression that thoughts impinge on one another and so at least minimally determine each other.[45] Kant argued in his first two Critiques that moral rational agency enjoys a freedom from ordinary causation, but that argument cannot help here: in narrative, the interior chain of thoughts is always liable to resemble the exterior chain of events.[46] This observation represents, in fact, the narrative version of Hobbes's philosophical claim that deliberative reasons exert causation on the will as much as do bodily appetites and external influences.

Compatibilists tend to be narrative thinkers. Daniel Dennett, for example, considers the example of Martin Luther's assertion, in breaking with the Church of Rome, that "I cannot do otherwise." For Dennett, this claim of necessity represents the most deliberate form of moral choice because it follows from a series of prior deliberations, habits, and resolutions on Luther's part. We must place his statement in its narrative context to appreciate it as a responsible act of volition.[47] Libertarians, by contrast, tend to be antinarrative thinkers. Robert Kane deems it a fatal mistake to think of human choice as occurring within a completed story; instead, he offers the analogy of a heroine facing a crisis "in the middle of a novel," whose character is "is not yet developed . . . in sufficient detail to say exactly how she will react." Kane insists that, as choosing agents, we never have a "fully formed" narrative character.[48] Free will here depends on denying narrative's ability to predict the outcome of a choice, a refusal of the finished story.

Perhaps Kane is right: real life is never a finished story, because life is not a story. But literary stories are finished, so we can most coherently account for the *narrative* representation of deliberate choice in terms of compatibilism. The compatibilist perspective, as derived from Hobbes, offers a compromise: our will enjoys freedom from compulsion but not from causation. We can do what we want, but we cannot will what we want. In this respect, compatibilism accepts a sort of middle ground between freedom and determinism required by narrative.[49] It recognizes that the narrative element (deliberation) that creates the effect of free agency also circumscribes this effect. Deliberation may be the minimum condition for the impression of narrative freedom, but this freedom does not simply increase as deliberation increases: deliberation also entangles the will. As a result, a character's choice can appear both intelligible and free (or free enough).

By contrast, applying a libertarian perspective to narrative would involve refusing this middle ground, making choice either radically undetermined (free) or deeply determined (compelled).[50] Either the moment of choice breaks free of the determining elements of narrative (volition becomes a detached product), or narrative leads up to and swallows the eventual choice (volition becomes a diffuse, determined process). In the final section of this essay I will suggest that this dichotomous model has important implications for the behavior of personifications, but for the moment let us note how peculiar the libertarian view would make choice in literal, verisimilar narrative. Either characters would be the absolute slaves of the story in which they appear, or their choices would make that story seem almost irrelevant. Yet most literary characters in fact appear to exercise volition in a *combination* of their personal agency and narrative circumstances. Anna Karenina chooses to have an affair with Vronski through her free will, but also because of the count's charisma, her husband's coldness, the stultifying society of St. Petersburg, and so on. Tolstoy's novel gives us the impression that she *can* voluntarily decide either to accept or resist Vronski's advances, but we also feel that narrative circumstances push her one way or another. She is free enough, but not too free.

Scholars who examine free will in *Paradise Lost* nearly always do so under the aegis of studying the poem's theodicy, and these examinations sometimes employ the philosophical categories of compatibilism and libertarianism. Two of the very best, Dennis Danielson and Stephen M. Fallon, consider the debate between Thomas Hobbes and John Bramhall, noting, surely correctly, that Milton's sympathies would have been with the libertarian Bramhall.[51] Yet whatever his theological commitments to absolute moral freedom, Milton the consummate narrativist saw at least this much: a choice too detached from the narrative chain of events risks obscurity, whereas a choice too diffused along this chain risks evaporation. Here we find the structural limits of narrative agency, and theodicean approaches to free will in *Paradise Lost* have underestimated these limits. Danielson, in the strongest (and most interesting) version of his libertarian interpretation, insists that Milton would rather leave choice unintelligible than risk its freedom: "There is finally no answer to the question *why*."[52] This is a bold recognition

of the problem of choice, though a narrative that actually allowed
for so radical a disjunction between choice and story would seem to
approach the realm of the absurd, on the order of Albert Camus's
L'étranger.

Indeed, I wish to argue that, despite his distaste for Hobbesian mechanics, Milton recognized—as an inevitable feature of
narrative—a form of determinism akin to that described by modern compatibilism, and that he placed it in tension with his libertarian commitment to free moral choice. Both views receive airtime
in *Paradise Lost*. When emphasizing the unfettered quality of the
will, Milton (like Bramhall) often associates will with power. Satan,
acknowledging to himself that he could have resisted his feelings of
ambition in heaven, concedes that he possessed "free will and power
to stand" (4.66). Raphael likewise explains to Adam that God "left
it in thy power, ordained thy will / By nature free, not over-ruled
by fate" (5.526–27). These passages insist on the potential power of
the will to overcome external influence or internal inclination that
would otherwise push it in a given direction—the libertarian will
breaks free of its constraints.

Yet when emphasizing the deliberate quality of the will, Milton
usually couples it with the idea of reason. God adduces humankind's "will and reason (reason also is choice)" (3.108); Raphael
warns Adam to "take heed lest passion sway / Thy judgment to do
aught, which else free will / Would not admit" (8.635–37). Critics
have tended to misunderstand the equation between reason and
choice in these passages, assuming that reason simply makes the will
free per se.[53] Yet reason or judgment, in the process of enabling
moral choice (by apprehending the existence of options beyond
mere passion or instinct), in fact *guides* the will to choose rightly,
ideally *limiting* its freedom to select evil. To say that the "free will /
Would not admit" certain passionate inclinations so long as "judgment" functions properly amounts to saying that judgment does
more than merely provide neutral data for the will to consider;
rather, the deliberative process of reason directs the will—prompts
it and pushes it. Thus Milton has God describe the rebel angels as
those "who reason for their law refuse" (6.41). Reason's law is in

fact philosophical compatibilism, ideally determining the will to (voluntarily) choose the good.[54]

And it's not only the notion of reason that implies the compatibilist view of determinism in the narrative. Consider the language of *caution* and *mindfulness* that peppers the poem's discourse about the possibility that Adam and Eve might succumb to temptation. God asks Raphael to warn Adam "to beware / He swerve not too secure" (5.237–38), and Adam assures the angel that "we never shall forget to love / Our maker, and obey him" (5.550–51). Adam later urges Eve to admonish her faculty of reason: "But bid her well beware and still erect / Lest by some fair appearing good surprised / She dictate false and misinform the will / To do what God expressly hath forbid" (9.353–56). When Eve begins speaking to the serpent, the narrator calls her "unwary" (9.614), and after the Edenic couple have transgressed the poet points out that "still they knew and ought t' have remembered / The high injunction not to taste that fruit" (10.12–13). These passages amount to a consistent piece of advice: remember to be careful.

Milton critics have sometimes sought to interpret this language of mindful caution in terms of the poem's insistence on free choice, but it is actually rather hard to do so coherently.[55] We find nothing remarkable in saying that people ought not to forget or be careless about their obligations. If they do forget, we fault them for doing so. But it is very odd to say in such a case that someone *chooses* to forget, or *chooses* to be careless. Forgetfulness and carelessness are things we let happen to us without full consciousness of doing so, not things we decide to do. These faults seem involuntary, yet we hold people responsible for them. And by placing this language of carelessness throughout his poem, Milton provides a way to understand Adam and Eve's choice to transgress. Again, a narrative negotiation between choice and circumstance seems in operation. We certainly don't have the impression that carelessness *compels* Eve to eat the fruit: she wants to eat it. But we do assume that carelessness *impinges* on her choice: she eats the fruit as a result of faulty deliberations and an incautious trust in what the serpent said. To claim this does not amount to a philosophical statement about determinism; it is simply the way we make sense of narrative action.

I've argued that Milton exhibits a quiet tolerance for the Hobbesian-compatibilist position to a degree unappreciated by most critics, and my argument hinges on Milton's recognition of certain structural constraints built into narrative form. But what about the archangel's choice to rebel in heaven—does Milton employ a compatibilist middle ground in this episode? He could have arranged things as Vondel does. He could have created an angel possessed with all the virtues and foibles of human beings—resentment, doubt, pride, sympathy, et cetera—and included impinging circumstances, such as peer pressure and new duties. Readers would locate the cause of the choice to rebel in the angel's circumstances and his character and would probably not worry much about how the angel got that character. The angel's choice would seem free but also intelligible.

But, as we have seen, Milton doesn't do this. He declines to turn his angel into a flawed tragic hero, as Vondel does, and he does not turn him into a daemonic personification, as Prudentius does. Nothing happens in the episode that might plausibly prompt the angel to begin considering rebellion: no serpent pressures him to revolt, no figure of Envy pricks him from the outside. Milton supplies nothing but the angel and his envy, along with the awkward question of where he got his envy from. Milton in this episode eschews the compatibilist compromise between free agency and causal circumstance that operates elsewhere in his poem. Compatibilism seeks to make free will less strange, showing how the will works by placing it in a series of causes. But Milton keeps the angel's choice strange, which is to say he tries to keep it radically free. The buck stops with the angel, who can't pass it on to his maker. Yet radical freedom keeps threatening to slip into narrative coercion. There's no middle ground: either the narrative compels the angel toward rebellion, or the angel's choice to rebel is divorced from any narrative or deliberative circumstances that might allow us to understand it as a choice.

This strangeness is the cost of avoiding "that seductive argument" which Prudentius detested. Milton doesn't hide this strangeness, awkward though it is. If anything, he emphasizes it by presenting the angel's story in a narrative flashback. If we think in terms of plot chronology, then we first see the angel before any narrative has a chance to intelligibly predict his choices: he is a radical version of Robert Kane's unformed character in a perpetually unfinished novel. This is why Milton gives the angel no name: no legible agency yet exists in him. On the other hand, if we think in terms of *récit*, then the narrative has long since named this angel Satan, making his prideful choices in heaven seem determined by his prideful, completed character. Significantly, the statement by Abdiel that we earlier took as the affirmation of the rebel angel's free choice—"I see thy fall / Determined" (5.878–79)—can also be read, because of its passive construction, as an indication of compulsion. This ambiguity results from Milton's insistence on literal agency in a heavenly narrative, with alternate possibilities fully intact, his refusal to turn the rebel angel into a mere "principle of evil."

Milton's Sin

Yet Milton had already come close to doing this earlier in the poem. We should see Raphael's narrative in book 5 as Milton's *second* try at representing the angelic will to sin. In it, Milton registers the necessity of accounting for the literal, mental process of transgression, even in a context (heaven) that deprives him of the usual narrative props that motivate sinful volition. His first try occurs in book 2, in Satan's encounter with the allegorical personifications Sin and Death at the Hell Gate. Milton clearly aligns these two episodes, having Sin's account of her sudden birth from Satan—"Out of thy head I sprung" (2.758)—anticipate Satan's claim of autonomy as a "birth mature" (5.862) in book 5. Yet whereas Raphael's literal narrative yields an uneasy oscillation between libertarian freedom and narrative coercion, the allegorical episode in book 2 represents volition in a much more radical relationship to narrative, one that simultaneously subjects and releases the will. In doing this, Milton avails himself of the curious effects of prosopopoetic agency.

I discussed in chapter 1 the degree to which personifications simultaneously appear deeply compelled and radically free. The character Vanity cannot do otherwise but behave vainly, but on the other hand nothing can stop her from choosing this behavior. She is her own master, free from the ordinary constraints of narrative circumstance. If this latter dimension of allegorical agency—the volitional realization of conceptual essence—constitutes a kind of agency, it is a kind quite different from the *deliberate* freedom we associate with literal characters. The point, then, is not that personifications are really just as free as other characters. Rather, personifications can make us notice the compromise that literal characters make with narrative determinism, because personifications eschew this compromise. Literal characters express their free will in a compatibilist manner, interacting with and reflecting on narrative circumstances that make manifest their options but also impinge upon their choices. They live in narratives that require a negotiation between the involuntary and the voluntary, allowing for the potential of the former to influence the latter.

Personification allegory, however, radically disentangles the voluntary and involuntary, placing them on either side of an uncrossable threshold. Personifications almost never undergo a process of cognition when choosing. Their mental activity of choice is usually represented as happening all at once—in what we can describe equally as a sudden volitional discharge or as an involuntary daemonic compulsion. To return to Prudentius's serpentine angel of primordial sin: the *free* will kicks itself free of cognitive process in the way that the Sinful serpent kicks itself free of the impinging goodness of heaven and chooses evil. Conversely, the free *will* derives from a cognitive and narrative process in the way that the sting of Envy inexorably inclines the Sinful serpent to choose evil. No compatibilist middle ground can mediate these two extremes.

The divided agency of personification sheds considerable light on Milton's use of the allegorical character of Sin. Most commentators conclude that this figure represents a kind of ontological diminishment, the consequence of choosing evil.[56] Yet Milton carefully links Sin, as I have already noted, with the precise moment of the rebel angel's choice to claim self-creation in heaven. She is *simultaneous* with this act of will, not a consequence of it. Her appearance reinscribes that literal act of deliberative agency in terms of a division between determinism and radical freedom. Milton does this in anticipation of the problem of sinful choice in book 5, which threatens to diffuse the moment of choice along the entangling process of narrative. We can better appreciate the care with which Milton sets up this reinscription if we compare his account with that of one of his primary sources, Phineas Fletcher's *The Locusts* (1627).

Both poets place Lucifer and Sin within a conceptual genealogy, where one term begets another, which begets another. Yet Fletcher associates his allegorical Sin with Adam and Eve's fall rather than with Lucifer's, shifting the emphasis from agentive origin to consequence. That is, he pushes Sin down the causal chain rather than up toward etiology, making her the *effect* of a prior choice. As with Milton, we come across Sin at the Hell Gate:

> A shapeless shape, a foul deformed thing,
> Nor nothing, nor a substance: as those thin
> And empty forms, which through the air fling
> Their wandering shapes, at length they're fastened in
> The Crystal sight. It serves, yet reigns as King:
> It lives, yet's death: it pleases, full of pain:
> Monster! ah who, who can thy being feign?
> Thou shapeless shape, live death, pain pleasing, servile reign.
>
> Of that first woman, and th'old serpent bred,
> By lust and custom nursed; whom when her mother
> Saw so deformed, how fain would she have fled
> Her birth, her self? But she her dame would smother,
> And all her brood. . . .[57]

Sin's determination to harm Eve's future "brood" (fallen humankind) suggests that Sin herself has begotten the allegorical figures we meet a few stanzas later: Sickness, Languor, Grief, and Pangs (1.15–16). The evil choices of fallen humankind are to some degree already determined by this genealogy of misery. Yet the allegorical chain moves not only downward but also upward, enveloping and transforming its historical (literal) origin, Eve. Fletcher describes Eve's transgression as a symbolic sexual coupling with Satan ("th'old

serpent"), so the "lust" that nurses Sin attaches itself to Eve, as if
Sin resulted not from Eve's free will but rather from her lustful essence.[58] Eve's literal agency tacitly transforms into allegorical essence, something like Feminine Lust.

So far the allegory behaves as conventional accounts of personification would lead us to expect, rewriting deliberative agency
as daemonic energy, making choices seem like bursts of volition.
Yet when we move past Eve, further up the genealogical chain to its
origin, Lucifer, we encounter a scenario that splits agency between
choice and compulsion. Fletcher's angel, "swollen with pride, but
more with rage, and hate" (1.18.4), is as much personification as
literal character when we meet him in council a few stanzas later.
Indeed, "swollen" aptly exemplifies "daemonic possession" under
which allegorical personifications operate. Yet Lucifer's essentialist
will to evil differs from that of Sin or Eve because no prior allegorical
genealogy can determine it: Lucifer's evil agency in heaven precedes
all others. This agentive anteriority causes Fletcher's description of
Lucifer's fall to vacillate between freedom and constraint:

> Thus fell this Prince of darkness, once a bright
> And glorious star: he willfully turned away
> His borrowed globe from that eternal light:
> Himself he sought, so lost himself: his ray
> Vanish't to smoke, his morning sunk in night,
> And never more shall see the springing day.
>
> (1.20.1–6)

The passage makes clear the angel's volition—"he willfully turned
away"—overcoming any circumstantial or mental context for his
choice: Lucifer simply wills, all on his own, to his own detriment.
Any attempt to explain rationally why Lucifer rebelled disappears
into paradox: "Himself he sought, so lost himself." On the other
hand, the poet has already made it perfectly clear why Lucifer transgressed: he was "swollen with Pride," and transgression is the kind
of thing Pride does, much as Sin sins because she's Sin. They don't
choose between options; instead, they will what they are. This is
why Fletcher makes "Prince of Darkness" the grammatical subject

of "fell"—an incorrect attribution, historically speaking, since the falling was the cause, not the effect, of the darkness. Yet the error represents an apt instance of the manner in which personification allegory confuses action with consequence. Thus, to the degree he is pulled into prosopopoeia, Fletcher's Lucifer is radically free *or* ontologically compelled; there is little deliberative or narrative room in between.

We can see some of the same dichotomous features in Milton's Sin. With Sin's birth from Satan, the will kicks itself free from any prior, entangling process of cognition. Sin carefully sets up the circumstances, describing Satan

> In heaven . . . at the assembly, and in sight
> Of all the seraphim with there combined
> In bold conspiracy against heaven's king. . . .
>
> (2.749–51)

The stage is richly set with details that we will see recapitulated in book 5, Satan's "bold conspiracy" here anticipating his "bold discourse" (5.803) in Raphael's telling. But how did he come to choose bold conspiracy? His envy? His resentment? A miscalculation of logic? As Sin explains, it just happened:

> All on a sudden miserable pain
> Surprised thee, dim thine eyes, and dizzy swum
> In darkness, while thy head flames thick and fast
> Threw forth, till on the left side opening wide,
> Likest to thee in shape and countenance bright,
> Then shining heavenly fair, a goddess armed
> Out of thy head I sprung. Amazement seized
> All the host of Heaven; back they recoiled afraid
> At first, and called me *Sin*, and for a sign
> Portentous held me. . . .
>
> (2.752–61)

Sin's sudden appearance replaces the psychological process of transgression with an instantaneous disclosure of daemonic energy, akin to Theresa Krier's account of the daemonic free movement across an interval. Satan chooses, all in a moment, free from the burden of explanatory contexts. Yet at the same time this act of willing so dislocates itself from any prior deliberation—emphasized by the language of "sudden," "surprised," and "amazement"—that choice here verges on trauma, and it is scarcely right to say that it is *Satan* who wills. Rather, volition happens to him, and he is daemonically possessed by sin, like Phineas Fletcher's Lucifer "swollen with pride." What book 5 presents as an ambiguous combination of causality and volition, book 2 presents as radically divided volition, free from narrative and yet subjected to essence.[59]

Yet Sin's association with the *first* wicked angelic choice also signals Milton's revision of Phineas Fletcher's Sin. That personification was a second-generation consequence of Lucifer's "willful" choice to sin, already interpolated by a genealogical chain. (Lucifer/Pride rebels, then Satan/Pride couples with Eve/Lust, who gives birth to Sin.) Milton's Sin, by contrast, emerges simultaneously with the rebel angel's choice. The poet intends her as an escape from time, eluding the diffusion of choice into narrative by using her as what we might call a *volitional radical*.[60] This escape does not so much stretch out the moment of choice—what Leslie Brisman describes as the "simultaneous ongoingness" of decision[61]—as it makes choice a singularity divorced from the contextualizing pressures of time itself. Vondel describes this aptly: "Time grants no respite," the anguished Lucifer says as he wavers between repentance and defiance, "and this instant now / Is no sufficiency of time, if one / May give the name of time to this brief moment / Between salvation and eternal doom."[62] Vondel's Lucifer compresses the instant of choice so tightly that it loses duration altogether.

Vondel (and Milton) recognize that this atemporal model will finally not work in narrative, since narrative makes choice meaningful by allowing the voluntary to interact with the involuntary over a period of time. Yet as a personification Sin does not exactly need to interact with the fictional elements in the narrative in order to acquire a meaningful identity, which she derives instead from an order of nonfictional ideas. Her meaning and being are identical the moment she emerges into the narrative. As a volitional radical, she isolates the rebel angel's choice from any deliberative or circumstantial process that would seek to determine it, and it is impossible to fix for certain her own temporal relation to this choice. Sin's appearance *causes* Satan's choice, as an agent herself ("a goddess armed"), and is also a *consequence* of the choice that Satan himself made ("a sign / Portentous").

Sin's double nature responds to the deliberate ambiguity of the narrative context that Milton supplies: "in bold conspiracy." At what point in a conspiracy does the *intention* to transgress become the *choice* to transgress? If we identify conspiracy with choice, Sin's appearance allegorically reflects what Satan has already willed. If we identify conspiracy with deliberation, Sin's appearance compels Satan finally to cross the volitional threshold from intention to choice.

Yet Sin remains an unusual personification, since after her fall from heaven Milton provides her with a psychological autonomy unexpected in an allegory. She appears to reflect on her decision to disobey God and open the gates of hell: "What owe I to his commands above / Who hates me . . . ?" (2.856–57). She also relates that, having just arrived in hell but before birthing Death, "Pensive here I sat / Alone" (2.777–78). What is she thinking about? Defeat? Revenge? Fear? Regret? For just a moment, Sin is psychologically abstracted from her conceptual being, like the "stupidly good" (9.465) Satan momentarily smitten with Eve's innocence.[63] Presenting Sin as a deliberating agent creates an odd effect: To what other choice could Sin's deliberations lead her except to sin? Why would Sin bother to deliberate at all?

These questions point to the manner in which Sin's reasoning process forces us to suspend temporarily our commonsense association of deliberation with freedom. In the case of the allegorical Sin, deliberation either *causes* her choice (her wicked thoughts ensure her wicked choice) or is *irrelevant* to her choice (even if she thought nice thoughts, Sin would still choose to sin). Sin's psychological depth amounts to a libertarian parody of the compatibilist compromise that deliberating characters, for the sake of intelligible choices, make with narrative determinism. At the moment of her birth, Sin circumvents this compromise by detaching the rebel angel's choice in heaven from any process that might explain it and so constrain it. This choice is supremely intelligible (the angel sins because he's sinful) and completely arbitrary (Sin happens to come upon the angel rather than Obedience).

This interpretation may seem to let Satan off the hook, marginalizing his "literal" agency and moral responsibility in heaven. Yet Milton intends Sin, not simply to represent Satan's evil status, but to expose the narrative limits of moral choice itself by pushing agency toward its two logical extremes. The allegorical interlude of book 2 thus seeks not so much to reaffirm the free-will theodicy of *Paradise Lost* as to reflect on the poem's narrative operations. (Consider, for example, how hopeless it would be to try to reconcile God's assertion that "Freely they stood who stood and fell who fell" [*PL* 3.102] with Sin's inclusion in "the general fall" [2.773] of the rebel angels from heaven into hell.) Certainly, when Sin and Death appear later in the poem, as God's "Hell-hounds" (10.630), they have been reabsorbed into the moral-punitive fabric of the poem's ethical cosmos. But in this initial episode Sin teaches us how to think about narrative agency, preparing us for the problematic mix of causality and freedom in heaven, and also for the gentler narrative determinism in Eden. The episode prompts us to recognize that, if in narrative Adam and Eve cannot be radically free (lest they become personifications), they are free enough for moral responsibility.

Milton thus uses personification allegory to intimate the limits of literal agency but also to guarantee a workable version of that agency, recognizing the risk of too absolute a demand for freedom in narrative. Victoria Kahn has written suggestively along these lines about the Sin and Death episode, which she sees as an effort "to negotiate between two allegorical extremes": "One in which everything is a function of the self, with the result that all experience is narcissistic; the other in which everything is a function of God and external circumstance, in which case experience—and education— are impossible. . . . If reading is to be possible, then the text must be conceived of as a thing indifferent in the precise sense that it offers an occasion for ethical deliberation."[64] This account of textual indifference, requiring a middle ground between narcissism and external causation, resonates with the compatibilist middle ground between arbitrary free choice and narrative compulsion. Kahn here admirably lays out the allegorical stakes of moral interpretation, in Milton's view, for both prelapsarian Adam and Eve and postlapsarian humanity.

Yet Kahn underestimates the special narrative circumstances to which Milton applies the Sin and Death episode, a narrative presenting the unique problem of angelic sin, which, unlike Eve's choice, is "Self-tempted, self-depraved" (*PL* 3.130). As we have discussed, heaven provides Satan with no indifferent tableau for neutral interpretation, so in representing the rebel angel's act of volition Milton is deprived of the usual narrative props that allow him to explain Edenic and postlapsarian choices. On the contrary: Milton's heaven, unlike his Eden, is exactly that narrative milieu in which interpretation risks evacuation into either pure narcissism or pure external determination. In this respect, it is significant that Milton chooses to represent Satan's transgression only in flashbacks told by characters in the poem, narratives overtly marked as *versions* of the event. No neutral telling can encompass the psychological impasse of the angelic will to sin. Either Milton must rely on a literal version (book 5) in which inexplicable involuntary circumstances such as "envy" threaten to overdetermine the free choice to transgress, or he must rely on an allegorical version (book 2) in which voluntary and involuntary are culled apart from one another in the most extreme fashion.

The allegory of Sin is Milton's concession, before he gives us the literal narrative in book 5, to John Calvin's judgment about the intricacies of angelic sin: "It were better, if not entirely to pass them in silence, at least only to touch lightly upon them."[65] Milton does touch upon them but uses allegory to isolate the contradictory pressures of causal circumstance and freestanding choice within any narrative of angelic transgression. As the *agent* of that transgression, Sin frees the will from narrative causality by rendering choice inexplicable. As the *sign* of that transgression, Sin entangles the will within the causation of allegorical genealogy, whereby her existence leads to Death and to the manifold, involuntary miseries that later pervert the will of postlapsarian humanity. This allegorical genealogy also stretches upward along the causal chain, enfolding Satan as its conceptual source. Milton anticipates this effect of allegorical genealogy as Satan flies toward his fateful encounter with Sin and Death, when, for the first time in the poem, he becomes the name he has. The narrator calls him "the *adversary* of God and man" (2.629), which is to say in Hebrew, *Satan*.

EPILOGUE

Premodern Personification and Posthumanism?

This book has told a story of the will through the literary device of personification, working from the assumption that no literary device is better designed to tell this story. The personification of Sin oscillates between its roles as the cause of the will and the sign of the will. The personification of Love traces the fine line separating voluntary self-surrender and compelled dispossession. Despair transmits spiritual hopelessness to others as an act of will and enacts it himself as an existential state unmanageable by the will. Conscience forces the sinner to come out of herself and formulate an exterior perspective on her sinful will. In each case, prosopopoeia extends and augments the actor's agency and also renders that agency partly independent of the actor.

Describing the relationship between personification and will in this manner obliges us to relinquish the rubric of the "person" as the touchstone for understanding premodern literary personification. Prior to the eighteenth century, personification did not produce a troubling confusion between humans and things, precisely because humans were still deeply imbricated with things. The premodern self had what this book has called a transactional relationship with its surroundings, making the distinction between human and nonhuman less urgent than it became in modernity. Laurie Shannon and others have demonstrated, for example, the degree to which the category of human in the Renaissance was not yet fully separated from the category of animal.[1] Furthermore, in obvious ways the medieval notion of the "chain of being" distinguished humans from nonhumans but made it impossible for humans to be fully separate from the animals, plants, and minerals that surrounded them.

Another way of putting this, for my purposes, is that the concept of the "person" did not yet underwrite the category of the human. When George Puttenham claims that poets use prosopopoeia when they "attribute any human quality, as reason or speech, to dumb creatures or insensible things, and do study (as one may say) to give them a human person," the "person" in this sentence retains a strong affiliation with *persona*, the mask through which an actor speaks.[2] Human beings do not constitute a fully separate category so much as they possess important, distinctive qualities, such as rationality and speech. (We find a similar arrangement, in fact, in Boethius's famous sixth-century definition of a person as "the individual substance of a rational nature": persons are individual and rational, but like nonpersons they are substances with a nature.)[3] When poets personify foxes, rivers, or the emotion of joy in a human figure, the crossing of a threshold certainly does occur—from nonrational to rational, voiceless to voiced, literal to figurative ("as one may say"). But this crossing is not, fundamentally, over a threshold between the inhuman and a special category of personhood.

Premodern literary personifications were not, then, uncanny or inchoate versions of persons; instead, as this book has argued, they were pieces of agency. Conscience, Despair, and Sin are psychic states residing within Philologus, Redcross Knight, and Satan, states that have transformed into actions external to these characters. The personifications extend the agency of these characters into the landscape, but the characters then have trouble managing the personifications, who in some cases seek to harm them. Yet such malfunctions do not result from a leakage between inside and outside, because this leakage is the condition of agency in the first place. In the premodern model, the goal is not to avoid being possessed by outside energies; rather, the goal is to be possessed by good energies instead of bad ones. Granted, by the late Renaissance a sealed barrier between mind and landscape was at least thinkable: Marlowe calls it despair, and Descartes calls it the ego—and in both cases this sealed self implies the absence of personification, as we have seen. Yet such formulations were rare, and prosopopoeia remained an intuitive representation of agency through most of the seventeenth century.

Since this account of personification rejects notions of the autonomous will and novelistic character as relevant criteria in the premodern milieu, to what degree is it congenial to or revived by recent critical projects such as ecocriticism, biopolitics, actor-network theory, or object-oriented ontology, all of which have been associated with the phenomenon of posthumanism? Do premodern prosopopoeia anticipate posthumanist agency? In several ways, they do. The "post-" in posthumanism tends to refer to the era following certain recent developments in modern society that oblige a revision of ordinary notions of identity or consciousness. For Donna Haraway and K. Katherine Hayles, the emergence of cybernetics and computer information technology collapses the distinction between human minds and thinking machines.[4] For Timothy Morton, the phenomenon of global warming forces upon us an awareness of vast "objects" (climates, planets, even processes such as evolution) intermeshed with one another: "What is called *subject* and what is called *mind* just are interobjective effects, emergent properties of relationships between enmeshed objects."[5] According to Sheryl N. Hamilton, as I mentioned in the Introduction, a wide-ranging set of legal and technological developments—corporate law, human cloning, celebrity commodification—has given rise to a host of what she calls "liminal beings": "Liminal beings are unnatural subjects. Sometimes they seem to straddle our categories—simultaneously object and subject, for example. Other times they reveal our categories for the constructed fictions that they are, exposing them as untenable at best, absurd at worst."[6] To the degree that such views conceive of human identity and agency as multisourced, hybrid, and in commerce with nonhuman presences, they do indeed recall the transactional behavior of premodern prosopopoetic agents.

This is perhaps why personification has played a significant role in posthumanist thinking and writing, which often sees the trope as openly flaunting the strict divide between human and nonhuman.

Hamilton suggests that cultural "technologies of personification," rather than turning liminal beings into persons, transforms them into *personae*: "Personae are lumpy, incomplete, and always simultaneously less and more than persons."[7] Ecocritics have also appealed to personification in order to contest anthropocentric assumptions about human superiority and uniqueness.[8] Actor-network theory argues that humans and nonhuman entities alike rely on prosopopoetic "figuration" in order to emerge as agents in the first place.[9] Indeed, Bruno Latour denies that free action requires the absence of interaction: "As to emancipation, it does not mean 'freed of bonds' but *well*-attached. . . . Freedom is getting out of bad bonds, not an absence of bondage."[10] There is not an uncrossable distance between this claim and some of the scenarios we have contemplated in this book: the Lover in conversation with Resistance, Fair Welcoming, and Friend; Philologus speaking with Spirit and Sensual Suggestion; Amoret surrounded by Cupid, Despite, Cruelty, and Britomart; Faustus listening to Mephistopheles and the Old Man; Satan's interactions with Sin and Death. Personification assumes that possession is inevitable; the relevant issue is what kind of possession one undergoes.

Indeed, "possession" becomes a kind of interpretive procedure in the work of Julian Yates, the critic who has perhaps most resourcefully used the trope of prosopopoeia to translate posthumanist thinking into Renaissance studies. Yates examines early modern objects that we ordinarily think of as the instruments of human beings, such as oranges and sheep, and treats them as quasi-agents that produce their own trajectories and stories. In studying objects in this way, Yates understands himself "to take up the rhetorical figure we call *prosopopeia*, the speaking thing of 'property,' the fetish, and inhabit it."[11] Inhabiting personification obliges us to extend agency to the nonhuman sphere: "What happens if we recast the *prosopopeia* that renders sheep talkative, preserving the non- or allohuman perspective it marshals?"[12] And, as in the accounts of personification we have noted in posthumanist writing, Yates suggests that prosopopoeia, by extending personhood to nonhumans, potentially ends up transforming us (the interpreters and readers) into hybrid persons/nonpersons: "Is it possible to engineer a reverse-*prosopopeia*, for example, and ask what it would entail to read as an orange?"[13] In this dispensation, the human agent or interpreter becomes a point within a network of actions and information, along with a whole host of nonhuman things—"all of us, just like Dolly [the cloned sheep], no more than various prosopopeias, or metaphorical agents engaged in acts of transport."[14]

Work such as Yates's has impressive potential to alter the way we think of ourselves as scholars in relation to what we understand as the early modern archive. It is worth noting, however, that Yates's primary interest is not in how early modern people experienced or read personifications but rather in how we post-Dolly modern interpreters might transform our sense of ourselves from "persons" studying "objects" to the fellow travelers of these objects. Yates imagines this altered understanding as both an epistemological and an ethical improvement, and in this he follows a central strain of posthumanist thinking. Posthumanists argue that personhood, the reputed guarantor of rights, dignity, and equality, in fact ends up excluding a host of potential participants. As Cary Wolfe has written, "The philosophical and theoretical frameworks used by humanism to make good on those commitments reproduce the very kind of normative subjectivity—a specific concept of the human—that grounds discrimination against nonhuman animals and the disabled in the first place."[15] To eschew this normative subjectivity, then, is a moral obligation. Likewise, Giorgio Agamben insists in his book *The Open: Man and Animal* that "it is more urgent . . . to ask in what way . . . has man been separated from non-man, and the animal from the human, than it is to take positions on the great issues, on so-called human rights and values."[16] This questioning of the divide between man and his others ends up, for Agamben, imposing a moral responsibility of astonishing scope: "the taking on of biological life *itself* as the supreme political (or rather impolitical) task."[17]

It is here that a difference in scale between premodern personification and posthumanist ethics becomes apparent. "Biological life itself" is not a human measure; instead, it is a geologic measure.

I confess that I am not sure what it would mean to be morally answerable for the category of biological life, since it is not in our power to influence the existence of life *as a category*, any more than it is in our power to preserve or extend the existence of a distant star. Perhaps we are morally responsible for that star; perhaps that is an implication of posthumanist thinking. But however one responds to this ethical imperative, the point at issue here is that premodern personification operates on an entirely different scale. In animating the landscape with affect, giving faces to abstract concepts, and conjuring the interior energies of the self to appear outside the self, literary prosopopoeia interprets the world according to human proportions—with "human" here in open commerce with the nonhuman. Personification in fact refuses an interpretation of the earth as ever entirely nonhuman or geologic. Instead, it renders the earth intimate to human beings, although intimacy in this case includes fear, discomfort, despair, and sin.

So the literary phenomena studied in this book do have an affiliation with posthumanist personae, but there is also a limit to that affiliation. Posthumanism assumes, to varying degrees, an autonomous selfhood in need of dismantling. The premodern self was, in profound and far-reaching ways, a transactional construct whose primary concern was not the anxious delineation of self from nonself. Personification, which confuses internal with external and cause with effect, did not dismantle this transactional self but rather reflected and affirmed it. The destabilizing role that modern personification may play in post-Renaissance conceptions of selfhood is certainly fascinating, but this was not the function or effect of premodern personification.

The Renaissance period saw the final configurations of this premodern self, and it was the last era before literary personification morphed from an expression of will to an imperfect approximation of the person. Since then, this imperfect person has been described as a clinical compulsive (Angus Fletcher), an uncanny ghost (Paul de Man), a figure of metaphysical violence (Gordon Teskey), a fanatically self-involved agent (Steven Knapp), and so on. It has also emerged, in posthumanist thinking, as a figure of remarkable utility and mobility, translating the person into a persona, reestablishing a lost affiliation with a range of nonhuman things. Yet in the Renaissance this affiliation was still more or less in place; it did not need to be reestablished. Literary personifications coordinate that agent's relation to the forces surrounding him or her in the landscape. These forces *are* human scale, not "biological life itself" or forces of a thousand millennia. But they are *not* human in the sense of excluding the nonhuman. They translate the landscape into chunks (some benevolent, some frightening, some ambiguous) that allow for interaction with the human agent. The energy of prosopopoeia derives from both the self and the nonself, but it always wears a face.

NOTES

Introduction

1. Saul, "On Treating Things as People."

2. Ashman and Winstanley, "For or against Corporate Identity?"

3. De Man, "Epistemology of Metaphor," 19.

4. Latour, *We Have Never Been Modern*, 136–45. For an extension of Latour's ideas into Renaissance studies, see Julian Yates, "What Are 'Things' Saying?"

5. Keenleyside, "Personification for the People," 466.

6. Hamilton, *Impersonations*, 222.

7. A paradigmatic, if extreme, account of modern personhood comes from Immanuel Kant, whose definition turns on the distinction between persons and things: "The fact that the human being can have an 'I' in his representations raises him infinitely above all other living beings on earth. Because of this he is a person . . . i.e., through rank and dignity entirely different from *things*, such as irrational animals, with which one can do as one likes"; see *Anthropology*, 15.

8. Knapp, *Personification and the Sublime*, 4. Knapp suggests that personifications' "radical self-absorption" makes them ideal embodiments of the Kantian sublime, whereas their conspicuous fictionality and improbability fulfill the Kantian requirement that the subject recognize the inaccessibility—for empirical actors—of this ideal agency.

9. "The aim of this book . . . has been to prove that literary personification is a code-specific *langue* that cannot impel, at the point of specific textual instantiation, the narrative of its own making without the narrative of its own unmaking"; see Paxson, *Poetics of Personification*, 165.

10. Lakoff and Turner, *More Than Cool Reason*, 72–80.

11. For examples of this popularity in dramatic literature, see Brown, *Persistence of Allegory*, esp. 125–37.

12. Dubos: "These allegorical personages ought not, methinks, to be principal actors themselves. Personages known to be imaginary entities,

and incapable of being actuated with passions like ours, can never interest us much in their adventures. The resemblance of truth cannot be too strictly observed in painting, no more than in poetry" (see *Critical Reflections*, esp. 1:154–55). Johnson: "But such airy beings are, for the most part, suffered only to do their natural office, and retire. Thus Fame tells a tale, and Victory hovers over a general, or perches on a standard; but Fame and Victory can do no more. To give them any real employment, or ascribe to them any material agency, is to make them allegorical no longer, but to shock the mind by ascribing effects to non-entity" ("Milton," in *Lives*, para. 256). Lord Kames: "The impression of real existence, essential to an epic poem, is inconsistent with that figurative existence which is essential to an allegory; and therefore no means can more effectively prevent the impression of reality, than to introduce allegorical beings co-operating with those whom we conceive to be really existing" (Home, *Elements of Criticism*, 2.394).

13. Some of the most influential nineteenth-century complaints about personification come from Samuel Coleridge, who accuses allegorical agents of alienating the senses, translating "abstract notions into a picture-language which is itself nothing but an abstraction from the objects of the senses" ("The Statesman's Manual," in *Collected Works*, 6:30). William Wordsworth explains that the poetry of the *Lyrical Ballads* will include little personification because he wishes "to adopt the very language of men; and assuredly such personifications do not make any natural or regular part of that language" ("Preface to the *Lyrical Ballads*," 250–51).

14. For a survey of eighteenth-century examples, see Sitter, *Cambridge Introduction*, 157–77. For a twentieth-century example, see Harris, *Mr. World*.

15. Lisa Freeman has written a study of literary character in eighteenth-century theater that argues that "in turning to 'character,' the stage registered a kind of resistance to and critique of the illusion of transparency and plenitude that the novel offered in 'the subject'" (*Character's Theater*, 8).

16. Blackwell, *Secret Life of Things*; C. Lupton, *Knowing Books*, esp. 47–69.

17. This is one of the implications, for example, of Knapp's *Personification and the Sublime*.

18. Spenser, *Faerie Queene* 3.10.59.

Chapter One   Personification, Energy, and Allegory

1. For histories of the Greek term *prosōpopoiia*, later Latinized as *prosopopoeia*, see Stafford, *Worshipping Virtues*, 3–10, and Paxson, *Poetics of Personification*, 8–29.

2. Demetrius, *On Style*, 265–66.

3. Quintilian, *Institutio oratoria* 9.2.1.

4. Ibid. 6.1.26.

5. Ibid. 9.2.36–37.

6. Fraunce, *Arcadian Rhetorike*, sig. G2r.

7. Alexander, "Prosopopoeia," 103.

8. Erasmus, *On Copia of Words*, 47, 50. This translation incorrectly transcribes the term of amplification as *energeia*; the correct term is found in Erasmus, *De copia verborum*, 202.

9. Puttenham, *Arte of English Poesie*, 246.

10. Both passages from Peacham, *Garden of Eloquence*, 136.

11. Ibid., 137.

12. Hoskyns, "Direccions for Speech," 163.

13. Luther, *Commentarie*, fol. 175v.

14. Tuckney, *Thanatoktasia*, 57.

15. Sidney, *Apology for Poetry*, 12.

16. Plato, *Symposium* 202e, in *Collected Dialogues*.

17. On the history of the relation between the daemon and Genius, see Nitzsche, *Genius Figure*, esp. 21–41.

18. Plutarch claims that daemons link the mortal and divine worlds and that these spirits attend to sacred rites and mysteries so that the gods themselves need not attend to every small appeal; see *Obsolescence of the Oracles*, esp. 417.13. Bernardus Silvestris, although using the term *angelus* rather than *daemon*, describes how these intermediate spirits "report the needs of man to God, and return the gifts of God's kindness to men, and so seek to show at once obedience to heaven and diligence in the cause of man"; see *Cosmographia*, 107. Ficino says that daemons, whom he also calls "angels," do friendly service to men, carrying the gifts of the planets (e.g., Jovian daemons bring power of governing, while Martian daemons give us greatness of soul) down to men on earth; see Ficino's *Commentary on Plato's "Symposium,"* 184–87.

19. According to Plato, as souls prepare for reincarnation they select a daemon who will lead them through their next life; see *Republic* 617d–

618b. Apuleius associates the daemon with our conscience and offers Socrates's praise of his invisible guiding spirit as a famous example of the guardian daemon; see *God of Socrates*, 195–216. For Plotinus, our guardian daemon resides just above us, in the intelligible realm, and seeks to guide our soul to virtue; see *Enneads* 3.4 ("On Our Allotted Guardian Spirit").

20. Euripides's tragedies feature daemons such as Necessity (in *Alkestis*), Ambition (in *The Phoenician Women*), and Madness (in *Herakles*) who threaten to possess and overwhelm the human protagonists of those plays. Yet the human agents are not always passive victims; sometimes their own dispositions summon the daemons. Just before Madness possesses Herakles, he is ripping off the head of the tyrant Lycus; see *Herakles*, in Euripides, *Complete Greek Tragedies*, 562–82. Porphyry understands daemons, both good and bad, to inhabit the material world, which for him provides a reason not to eat animal flesh: you might inadvertently consume the effluence of a daemon whose nature is uncongenial with yours (see *On Abstinence*, esp. 74–76). Leone Hebreo elaborates on Plato's claim that *Eros* is a daemon by detailing the manner in which this spirit comes upon lovers from outside and possesses them; see Hebreo, *Philosophy of Love*, esp. 153–56.

21. Cicero, *Nature of the Gods* 3.51–52.

22. Augustine, *City of God* 8.14–9.13.

23. Harington, *New Discourse*, 11–12.

24. Padel, *In and Out*.

25. Taylor, *Secular Age*, esp. 29–43.

26. Reiss, *Mirages of the Selfe*, esp. 93–97.

27. Paster, *Humoring the Body*. See also Paster, Rowe, and Floyd-Wilson, introduction to *Reading the Early Modern Passions*, 1–20.

28. Compare James Simpson's comments about the analytical focus of personification, which ends up exceeding the boundaries of a single individual: "Personification analyzes force, isolating as it does the powers that govern particular fields of action. . . . [Personification] concedes that the phenomenal world can be grasped only in conceptual terms, terms that recognize the presence and impersonal force of systems that drive individual action" ("Power of Impropriety," 149).

29. Aers, "*Piers Plowman*," 120.

30. Spenser, *Faerie Queene* 2.5.10.

31. Berlin, "Two Concepts of Liberty," 203.

32. Fisher, *Vehement Passions*.

33. For a survey of this association, see O'Reilly, *Studies in the Iconography*.

34. Guillaume de Lorris, *Romance of the Rose*.

35. Bunyan, *Pilgrim's Progress*, 36.

36. Bloomfield, "Grammatical Approach"; Paxson, "Queering 'Piers Plowman,'" 24; Newman, *God and the Goddesses*, 33–35.

37. Krier, "Daemonic Allegory."

38. For Krier's account of allegory and thinking, see "Psychic Deadness in Allegory."

39. Jefferson to John Quincy Adams, October 12, 1813, in *Papers of Thomas Jefferson*, 6:548–51.

40. Kant, *Critique of Judgment* 46.307, trans. Pluhar, 308.

41. Kant, *Groundwork* 4.428.

42. Simpson, "Power of Impropriety," 157n36. Simpson observes that "the literary form of certain medieval (and post-medieval) works is correlative with the form of the psyche whose integration is imagined in those works: as the soul comes to its own fullness, so too does the narrative end." See also Simpson's comments in *Sciences and the Self*, 272.

43. Quoted in Aquinas, *Summa theologica* 1.29.3.

44. Pfau, *Minding the Modern*, 80.

45. Spaemann: "With the concept of a person . . . we come to think of the particular individual as being more basic than its nature. This is not to suggest that these individuals have no nature, and start out by deciding for themselves what they are to be. What they do is assume a new relation to their nature; they freely endorse the laws of their being, or alternatively they rebel against them and 'deviate'"; see *Persons*, 33.

46. Pfau, *Minding the Modern*, 83.

47. Ibid., 182.

48. For an account of personification that associates it with catachresis rather than metaphor, see Nishimura, "Personification."

49. Sutcliffe, *Ful and Round Answer*, 26–27.

50. For example, this is a central theme in Murrin, *Veil of Allegory*. Likewise, James Simpson has observed that "prosopopoeia is, after all, an extremely explicit literary procedure, designed for the maximum degree of clarity, quite unlike allegory proper, which 'says one thing and means another'"; see *Sciences and the Self*, 58.

51. Robert Worth Frank Jr. argued some time ago about personification allegory that "only the action is allegoric, and often not that (or only in a most limited way). Characters are never allegoric. They are literal; they

mean what their names say they mean"; see "Art of Reading," 243. Likewise, Stephen Barney suggests that still images of personifications approach allegory only insofar as we imagine them as a snapshot of a moving narrative; see *Allegories of History*, 29. Thomas Maresca insists that "allegory has nothing to do with personification. Corollary: *The Pilgrim's Progress*, for example, is not an allegory. Corollary: an accurate theory of allegory cannot start accepting such texts as *The Pilgrim's Progress* as bona fide allegories"; see "Saying and Meaning," 257.

52. Jon Whitman argues that although one does not need personification to produce an allegory, personification remains "the most striking kind of compositional allegory"; see *Allegory*, 6. Maureen Quilligan has suggested that personification offers "one of the most trustworthy signs of allegory" because it illustrates so clearly the activity of wordplay that characterizes allegorical writing in general; see *Language of Allegory*, 42. Similarly, Isabel G. MacCaffrey has described allegory's tendency to turn adjectival characters (the shamefast man) into noun-characters (Shamefastness); see *Spenser's Allegory*, 84.

53. Borris, *Allegory and Epic*, 31.

54. J. Anderson, *Reading the Allegorical Intertext*, 189.

55. Goethe, *Maxims and Reflections*, 159.

56. Goodman, *Languages of Art*, 3–10. Subsequent page citations to this work are given parenthetically in the text.

57. On the possibility of both realist and nominalist personifications, see L. Griffiths, *Personification in "Piers Plowman,"* 41–46.

58. Dante, *Vita nuova*, 54, 22.

59. *Sign* is the term generally used in scholarship about literary and biblical allegory, and it captures Goodman's sense of the denotative label as both referential and arbitrary.

60. Prudentius, *Psychomachia*, lines 40–52. Many modern commentators have been surprised by the violence of Chastity's behavior. For a canvass of such views, see Van Dyke, *Fiction of Truth*, 32–34.

61. The converse condition also applies: just as allegorical signs cannot be self-contradictions, they cannot be tautologies. It is unclear what the Armor of Armored Protection signifies, in an allegorical sense.

62. Puttenham, *Arte of English Poesie*, 155.

63. Prudentius, *Psychomachia*, lines 109–10.

64. Ibid., lines 121–53.

65. Here I must part ways with Lavinia Griffiths (*Personification in "Piers Plowman"*), who repeatedly associates exemplification with the

impression of psychological and social resemblance between personifications and real people, a "gesturing to the world of common experience" (54), movement "from a metaphysical to a psychological sphere" (57), and "a different sort of psychological accuracy to that found in icon or emblem" (57).

66. Spenser, *Faerie Queene* 1.1.14–25; Bunyan, *Pilgrim's Progress*, 115–17.

67. Guillaume de Lorris, *Romance of the Rose*, lines 3317–40. Langland, *Piers Plowman* B:5.60–506, ed. Schmidt, 184–244.

68. Langland, *Piers Plowman* B:15, 15.15–40, ed. Schmidt, 570–72. Of this moment in the poem James Simpson comments, "Even as pure exposition one may have wished for a more systematic fit between this sequence of names and the preceding action of the poem from Passus 8" ("Power of Impropriety," 157).

69. V. Kahn, "Revising the History," 554.

70. Knapp, *Personification and the Sublime.*

71. Jewett, *"Fall of Robespierre,"* 434.

72. As Jacque Bos demonstrates, before the late seventeenth century the term *character* signified a *type* of person, not an individual. See "Individuality and Inwardness."

73. Fowler, *Literary Character.*

74. See, for example, Curran, *Character*, and the range of essays in Yachnin and Slights, *Shakespeare and Character.*

75. De Man, "Autobiography as De-facement."

76. J. Miller, *Versions of Pygmalion*; Garber, "Hamlet."

77. De Man, "Hypogram and Inscription," 48.

78. Ibid., 49, 49–50.

79. Riffaterre, "Prosopopeia," 108.

80. Ibid., 123.

81. Paxson, "Queering *Piers Plowman*," 21–29.

82. Peacham, *Garden of Eloquence*, 136.

83. Wofford, *Choice of Achilles*, 303. Subsequent page citations to this work are given parenthetically in the text.

84. Dolven, "Spenser's Sense," 139–40. Dolven's analysis is very subtle, and he carefully avoids an argument "that might simply equate allegory and punishment. One could say, after all, that allegory is about *thinking*—and that it is no more violent or punitive than extended analogy" (134).

85. Ibid., 138, my emphasis.

86. Raskolnikov, *Body against Soul*, 5, 14.

87. Ibid., 46–47.

88. Ibid., 54, my emphasis.

89. A. Fletcher (1930–2016), *Allegory*, 68. Subsequent page citations to this work are given parenthetically in the text. Fletcher recently reaffirmed this estimation: "The key to understanding how allegory works is to focus on its mode of agency, and here we find that from ancient times to the present, under various guises, the demonic—not necessarily bad—is the embodiment of primordial agency; the *daimons* of Greek myth have a unique power to act without impediment, obeying a system of absolute, single-minded, purified intention"; see his "Allegory without Ideas," 9.

90. The question of whether this appeal to common humanity is designed to mask social differences in class or sex falls outside the range of my inquiry here.

91. Theresa Krier is the critic who has seen this most clearly: Fletcher's view of personification "seems to imply that a character starts out by inviting us to think of her as a person with psychic complexity and temporality—as a subject—then turns out to be a reduced person"; see "Daemonic Allegory," 331.

92. E.g., Aristotle, *Poetics* 10.1452a.

93. E.g., "The most important of these things is the structure of events, because tragedy is mimesis not of persons but of action and life. . . . So it is not in order to provide mimesis of character that agents act; rather, their characters are included for the sake of their actions" (*Poetics* 6.1450a14–16, 20–21).

94. E.g.: "Since mimetic artists represent people in action, and the latter should be either elevated or base (for characters almost always align with just these types, as it is through vice and virtue that the characters of all men vary), they can represent people better than our normal level, worse than it, or much the same" (*Poetics* 2.1447b30–1448a5); and also: "Since, then, the structure of the finest tragedy should [represent] fearful and pitiable events . . . it is clear that neither should decent men be shown changing from prosperity to adversity, as this is . . . repugnant, nor the depraved changing from adversity to prosperity, because this is the least tragic of all" (8.1452b30–37).

95. "Character is that which reveals moral choice [*proairesis*]—that is, when otherwise unclear [from the action], what *kinds* of thing [*tis*] an agent chooses or rejects" (Aristotle, *Poetics* 6.1450b8–9, my emphasis).

96. Teskey, *Allegory and Violence*, 14–17. Subsequent page citations to this work are given parenthetically in the text.

97. "What excites interest in allegorical agents is their seeming to be built up out of the material remains of the past in a manner that violates the original state of those remains. There thus seems to be a struggle occurring inside such agents" (45); "The agents in the narrative of an actual allegorical work must draw what power of action they have from something that is below the threshold of what the imaginary order can acknowledge. Hence, the very power of a narrative figure to act, a power that is the unsuppressed remnant of allegory's negative other, surrounds the figures in the narrative with a nimbus that seems to rise like a mist from the ground" (55).

98. Teskey, "Death in an Allegory," 66 and 82–83.

99. Coleridge, *Collected Works*, 2:102. See Teskey, *Allegory and Violence*, 36, 44–45.

100. In allegory, local daemonic power "is incorporated in the system as a whole, as meaning, and is referred ultimately to a singularity that is outside the system. It is this constant referentiality of the numinous to a point outside the system that makes the work as a whole an interpretable text" (Teskey, *Allegory and Violence*, 39). "Only when we pass from the culture of the numen to the culture of the sign do we encounter appropriate conditions for allegorical expression. For under polytheism the relations among terms in any system of thought, as we saw in Hesiod, were determined genealogically rather than logically. . . . Under the logocentric conditions of medieval Christianity, by contrast, the removal of the divine to a transcendental location, outside the system, guaranteed the articulate coherence of all area and levels of thought" (50–51).

101. For a brief but dense review of some of the scholarly literature, see Whitman, *Allegory*, 269–72. Roger Hinks notes that daemons, unlike medieval personifications, were sometimes worshipped in the ancient world, but he also cautions that "the intrinsic difference between a daemon and an allegorical abstraction, great as it is, cannot easily be conveyed by externals; and the iconography of these personages does not always indicate clearly whether we are intended in any given case to think of the figure represented as a genuine mythical being or as a conscious personified abstraction" (*Myth and Allegory*, 111). E. H. Gombrich likewise suggests that "it is rarely possible [in ancient art and literature] to say at any particular point whether we are confronted with an abstraction or a divinity, not to say a demon" ("Personification," 249). Paxson accepts the difference between numinous agents and personification but concedes that "the distinc-

tions among gods, ghosts, genii, fantastic creatures, and personification characters were not always clear even to the principal theorists of classical, medieval, or Renaissance rhetoric" (*Poetics of Personification*, 7). Timothy Reiss is not sure, in certain cases, whether we should read daemons "as allegories of . . . a relation between human to universal logos" or as a literal "physicalizing of the passibility" that he thinks characterizes premodern conceptions of self (*Mirages of the Selfe*, 246).

102. Stafford, *Worshipping Virtues*, 2. See also the range of essays in Stafford and Herrin, *Personification in the Greek World*.

103. Newman, *God and the Goddesses*.

104. A classic study in this regard is Carlo Ginzberg's *Cheese and the Worms*.

105. L. Wager, *Life and Repentance*, sig. f3v.

106. Hebreo, *Philosophy of Love*, 119, my emphasis.

107. In this regard, see A. D. Nuttall's criticism of C. S. Lewis's sharp distinction between symbolism — supposedly rich and vivid with concrete detail — and allegorical personifications — supposedly abstract and vapid. He suggests, for example, that the distance between Dante the symbolist and Guillaume the allegorist is less than many commentators have allowed: "Dante did believe that there was a place of torment, just as Guillaume de Lorris believed that different forces really did contend in his lady's mind. But neither of these things could be described except by way of allegory" (*Two Concepts of Allegory*, 31).

108. Lewis, *Allegory of Love*, 52. Lewis makes this claim in the course of comparing the mythologically motivated deities of Virgil's *Aeneid* with the abstract functions filled by the deities of Statius's *Thebaid* (48–56).

Chapter Two   THE PROSOPOPOETIC WILL

1. Aristotle, *Physics* 8.5.256a8–11.

2. Ibid. 8.2.253a7–20. Aristotle does elsewhere talk about animals as "self-moving," but in such cases he appears to be trying to distinguish inanimate objects, which have no internal capacities for motion, from animate creatures for whom external triggers set their internal capacities into action. On this point, see Furley, "Self-Movers."

3. Aristotle, *Nicomachean Ethics* 3.2–4.1111b–1113b. Quotations from the original Greek come from the Loeb edition.

4. Ibid. 7.4.1148a9.

5. The question among modern commentators of whether Aristotle posits a notion of will is ongoing. Gilbert Ryle sees no such notion in the philosopher and highly approves (*Concept of Mind*, esp. 64). G. E. M. Anscombe and Hannah Arendt agree that Aristotle lacks a concept of will but think that this indicates a deficiency in Greek thought (Anscombe, *Intention*, esp. 150, and Arendt, *Life of the Mind*, 15–19). Anthony Kenny and Albrecht Dihle argue that Aristotle does indeed imply a theory of will, but one far different from the modern notion of volition (Kenny, *Aristotle's Theory of Will*, and Dihle, *Theory of the Will*, 55–60).

6. On this point, see Gary Watson, *Agency and Answerability*, 129–30.

7. Long, "Freedom and Determinism."

8. Epictetus, *Discourses* 1.23.

9. Seneca, *De ira* 2.4.1, in *Moral Essays*.

10. Lucretius, *De rerum natura* 4.884–85.

11. It's worth noting that this moment in *De rerum natura* offers one of the earliest examples in philosophical Latin of describing *voluntas* as *libera*; see C. Kahn, "Discovering the Will," 248.

12. On this point see Michael Frede, *Free Will*, 13.

13. Lucretius, *De rerum natura* 2.263–65.

14. Cicero, *De fato* 9.18.

15. Ibid. 9.25.

16. For an account of some of the variety in ancient personification, see Lowe, "Personification Allegory," 414–35.

17. Kant concedes that in empirical terms "no given action . . . can begin absolutely of itself." But reason, which operates according to the world of intelligibility rather than the world of sense, plays by different rules: "In reason itself nothing begins; as unconditioned condition of every voluntary act, it admits of no conditions antecedent to itself in time. Its effect has, indeed, a beginning in the series of appearances, but never in this series an absolutely first beginning" (*Critique of Pure Reason*, 476).

18. Kant, *Groundwork* 4.451.

19. Ibid. 4.557.

20. Mill, "On the Freedom," 452.

21. Bergson, *Time and Free Will*, 169–70.

22. Sartre, *Existentialism Is a Humanism*.

23. Arendt, *Human Condition*, 175–80.

24. Chisholm, "Human Freedom," 31.

25. See Nietzsche's skeptical remarks about free will in *Beyond Good and Evil*, sec. 21.

26. Scholars sometime nod to Alexander of Aphrodisias (late second century), who, in his disagreements with the Stoic doctrine of determinism, rejects even internal determinism and perhaps therefore implies a model of volition detached from judgment and intellect. Likewise, Greek philosophers of the second and third centuries begin using the term *autexousion* (from *exousia*: power, authority, license), by which they seem to mean a human capacity to choose good or evil. Tertullian, in his Latin treatise *De anima* (210 AD), defines this Greek term as "the free power of decision [*liberum arbitrium*]. . . . By nature there is within us *to autexousion*" (*De anima* 21.6; my translation). Tertullian does not mention of *voluntas* here, but he appears to think that "the free" is in us as a capacity.

27. Arendt, *Life of the Mind*, 84. See also Dihle, *Theory of the Will*, 125–28.

28. E.g., see Frede, *Free Will*, 168–72. R. A. Gauthier has dismissed Augustine's account of volition as derivative: "If no one has ever defined the Augustinian conception of will, that is simply because his conception does not exist: of all the traits of the 'will' in Augustine, there is not a single one that is not found earlier in the Stoics" (quoted in C. Kahn, "Discovering the Will," 238).

29. Augustine, *On the Free Choice* 1.11. Subsequent citations to this work are given parenthetically in the text by division number. Latin quotes from Augustine come from *De libero arbitrio*.

30. On the question in Augustine's thought of the human freedom to act on second-order desires about one's will, see Stump, "Augustine on Free Will."

31. Aers, *Salvation and Sin*, esp. 1–24.

32. E.g., when God punishes a sinner, he seems to say, "Why have you not used free will for the purpose for which I gave it to you, to act rightly?" (*On the Free Choice* 2.6).

33. Augustine, *De libero arbitrio* 2.203.

34. "Our will is not a will unless it is in our power. And since it is indeed in our power, it is free in us" (Augustine, *On the Free Choice* 3.33).

35. Augustine, *Confessions* 8.9.

36. Lombard, *Sentences*, bk. 2, dist. 25.

37. Simpson, *Sciences and the Self*, 169.

38. E.g., see Simpson's discussion of reason, will, and genius in Gower's *Confessio amantis* (*Sciences and the Self*, 179–85).

39. See Korolec, "Free Will and Free Choice," 629–41; and Kent, *Virtues of the Will*, 98–108.

40. "The root of liberty is the will as the subject thereof; but it is the reason as its cause. For the will can tend freely towards various objects, precisely because the reason can have various perceptions of good. Hence philosophers define the free-will as being 'a free judgment arising from reason,' implying that reason is the root of liberty" (Aquinas, *Summa theologica*, 2[1].17.4).

41. "For every movement of the will must be preceded by apprehension, whereas every apprehension is not preceded by an act of the will" (Ibid. 1.82.4). Also, see Aquinas's calm response to Augustine's perplexity about how the will can command itself to act but then fail to act (2[1].17.6).

42. As Kent notes, "*Libertas voluntatis* thus became a kind of rallying cry for opponents of Thomism as well as opponents of radical Aristotelianism" (*Virtues of the Will*, 105).

43. Bowers pursues this link in his *Crisis of Will*.

44. Henry of Ghent, *Quodlibetal Questions*, 32–50.

45. Ibid., 26.

46. See Spruyt, "Duns Scotus's Criticism," 139–54.

47. Duns Scotus, *Duns Scotus on the Will*, 155, 167–69. Subsequent page citations to this work are given parenthetically in the text.

48. William of Ockham's oft-quoted definition of freedom is as follows: "Freedom is the power by which I can indifferently and contingently posit diverse things, in such a way that I am both able to cause and able not to cause the same effect when there is no difference anywhere else outside that power" (*Quodlibetal Questions* 1.16).

49. Ibid. 7.14.

50. Ibid. 4.1 [300].

51. Adams, "Ockham on Will," 245.

52. Henry of Ghent, *Quodlibetal Questions*, 61.

53. Gillespie, *Theological Origins*, 22.

54. Pfau, *Minding the Modern*, 168.

55. Ibid., 175.

56. Aers, *Salvation and Sin*, 43. It should be noted that Aers does not have a stake in linking Ockham to modern conceptions of the will in the way that Pfau and Gillespie do. Indeed, Aers points out (*Salvation and Sin*, 35) Martin Luther's subsequent attacks on the nominalist doctrine of *facientibus quod in se est, Deus non denegat gratiam*.

57. Anselm, *De casu diaboli*, secs. 12–14.

58. Normore, "Ockham, Self-Motion," 294.

59. E.g., Ockham distinguishes "the case of a natural agent, whether it be corporal or spiritual" from "the case of a free agent such as the will" (*Quodlibetal Questions* 1.16). Cf. *Quodlibetal Questions* 1.17, 2.2, 2.9, 2.11, 3.22, 4.1, 4.2, etc.

60. Hobart, "Free Will," 6.

61. Augustine, *Confessions* 8.11.

62. Ibid.

63. Burckhardt, *Civilisation of the Renaissance*, and Cassirer, *Individual and the Cosmos*. For a review of this debate's literature, see Baldwin, "Individual and Self," 341–64.

64. For a literary study that does appear to assume a constitutive relationship between will and self in the Renaissance, see Wojciehowski, *Old Masters*.

65. Ficino: "The intellect grasps the object through a kind of imagery, but the will strives to transfer itself to its object by natural impulse" (*Letters*, 175). Sander praises man, "in whose soul is free will and power to govern, agreeable to the nature of angels and heavenly spirits" (*Supper of Our Lord*, fol. 19). Bramhall: "So as, whatsoever obligation the understanding does put upon the will, is by the consent of the will, and derived from the power of the will, which was not necessitated to move the understanding to consult" ("Defence of True Liberty," 46).

66. Valla, *Dialogue on Free Will*, 170–74.

67. See Valla, *Dialectical Disputations*, esp. 1:9–10.

68. Pomponazzi, *Libri quinque de fato* 2.7.1.34–39. And see the discussion in Antonino Poppi, "Fate, Fortune," esp. 653–60.

69. Pomponazzi, *Libri quinque de fato* 3.4–6.

70. Ibid. 3.8.10.

71. Braden, *Renaissance Tragedy*; Schoenfeldt, *Bodies and Selves*.

72. Charron, *Of Wisdome Three Bookes*, 69.

73. Spenser, *Faerie Queene* 1.2.12 and 2.12.53.

74. Of course, the power of Reason (represented in Spenser's poem by the Palmer) plays a role in controlling willfulness. But Reason needs the Will to carry out its judgments, the very act of will that we see Guyon perform here.

75. Shakespeare, *Julius Caesar* 2.2.71–72, in *Riverside Shakespeare*.

76. Wright, *Passions of the Minde*, 57–59.

77. Hooker, *Of the Laws* 1.7, ed. McGrade, 1:59.

78. Ibid. 1.7.7, ed. McGrade, 1:59.

79. Sidney, *Apology for Poetry*, 17.

80. Luther: "A work can only be called contingent when *from our point of view* it is done contingently and, as it were, by chance and without our expecting it, because our will or hand seizes on it as something presented to us by chance, when we have thought or willed nothing about it previously" (*On the Bondage*, 119; subsequent page citations to this work are given parenthetically in the text). Likewise, Calvin insists that it is absurd to think an event can happen without the direct intervention of God, "because it would happen at random. For which reason, he also excludes the contingency which depends on human will" (*Institutes* 1.16.8; see also 1.16.2–3; subsequent citations to this work are given parenthetically in the text by division numbers).

81. Calvin insists that God dispenses with natural causality at his whim: God's power, "in overruling all things, works at one time with means, at another without means, and at another against means" (*Institutes* 1.17.1).

82. Luther explains that we willingly sin not through external compulsion but through the inclination of our own nature: "When a man is without the Spirit of God he does not do evil against his will, as if he were taken by the scruff of the neck and forced to it, like a thief or a robber carried off against his will to punishment, but he does it of his own accord and with a ready will" (*On the Bondage*, 139).

83. Ibid., 232.

84. See Luther, *On the Bondage*, 142; Calvin, *Institutes* 2.2.7.

85. On this point, I suspect Lisa Freinkel overstates her case when she suggests that for Luther "Every act of will, precisely by dint of being willful, contains that about which we are unwilling: the volition or inclination that we do not choose, nor cannot change" (*Reading Shakespeare's Will*, 134). The inability to choose our preferences does not mean that the acts of will based on those preferences are unwilling.

86. E.g., see Calvin's retention of the vocabulary of medieval faculty psychology in *Institutes* 1.15.6–7 and 2.2.23–26.

87. Freinkel: "For Luther, our failure lies not in the body's irrational resistance to the rational commands of the will, but rather in the inherent irrationality of the will itself" (*Reading Shakespeare's Will*, 245).

88. See James, *Passion and Action*.

89. Descartes, *Passions of the Soul*, 47.

90. Descartes, *Meditations*, 121.

91. Hobbes, *Leviathan*, 1.6.49. Subsequent citations to this work are given parenthetically in the text by division numbers.

92. "Personate, v," def. 4a. OED Online.

93. Henry S. Turner has suggestively identified the signifying template of corporations to be one of form rather than content: "The corporate person . . . [is] empty, a formal shell that can in principle become animated by *any* purpose and by any member. The corporation lives through the personations that *we* undertake, as we begin to move and speak on its behalf. . . . The legal person presents us with the structure of *allegory without content*, a purely formal structure for action that waits to be animated by the particular bodies, substances, and circumstances that will endow it with identity, rather than appearing to us as already conceptually full"; see Turner, "Corporate Persons." (My thanks to Professor Turner for sharing the prepublication version of this article with me.)

94. Lucan, *Pharsalia* 1.183–92.

95. James, *Passion and Action*, 106.

96. Descartes, *Passions of the Soul*, 289.

97. Hanna, "Persons and Personation," 177–91.

98. Wright, *Passions of the Mind*, 58.

99. La Primaudaye, *Second Part*, 208.

100. Schwarz, *What You Will*. Subsequent page citations to this work are given parenthetically in the text.

101. P. Fletcher, *Purple Island*, 6.60. Subsequent citations to this work are given parenthetically in the text by canto and line numbers.

102. Spenser, *Faerie Queene* 2.4.1–33.

103. Ibid. 2.4.32.

Chapter Three CONSCIENCE IN THE TUDOR INTERLUDES

1. Plato, *Apology* 31c–d, 40a; *Republic* 620e. Throughout this chapter, all English passages from Plato are taken from *Collected Dialogues of Plato* (ed. Hamilton and Cairns) and will subsequently be cited parenthetically in the text.

2. Plotinus, *Enneads* 3.4 ("On Our Allotted Guardian Spirit"), esp. 3.4.3.1–21.

3. E.g., "We have renounced the hidden things of dishonesty, not walking in craftiness, nor handling the word of God deceitfully; but by

manifestation of the truth commending ourselves to every man's conscience in the sight of God" (KJV, 2 Cor. 4:2). Also: "For when the Gentiles, which have not the law, do by nature the things contained in the law, these, having not the law, are a law unto themselves: Which shew the work of the law written in their hearts, their conscience also bearing witness, and their thoughts the meanwhile accusing or else excusing one another" (Rom. 2:14–15).

4. E.g., see Pierce, *Conscience*.

5. Apuleius, *God of Socrates*, 208.

6. Ibid., 208.

7. Olympiodorus, *Commentary*, ed. Westerink, 17, my translation.

8. On the complex merging of Genius and the Greek daemon in Roman literature and philosophy, see Nitzsche, *Genius Figure in Antiquity*, esp. 21–41.

9. See the discussion in D. Baker, "Priesthood of Genius," esp. 279–80.

10. Bernardus Silvestris, *Cosmographia*, 107.

11. Ibid.

12. See Simpson, *Sciences and the Self*, 134–229.

13. Plotinus, *Enneads* 3.4.5.19–23.

14. Spenser, *Faerie Queene* 2.12.47.

15. Perkins, *Discourse of Conscience*, 9–10.

16. Aquinas, *Summa theologica* 1.79:12–13. For Aquinas, conscience does not even amount to a mental faculty; it is simply the *act* of applying principles to specific cases.

17. Slights, *Casuistical Tradition*; and L. Gallagher, *Medusa's Gaze*.

18. Lukacher, *Daemonic Figures*, 10.

19. For overviews of this dimension of the plays, see Spivak, *Shakespeare*, 206–11; and Norland, *Drama in Early Tudor Britain*, 37–47.

20. Jane Griffiths has linked the practice of name changing in the interludes to Renaissance skepticism about realist theories of language, on which, she argues, allegory depends. Griffiths thus concludes that the interlude genre "challenges the very allegorical mode on which the plays depend" ("Counterfeit Countenaunce," 20).

21. Beckwith, *Signifying God*, 154.

22. *Worlde and the Chylde*, lines 705–7, ed. Davidson and Happé. Subsequent line citations to this work are to this edition and are given parenthetically in the text.

23. Langland, *Piers Plowman*, 184.

24. Wanhope threatens Age in *Worlde and the Chylde*, line 852. In *Piers Plowman*, when Repentance chides Covetousness, the vice falls into "wanhope and wolde han hanged himselve" (B:5.279), at which point Repentance immediately comforts him.

25. Plato, *Meno* 77e.

26. Plato, *Laws* 861e–863a.

27. W. Wager, *Longer Thou Livest*, lines 1799–1802.

28. Wever, *Lusty Juventus*, lines 1025–26. On the debatable date of composition, see Thomas's introduction, xiii–xxx.

29. Wapull, *Tide Tarryeth No Man*, sig. G1r.

30. L. Wager, *Life and Repentance*, sig. G2r.

31. For example: *Nice Wanton*, lines 294–95; Fulwell, *Like Will to Like*, sig. E4r.; Wapull, *Tide Tarryeth No Man*, sig. A2v; W. Wager, *Enough Is as Good*, lines 405–6, in *Longer Thou Livest*.

32. Herdt, *Putting on Virtue*, 188.

33. A. Fletcher (1976–), "*Doctor Faustus*," 189. For bibliographic clarity, this is not the Angus Fletcher who authored *Allegory* and *The Prophetic Moment*.

34. Harsnett, "Sermon Preached."

35. Luther: "For the expression 'free choice' is too imposing, too wide and full, and the people think it signifies—as the force and nature of the term require—a power than can turn itself freely in either direction, without being under anyone's influence or control" (*Of the Bondage*, 142). Calvin: "[The sinner] acts voluntarily, and not by compulsion. This is perfectly true: but why should so small a matter have been dignified with so proud a title? An admirable freedom! That man is not forced to be the servant of sin, while he is, however, *ethelodoulos* (a voluntary slave); his will being bound by the fetters of sin" (*Institutes* 2.2.7).

36. Stachniewski, *Persecutory Imagination*, 296. Stachniewski is here discussing Marlowe's *Doctor Faustus* as illustrative of Protestant moral interludes, a genre he describes as the "Calvinist deformation of the morality tradition" (300).

37. Herdt, *Putting on Virtue*, 188.

38. Calvin, *Institutes* 3.3.5; Perkins, *Golden Chaine*, 128.

39. Perkins, *Reformed Catholike*, 14–15.

40. Perkins, *Treatise*, 378.

41. As Perkins writes in *Discourse of Conscience*, "God knows perfectly all the doings of man, though they be never so hid and concealed, and man by a gift given him of God, knows together with God, the same

things of himself: and this gift is named Conscience. . . . [God] gave him conscience to be his keeper, to follow him always at the heels and to dog him (as we say) and to pry into his actions and to bear witness of them all" (5, 9).

42. See the discussion in Zackman, *Assurance of the Faith*, 63–68.

43. Perkins, *Treatise*, 8.

44. Calvin would probably describe a desire like David's as "the beginning of repentance," the point at which one receives faith in divine forgiveness: "It is a gift of the Holy Spirit . . . to which none can attain by his own efforts," as he puts it in his *Commentary on Matthew* (in *Calvin's New Testament Commentaries*, 11:28, 2:223).

45. Perkins, *Reformed Catholike*, 317.

46. Ibid., 326.

47. Fleming, *Milton's Secrecy*, esp. 31–56.

48. Ibid., 50.

49. Ibid., 34.

50. Frankfurt, "Freedom of the Will," 5–20.

51. Calvin, *Institutes* 3.19.15.

52. Perkins, *Discourse of Conscience*, 6–7.

53. These two phrases come from Perkins: ibid., 145, and *Treatise*, 7.

54. Frankfurt, "Freedom of the Will," 16.

55. Ibid.

56. Watson, *Agency and Answerability*, 29.

57. Luther, *Of the Bondage*, 140.

58. Perkins, *Treatise*, 78–79; 92.

59. Ibid., 91–92.

60. When indicating the approximate date range of composition for the interludes, I rely on Grantley, *English Dramatic Interludes*.

61. Wapull, *Tide Tarrieth No Man*, sig. G2r. Subsequent citations to this work are given parenthetically in the text.

62. Fulwell, *Like Will to Like*, sig. C4v.

63. Wilks, *Idea of Conscience*, 75–76.

64. Woodes, *Conflict of Conscience*, lines 1914–15, 1983.

65. L. Wager, *Mary Magdalene*, sigs. B3r, E4v, F3r.

66. Wever, *Lusty Juventus*, lines 1010–12.

67. For example, see *Nice Wanton*, lines 25–35, and Wever, *Lusty Juventus*, lines 1–21.

68. W. Wager, *Enough*, line 275.

69. *Nice Wanton*, lines 279–80.

70. Ibid., lines 335–36.

71. Ibid., line 285.

72. After Christ banishes Infidelity from Mary's presence, she says: "Blessed be thy name, O father celestial. / Honor and glory be given to thee world without end. / O Lord, dost thou regard thus a woman terrestrial? / To thee what tongue is able worthy thanks to repend? / O what a sinful wretch, Lord, have I been? / Have mercy on me, Lord, for thy name's sake. / So grievous a sinner before this day was never seen. / Vouchsafe, therefore, compassion on me to take" (L. Wager, *Mary Magdalene*, sig. F4r). Jesus responds by asking her, "Canst thou believe in God, the maker of all thing [*sic*], / And in his only son, whom he hath sent?" (sig. F4r). The question seems a bit superfluous: Why would Mary so movingly ask forgiveness from a God in whom she did not believe?

73. "Wanton, adj. and n.," *OED Online*.

74. *Nice Wanton*, lines 79–81.

75. L. Wager, *Mary Magdalene*: the first passage comes from sig. B2v, the next three from sig. F1v.

76. See Cummings, *Literary Culture*, esp. 144–83.

77. Magnusson, "Play of Modals," 72. I have modernized the passage.

78. Ibid., 79.

79. Perkins, *Treatise*, 4 (my emphases).

80. W. Wager, *Enough*, line 1282, in *Longer Thou Livest*.

81. Ibid., line 1278.

82. Wever, *Lusty Juventus*, lines 1043–44.

83. Ibid., line 1048.

84. Woodes, *Conflict of Conscience*, Prol. line 60. Subsequent line citations to this work are given parenthetically in the text.

85. Bevington, "Christopher Marlowe's *Doctor Faustus*," 710.

86. I ask my readers to understand "stage" metaphorically here: there is no evidence that *Conflict of Conscience* was intended for performance.

87. On this quality of the play, see Bevington, "Christopher Marlowe's *Doctor Faustus*," 704–17.

Chapter Four DESPAIR IN MARLOWE AND SPENSER

1. Mâle, *Religious Art in France*, 99–119; and Barash, "Despair," 566–76. Jennifer O'Reilly notes that although one can find examples of a suicidal Ira opposed to Patientia as far back as Prudentius, she finds no

example of a Desperatio specifically opposed to Spes until the late thirteenth century; see *Studies in the Iconography*, 58.

2. Fisher, *Vehement Passions*.

3. Kierkegaard: "In the composite of the eternal and the temporal, man is a relation, in this relation itself and relating itself to itself. God made man a relation; to be a human being is to be a relation. But a relation which, by the very fact that God, as it were, releases it from his hand, or the same moment God, as it were, releases it, is itself, relates itself to itself—this relation can become in the same moment a misrelation. To despair is this misrelation taking place" (*Sickness unto Death*, 143–44).

4. Ibid., 30–35. For a discussion of this dimension of despair in Spenser, see Andrew Escobedo, "Despair and the Proportion," 75–90.

5. Kierkegaard, *Sickness unto Death*, 47.

6. Hooker, *Learned and comfortable sermon*, 7.

7. Spenser, *Faerie Queene* 2.7.41; subsequent citations to this work by book, canto, and stanza are given parenthetically in the text. This example is courtesy of Teskey, *Allegory and Violence*, 22.

8. Robert Parsons observes that "there be two things whereby sinners do stand in danger: the one in hoping too much (which is presumption); the other in hoping too little, which is desperation" (*Booke of Christian exercise*, 306–7).

9. See the discussion of examples in Barash, "Despair," 570–74.

10. William Willymat identified two kinds of despair: "the one a wicked kind of desperation of God's promises, power, goodness, and mercy towards sinners . . . the other an holy desperation of a man's own power in the obtaining of eternal life" (*Physic to Cure*, 3). Likewise, the preacher Edward Reynolds distinguished between a form of despair that is "regular and allowable, I mean that which in matter of importance drives us out of ourselves, or any presumption and opinion of our own sufficiently," and that which "riseth out of a groundless unbelief of the Power, or distrust of the Goodness, of a superior Agent (especially in those things which depend upon the Will and Omnipotency of God)" (*Treatise of the Passions*, 236–37).

11. Calvin is complex on this issue, since although he technically insists on the infallibility of elect assurance, he also admits that all assurance is tinged with doubt (*Institutes* 2.3.17). My thanks to Susannah Brietz Monta for calling my attention to this ambiguity.

12. Marlowe, *Doctor Faustus* A:1.3.78–82. Like many recent critics, I treat the two quarto editions of *Doctor Faustus* as a kind of *hendiadys*, one

play through two texts. Whenever I quote, I identify whether the passage comes from the A-text or the B-text.

13. For example, Marlowe may be thinking of the widespread belief that the primary torment of the damned is to suffer the absence of God. Spenser, for his part, is probably thinking of traditional depiction of Judas hanging himself.

14. Luther, *Of the Bondage*, 244.

15. Burton, *Anatomy of Melancholy* 3.403. Here and throughout, *Anatomy* is cited by partition and page number.

16. Perkins, *Works,* 1:365, 378.

17. Monta and Oliver, "Spenser, Wolfram," 9–30.

18. E.g., Luther writes, "Thus, [God] does not will the death of a sinner, according to his word; but he wills it according to that inscrutable will of his" (*Of the Bondage*, 201).

19. Skulsky, "Spenser's Despair Episode," 235.

20. Higgins, *First Part*, fol. 52r.

21. Ibid., fol. 53r.

22. On the possibility of Wolfram as a source, see Monta and Oliver, "Spenser, Wolfram."

23. For more details about the correspondence, see Kessler, "Analogue," 31–34.

24. Higgins, *First Part*, fols. 52r, 54r.

25. Ibid., fol. 54r.

26. Augustine, *City of God* 1.20, 26.

27. See Snyder, "Left Hand of God," 50.

28. Burton, *Anatomy of Melancholy* 1.29–39.

29. Dolven, "Spenser's Sense," 130.

30. Kierkegaard, *Sickness unto Death*, 18.

31. Ibid., 19.

32. Kierkegaard does not deny that suicide is a sin against God, nor that it sometimes follows as a consequence of despair. But suicide has no necessary relation to spiritual hopelessness. For example, Kierkegaard suggests that the ancients' failure to recognize suicide as a mortal sin against God constituted a kind of unconscious despair but that, as regards the act of self-killing in its own right, "it cannot be said that suicide is despair" (ibid., 46).

33. Imbrie, "Playing Legerdemaine with Scripture"; Goeglein, "Utterances"; Dixon, *Polliticke Courtier*; J. Anderson, "What I Really Teach."

34. Skulsky, "Spenser's Despair Episode."

35. Moss, "Spenser's Despair," 73–102.

36. For two further accounts of predestinarian theology and despair in Spenser, see Escobedo, "Despair," and B. Quitslund, "Despair."

37. For example, when Despaire suggests that "the lenger life, I wote the greater sin, / The greater sin, the greater punishment" (1.9.43), he recalls 1 John 1:8: "If we say we have no sin, we deceive ourselves, and the truth is not in us." A. C. Hamilton's gloss on Despaire's reference is characteristic of the rhetorical tradition: "Again, Despaire ignores the [scriptural] context, for John adds: 'If we acknowledge our sins, he is faithful and just, to forgive us our sins, and to clense us from al unrighteousness.'" No doubt, it does not serve the demon's purpose to mention 1 John 1:9. But in ignoring it he shows himself to be a good reader of the Elizabethan Thirty-Nine Articles of Religion. Article 15 explains that Jesus Christ on earth was without sin but that "all we the rest, although baptized and born again in Christ, yet offend in many things; and if we say we have no sin, we deceive ourselves, and the truth is not in us." The article gives us verse 8 without verse 9, just as Despaire does.

38. I'm quoting the 1590 reading of this line, rather than the 1596 reading that the Hamilton edition uses, because I think it most thoroughly communicates the tone of sympathy in Una's appeal. My thanks to David Lee Miller for calling my attention to the difference.

39. Skulsky, "Spenser's Despaire Episode," 228, 230.

40. Moss, "Spenser's Despair," 80. It should be noted that Moss has a keen sense of the problem here and is careful to observe of Una's intervention that "even this perfect moment of grace may not finally be sufficient, for despair—theological or psychological—is partly defined by the dependability of its own recurrence.... [Despair] will haunt Redcrosse even in the House of Holiness" (93–94).

41. Douglas Trevor offers a tour de force reading of Spenser's despair episode that distinguishes between salutary sadness and sinful melancholy: "The temptation to self-slaughter is so serious precisely because it reveals the difficulty of sustaining appropriate sadness without tumbling into self-destructive melancholy" (*Poetics of Melancholy*, 50). This account is alert to the interplay between positive and negative forms of despondency that characterize early modern notions of religious despair. But Trevor exaggerates the degree with which Redcross Knight leaves the bad version behind: "Redcrosse . . . fully recovers from this temptation [suicide] in the House of Holiness. . . . After his treatment in the House of Holiness, Redcrosse is no longer vulnerable to the kind of melancholy embodied in Despair" (49,

50). Yet Redcross continues to wish for death during his ordeal in the House of Holiness and then later during his fight with the dragon (1.11.28).

42. Marlowe, *Doctor Faustus* A:5.1.59.

43. Thomas P. Roche notes this absence of response and ascribes it to the protocols of allegorical fiction: "Redcross is . . . a saint to be proclaimed. There is no possibility for him to fail in the fiction. . . . In allegorical poems the conquest of a vice or a passion can only be a momentary victory because of the unending continuance in this world of the vice or passion" ("Menace of Despair," 87). The point about allegory offers great insight about Spenser's fiction, but it does not, it seems to me, cast any light on why Spenser declines to have Redcross literally repent, since he does not scruple to have him literally attempt suicide.

Darryl J. Gless, for his part, assumes an inner change within the knight: "Red Cross escapes Despair because something superrational has enabled him to believe, at least for the moment, that he enjoys a 'part' in 'heavenly mercies.' His subsequent actions appear to express a decisive inner alteration" (*Interpretation and Theology*, 145). But why does Spenser not allow the knight to express this superrational faith for the reader to hear? Again, my hesitation about this kind of reading is that it assumes that escaping suicide amounts to escaping despair, even if just "for the moment."

44. Carol Kaske, in her annotation on this line, claims that Despaire is lying about Terwin's guilty mind in an effort to deceive Redcross, since Trevisan said only that Terwin was in despair about love; see Kaske, *Faerie Queene*, 1.9.38. This is a possibility, given Despaire's rhetorical trickery. Yet the intensity of Terwin's and Trevisan's despair seems to have existential depth, and Spenser makes it clear, in the example of Malbecco, that erotic despair is linked to the religious variety.

45. Calvin, *Institutes* 2.4.2.

46. Beard, *Theater of God's Judgements*, sig. K5v.

47. Cole, "*Doctor Faustus*," 231–43.

48. *Historie of the Damnable Life.*

49. On this point, see, for example, Deats, "From Chapbook to Tragedy," 3–16.

50. See, *inter alia*, Sanders, *Dramatist*, esp. 214–17; Pittock, "God's Mercy Is Infinite," 310; and Cole, "*Doctor Faustus*," 41–43.

51. Marlowe, *Doctor Faustus* A:5.1.36–57. Subsequent citations to A- or B-text and part divisions are given parenthetically in the text.

52. L. Wager, *Life and Repentance*, sig. F1v.

53. In the B-text, Lucifer, not Faustus, dismisses the vices to hell, but Faustus's response, as in the A-text, treats these figures of objects for consumption: "O, how this sight doth delight my soul" (B:2.3.160).

54. Reiss, *Mirages of the Selfe.*

55. Taylor, *Secular Age,* 32.

56. Wapull, *Tide Tarryeth No Man,* sig. G2r.

57. This reading is courtesy the interpretation of Snow, "Marlowe's *Doctor Faustus,*" 71–72.

58. On the contradictory nature of the contract in this scene, see Wilson, *Theaters of Intention,* 205–7.

59. See Prieto-Pablos, "'What Art Thou Faustus?,'" 71–73; Hamlin, "Casting Doubt," 265; and A. Fletcher, "*Doctor Faustus,*" 202. (For bibliographic purposes, this Angus Fletcher is not the author of *Allegory: Theory of a Symbolic Mode.*)

60. Sanders, *Dramatist,* 217.

61. Stachniewski, *Persecutory Imagination,* 296.

62. Kiessling surveys critical views about this issue in "*Doctor Faustus,*" 205–11.

63. The Old Man immediately calls Faustus a "miserable man / That from thy soul exclud'st the grace of heaven" (A:5.1.11–12). At the beginning of the next scene, Lucifer with his demonic fellows says, "Faustus, we come to thee, / Bringing with us lasting damnation" (B:5.2.4–5). At the end of this same scene the good angel tells Faustus, "And now, poor soul must thy good angel leave thee. / The jaws of hell are open to receive thee" (B:5.2.119–20).

64. *Historie of the Damnable Life,* 73–74.

65. Woodes, *Conflict of Conscience,* lines 2108–9.

66. Ornstein, "Marlowe and God," 1379.

67. Perkins, *Treatise,* 105–6.

68. King-Kok Cheung offers a reading of *Doctor Faustus* that considers the mutually implicating qualities of despair and contrition, with reference to Kierkegaard ("Dialectic of Despair"). Unfortunately, Cheung bases his interpretation on a puzzling distinction between "religious" and "existential" despair that he never makes clear. For Kierkegaard, religious despair is always existential.

69. David Bevington comments, "In a sense [Faustus] never really tries to repent, for he knows his own disposition too well" ("Marlowe and God," 23). A. D. Nuttall, by contrast, suggests that the lines amount to repentance in a way that critiques Calvinist theology: "Faustus clearly re-

pents in the sense that he wishes he had not done what he has done, and he calls on Christ; why then does not Christ respond and save him?" (*Alternative Trinity*, 30).

70. Faustus's other conditional statements all pertain to external events rather than to acts of will that *he* would undertake if the right conditions obtained. For example, when he says, "God will pity me, if I repent" (A:2.3.15–16), his prediction about God may or may not be correct, but the statement says nothing about his own intention or wish to repent. This is likewise the nature of his final conditional statement in the play: "O God, if thou wilt not have mercy on my soul, / . . . / Impose some end to my incessant pain. / Let Faustus live in hell a thousand years, / A hundred thousand, and at last be saved" (A:5.2.92–96). He imagines the conditions of fatality being hypothetically otherwise; he does not imagine himself hypothetically doing something depending on the conditions of fatality.

71. Despite the absence of the word *if*, I assume that the modal *would* in these lines has a conditional force beyond the optative sense of *I wish to weep* or *I wish to raise my hands.*

72. Sanders, *Dramatist*, 237–38.

Chapter Five   Love and Spenser's Cupid

1. Smith, "Premodern Sexualities," 319.

2. Halperin, "Love's Irony," 52.

3. Plato, *Symposium*, 203b–c. Throughout this chapter, all English passages from Plato are taken from *Collected Dialogues of Plato* (ed. Hamilton and Cairns) and will subsequently be cited parenthetically in the text. This collection reprints R. Hackforth's translation of the *Phaedrus* (1952) and Michael Joyce's translation of the *Symposium* (1935). All passages and phrases from the original Greek are from *Platonis opera* (ed. Burnet).

4. Spenser, *Hymn in Honour of Love*, lines 50–56, in *Yale Edition.*

5. E.g., see Sheffield, *Plato's "Symposium,"* 66–68; and D. Anderson, *Masks of Dionysos*, 67–68.

6. See, for instance, *Cratylus* 398b, *Republic* 496b–c; *Euthyphro* 3b; and *Apology* 20d–e, 24b–c, 26b.

7. Plotinus, *Enneads* 3.5 ("On Love"), 166–203.

8. For a survey of these complaints, see Hyde, *Poetic Theology of Love*, 29–86.

9. Natale Conti canvasses a whole range of opinions, ancient and modern, about this matter in his *Mythologiae* 4.14.

10. Ficino and Leone, although identifying Love as a daemon or spirit, both offer elaborate allegorical interpretations of Diotima's story. See Ficino, *Commentary on Plato's "Symposium,"* 190–91; and Leone Hebreo, *Philosophy of Love*, 366–72.

11. Pietro Bembo's Perottino, although arguing for the cruelty of Love, observes that poets feigned Love as a god in an effort to educate and civilize their audiences: "The poets devised these fables, in which, as under a transparent glass, they veiled the truth. . . . Love, together with many other forces, was made a deity . . . to show that brutal race, under the name of *god*, what power this passion wielded over human minds" (*Gli Asolani*, 27–28).

12. For a magisterial account of the importance of Renaissance Platonic thought about daemons to Spenser's poetry, see J. Quitslund, *Spenser's Supreme Fiction*, esp. 227–66.

13. Regarding the poem's anti-Petrachanism, Heather Dubrow has suggested that *Faerie Queene* conceives of Petrarchanism as embodying "dangerous types of love" (*Echoes of Desire*, 258) and that certain episodes, such as the Mask of Cupid and Serena with the cannibals, signal the poem's distrust of Petrarch poetry: "To what extent, *The Faerie Queene* demands, does Petrarchanism use its own equivalents of ritual, notably literary convention, to excuse the violence found in many sequences?" (260).

14. Kingsley-Smith, *Cupid*, 29.

15. Hyde, *Poetic Theology of Love*, 144, 112.

16. Spenser, *Faerie Queene* 3.12.22. Subsequent citations by book, canto, and stanza are given parenthetically in the text.

17. Lewis, *Spenser's Images of Life*, 28.

18. Maurice Evans sees Spenser distinguishing between a worldly Cupid ("the traditional symbol of carnal desire") and a heavenly Cupid ("a higher Cupid . . . [representing] the highest power of the human intellect") ("Platonic Allegory," 135 and 139). Joanne T. Dempsey makes a similar distinction between worldly and celestial Cupids ("Angel, Guyon's," 40). Jane Kingsley-Smith (*Cupid*, 57) gives contrasting examples of what she takes to be the use and abuse of Cupid-art. William Nestrick posits a dichotomy between the natural (good) and artificial (bad) Cupid ("Spenser," 70). Hendrix ("'Mother of Laughter,'" 113–33) sees a dichotomy, not precisely between two Cupids, but between Cupid (fallen, marital love) and his mother Venus (golden age, peaceful love).

19. Hyde, *Poetic Theology of Love*, 207.

20. For a review of this commonplace, see Dandas, "Masks of Cupid."

21. "Definition of Love," lines 1–8, in Marvell, *Complete Poems*.

22. Junker, "Spenser's Unarmed Cupid," 59–83.

23. For a study of Spenser's juxtaposition of the armed and unarmed Cupids in terms of iconographic tradition, see Borris, "(H)eroic Disarmament."

24. D. Miller, *Poem's Two Bodies*, 170.

25. Shuger, *Renaissance Bible*, 176–81.

26. Elizabeth Story Donno offers an early, and very lucid, expression of this position: "The thematic stress of Book III, then, does not relate to a kind of Cupid or a kind of Love—good or bad, false or true—but rather to its compelling power manifested in the diversity of response . . . in diverse characters" ("Triumph of Cupid," 43).

27. Petrarch, "Triumph of Love" 4.89–90, in Petrarca, *Triumphs of Petrarch*; Googe, *Cupido Conquered*, lines 472, 493, in *Eclogues, Epitaphs*. Italian quotations from Petrarch will be from Francesco Petrarca, *Rime, Trionfi*.

28. Deneef, "Spenser's *Amor Fuggitivo*," 7 and 9. This essay is reprinted, in slightly revised form, in Deneef, *Spenser*, 157–77.

29. Deneef, "Spenser's *Amor Fuggitivo*," 13.

30. Foucault: "The *Symposium* and the *Phaedrus* indicate a transition . . . to an erotics centered on an ascesis of the subject and a common access to truth . . . an economy of pleasure ensured by the control that is exercised by oneself over oneself" (*Use of Pleasure*, 244; and see Foucault's remarks about Platonic Eros generally, 229–46).

31. For example, in his otherwise impressive essay on Platonism and the figure of Florimell, Patrick Cheney emphasizes the process of abstraction in the Platonic scheme ("'And Doubted Her,'" 310–40). William A. Oram likewise speaks about the abstractive and nonsomatic quality of Platonism: "the neoplatonic insistence on the image of the Lady in the place of the person. . . . The traditional neoplatonic ascent is solitary: the beloved is primarily a spur to the lover's spiritual development" ("Spenser's Crowd of Cupids," 93).

32. Platonism has made a comeback in Spenser studies in recent years, after a long period of relative quiescence inaugurated by Robert Ellrodt's *Neoplatonism in the Poetry of Edmund Spenser* in 1960. Recognizing that Ellrodt had defined "Neoplatonism" in a way that stacked the deck against finding it in Spenser, or in most poets, a number of scholars have set about

devising new Platonic lenses by which to interpret Spenser's poetry. Jon Quitslund has explored the topic of Spenser's fiction making in Platonic terms, and Kenneth Borris has done the same with the topic of authorship in Spenser. I intend to pursue a third avenue into Spenser's Platonism: the issue of erotic madness.

33. Pieper, *Enthusiasm and Divine Madness*, 49, 56.

34. Nehamas, *Only a Promise*, 7. The two uses of *sunousia* that Nehamas has in mind occur at *Symposium* 211d6 (*sunontas*) and 211d8 (*suneinai*).

35. I have made R. Hackforth's translation slightly more literal in order to avoid obscuring the verbs of rapture that I wish to highlight.

36. Discussing in the *Republic* why "Love has long since been called a tyrant," Socrates deplores "the feats and carousals and revelings and courtesans and all the doings of those whose souls are entirely swayed by the indwelling tyrant Eros" (573b and d). In the *Laws*, Socrates insists that the temperate life offers pains and pleasure "alike unexciting, its desires and passions never furious, but mild, whereas that of profligacy is uniformly rash. The pains and pleasures it offers are alike violent, its intense desires and frantic passions maddening in the extreme" (734a).

37. Halperin, "Love's Irony," 49.

38. Ibid., 52.

39. Again, I have made the translation slightly more literal in order to avoid obscuring the language of seizure.

40. Plotinus, *Enneads* 1.6 ("On Beauty"), 244–45.

41. Plotinus, *Enneads* 3.5 ("On Love"), 179.

42. Even at the upper rungs, when the lover's soul begins to contemplate the heavenly source of beauty, this soul, "ravished with the splendor of that light, begins to kindle and to pursue it so eagerly that it is almost drunk and beside itself in its desire" (Castiglione, *Book of the Courtier*, 353–54).

43. Ficino, *Commentarium in Phedrum*, in *Marsilio Ficino*, ed. Allen, 84.

44. Ficino, *Commentum cum summis capitulorum*, in *Marsilio Ficino*, ed. Allen, 141–42.

45. Leone, *Philosophy of Love*, 339–43. See the discussion of this dichotomy in Hyde, *Poetic Theology of Love*, 98–99.

46. "Love, once born, no longer submits to the orders and rule of reason which bore it; but recalcitrates at its parent, becoming, as you say, so

ungovernable as to harm and injure its votaries. For he who truly loves another unloves himself; which is against all reason and duty" (Leone, *Philosophy of Love*, 58).

47. Ibid., 61.

48. Ibid., 155, my emphasis.

49. The best modern discussion of this alignment remains Bataille, *Erotism.*

50. The question of where Spenser got his Platonism from—Plato himself, or Plotinus, or medieval Platonism, or Renaissance Platonists—has been extensively debated. I have little to add to the debate about specific sources except my impression that Spenser absorbed the main doctrines of Plato's erotic theories thoroughly enough that they emerge with some coherence in his poetry.

51. For touchstone studies of the Petrarchan and courtly sources of Spenser's love poetry, see Lewis, *Allegory of Love*, and Roche, *Kindly Flame.*

52. My notion of Spenserian rapture seeks to combine two critical views of the phenomenon: one from Gordon Teskey (*Allegory and Violence*), whose account of allegorical capture, as we discussed in chapter 1, relies on a model of repressive constraint, the other from Katharine Eggert ("Spenser's Ravishment"), which relies on a model of open-endedness, where the narrow-minded literalism of rape is replaced with a rich sense of poetic possibilities.

53. Berger, *Revisionary Play.*

54. Oram, "Characterization and Spenser's Allegory," 91–122.

55. In the case of Britomart, it is true that her mission to found a British dynasty comes from Merlin in 3.3, but Merlin merely helps determine what Britomart will do with her love; he does not help her decide whether she loves or not, a question that has already been definitively answered by the mastery of Eros in 3.2.

56. Sanchez, *Erotic Subjects.*

57. Ibid., 65.

58. Ibid., 66.

59. Ibid., 71.

60. However, I do not deny that the early modern terminology is quite ambiguous on this question. Spenser says that "Paridell rapeth Hellenore" (3.10.arg) even though Hellenore appears to accompany him willingly.

61. Loewenstein, "Echo's Ring," 291n12, emphasis in original.

62. Hieatt, "Room of One's Own," 147–64.

63. Spenser *can* find humor in casual love, as the examples of the Squire of Dames and Helenore and the Satyrs suggest. *The Faerie Queene* offers a range of sexual tonalities, not a single note.

64. On the question of Scudamour's sincerity and consistency as a lover, see Escobedo, "Sincerity of Rapture."

65. Versions of these ideas can be found in Wofford, *Choice of Achilles*, 295–371; Deneef, "Spenser's *Amor Fuggitivo*"; and Thomas Hyde, *Poetic Theology of Love*, 143–79. John C. Bean mounts a somewhat similar argument that opposes daemonic Eros to personal identity; see "Making the Daimonic Personal."

66. Roche, *Kindly Flame*, 72–88. Partly on this basis, Joseph Campana argues that Amoret's constraint signifies a masculine erotic subjectivity (*Pain of Reformation*, 183).

67. See the commentary in the variorum *Works of Edmund Spenser*, 298.

68. On this point, see Stephens, *Limits of Eroticism*, 32.

69. Petrarch, *Rime, Trionfi*, line 92. Googe, *Cupido Conquered*, lines 599–616, 683–90, in *Eclogues, Epitaphs*.

70. Petrarch, "Triumph of Cupid," lines 28–29, in *Triumphs of Petrarch*; Googe, *Cupido*, 621–24, in *Eclogues, Epitaphs*.

71. Petrarch, "Triumph of Chastity," lines 133–35, in *Triumphs of Petrarch*.

72. Googe, *Cupido*, lines 691–714, in *Eclogues, Epitaphs*.

73. Ibid., line 717.

74. Petrarch, "Triumph of Chastity," line 181 in *Triumphs of Petrarch*; Googe, *Cupido*, line 234, in *Eclogues, Epitaphs*.

75. For an account of this complex process in the *Trionfi*, with an argument that Spenser applies it to his *Hymnes*, see D. Miller, "*Fowre Hymnes*," 294–96.

76. Googe, *Cupido*, lines 771–72, in *Eclogues, Epitaphs*.

77. For discussion on this point, see Stephens, *Limits of Eroticism*, 29.

78. Silberman, *Transforming Desire*, 68.

Chapter Six   SIN AND MILTON'S ANGEL

1. T. Lupton, *Moral and Pitieful Comedie*, sigs. A4v–B2v.

2. Ibid., sig. B3r.

3. Ibid., sig. B3v.

4. Spenser, *Faerie Queene* 1.1.25–26 (subsequent citations by book, canto, and stanza are given parenthetically in the text); P. Fletcher, *Purple Island* (12.27–29) and *Locusts* (1.10–11); Milton, *Paradise Lost* 2.746–814 (subsequently abbreviated as *PL* and cited parenthetically in the text by book and line number).

5. Herodotus, *History* 3.109.

6. See Pheifer, "Errour and Echidna," 127–74.

7. Prudentius, *Hamartigenia*, 584. Subsequent page citations to this work are given parenthetically in the text.

8. Although identifying Satan as the source of human evil, Prudentius is anxious to deny that we can effectively blame Satan for the evil we practice, "when our sins grow out of our own minds and take their birth and source and power, their being and their strength, from the heart which begets them" (554–56).

9. See Anthony Dykes, *Reading Sin*.

10. Throughout this chapter I will avoid referring to Milton's rebel angel as "Lucifer," since, as John Leonard has discussed, Milton deliberately withholds Satan's prior name in heaven (*Naming in Paradise*, 86–104). This lack of naming also has consequences, as I will suggest, for the poem's sense of the angel's agency.

11. John Carey assumes precisely this, suggesting that Milton responded to the problem of illogical angels by "omitting any depiction of the unfallen Satan from his account" ("Milton's Satan," 136).

12. William Poole has written a monograph on Renaissance discussions about the fall of Adam and Eve and their relation to Milton, and Poole uncovers plenty of perplexities facing commentators. Why, for example, would the presumably sin-free Edenic couple choose to disobey God unless they had already fallen before the serpent tempted them? (*Milton and the Idea*, esp. 9–39). Yet whatever puzzlements emerged from the Genesis story, narrative elaborations of Genesis 2–3 regularly identify the serpent as the "cause" of the transgression. Milton makes this move at the beginning of his epic: "Th'infernal Serpent. He it was . . . " (*PL* 1.34).

13. Passages from R. Baker, *Apology*, sigs. H7r, H9r, H12r; from Grotius, *Adamus Exul*: "Quid in exitium ruiture tuum / Rerum authori parere negas, / Cumque obtigerit res quae potuit / Maxima, frustra majora paras?" (112); and from Heywood, *Hierarchy*, 335.

14. Revard, *War in Heaven*.

15. Heywood, *Hierarchy*, 339; R. Baker, *Apology*, sig. I1r.

16. "When we ask the cause of the evil angels' misery, we find that it is the just result of their turning away from him who supremely is, and their turning towards themselves, who do not exist in that supreme degree. What other name is there for this fault than pride?" (Augustine, *City of God* 12.6, trans. Bettenson, 477). Notice that Augustine is discussing the cause of the rebel angels' misery after their rebellion, not the cause of their choice to rebel. Pride didn't cause the rebel angels to turn away from God to themselves; rather, it is this turning.

17. Ibid. Augustine does note in the *City of God* (12.6, trans. Bettenson, 479) that our creaturely origin *ex nihilo*, rather than *ex dei*, does make possible wicked choices, but he does not think this explains why some creatures choose evil whereas others do not. Only free will can account for that. Nothingness is the initial condition of, not the cause of, the evil will.

18. Ibid. 11.13, trans. Bettenson, 446.

19. Ferry, *Milton's Epic Voice*, 130–31.

20. Of course, if Milton thinks voluntary loving is the same as feeling envious, then we could say that the angel chooses to experience envy. Yet "fraught with envy" sounds highly passive, especially compared to the sense of sustained commitment in the choice to "freely love." Furthermore, "as in our will" may act as a qualifier, designating that dimension of love that *voluntas* can command. Milton suggests that angels do experience involuntary feelings when he describes how Raphael "glowed / Celestial rosy red, love's proper hue" (*PL* 8.618–19). Love's proper hue: the glow belongs to love, not to Raphael's free will.

21. See also *De doctrina Christiana*: "It seems to some people that the good angels now maintain their position not so much by their own strength as by the grace of God. . . . It seems more reasonable, however, to suppose that the good angels stand by their own strength, no less than man did before his fall" (Milton, *Complete Prose Works*, 6:343–44).

22. *City of God* 11.13, trans. Bettenson, 445.

23. On this definition of sin, see Milton, *De doctrina Christiana* (*Complete Prose Works*, 6:382).

24. The only two personifications mentioned in the play, Mercy and Justice, never even appear onstage. See Vondel, *Lucifer*, trans. Clark, 49. Subsequent page citations are to Clark's translation unless otherwise noted and are given parenthetically in the text.

25. Hugo Bekker notes this problem and accounts for it by arguing that Vondel wants to emphasize the theme of mercy. Thus any indication that Lucifer has crossed the point of no return (until the very end) is mis-

taken, including Gabriel's straightforward report in act 3 (Vondel, *Lucifer*, 49) that God has decided to withhold mercy from the rebels (Bekker, "Vondel's 'Lucifer,'" 425–34). Yet his account of Gabriel's "mistake" is rather arbitrary, since nothing else in the play suggests that this angel makes erroneous reports about God's will.

26. Leonard, *Naming in Paradise*, 93.

27. Critics sometimes argue that any inconsistencies result from Abdiel's or Raphael's imperfect knowledge of divine will. But surely this claim amounts to saving the appearances: neither Milton nor his God gives any indication that these loyal angels get the story wrong.

28. In some cases a Miltonic character makes more than one crucial choice over his entire career, such as Samson's decision to trust Delilah. Yet, significantly, Milton opts to place this decision in the past and dramatizes instead Samson's single (heroic and horrific) choice to overcome his Palestinian enemies. Likewise, even if we say that the Lady "chooses" to trust the disguised Comus, Milton gives no indication that her ignorance of his libidinous intentions in any way constitutes a moral lapse, as would be the case in Spenser, for example. Instead, moral choice becomes relevant when the Lady, now aware of her captor's intentions, must definitively refuse his advances. The same situation applies to Eve's "choice" to follow the talking serpent to the Tree of Knowledge.

29. Teskey, "From Allegory to Dialectic," 9.

30. P. Gallagher, *Milton, the Bible*, 93.

31. Ibid., 89.

32. Fallon, *Milton among the Philosophers*, 218.

33. For a very different view of Milton's representation of free will in heaven, one that finds the poem's theodicy a failure, see Strier, "Milton's Fetters," 169–97.

34. Hobbes, *Leviathan* 21.2.

35. Bramhall, "Bramhall's Discourse of Liberty," 4.

36. Bramhall: "[Hobbes's] errour proceedeth from the confounding of *voluntas* and *volitio*, the faculty of the will, and the act of willing" (*Castigations of Mr. Hobbes*, 89). "The act of willing . . . takes not beginning from itself but from the faculty or from the power of willing, which is in the soul. . . . Man, who has a perfect knowledge and prenotion of the end [of an action], is most properly said to move himself" ("Defence of True Liberty," 61).

37. Hobbes: An inquirer into the matter of causation "shall find as much reason, if there be no cause of the thing, to conceive it should begin

at one time as at another, that is, he has equal reason to think it should begin at all times; which is impossible, and therefore he must think there was some special cause why it began then rather than sooner or later; or else it began never, but was eternal" ("Hobbes' Treatise," 39–40).

38. Bramhall: "Whatsoever obligation the understanding does put upon the will, is by the consent of the will, and derived from the power of the will, which was not necessitated to move the understanding to consult. So the will is the lady and mistress of human actions; and the understanding is her trusty counselor, which gives no advice but when it is required by the will. . . . Yea, though the understanding shall judge one of these means to be more expedient then the other, yet forasmuch as in the less expedient there is found some reason of good, the will, in respect of that dominion which it has over itself, may accept that which the understanding judges to be less expedient, and refuse that which it judges to be more expedient" ("Defence of True Liberty," 46).

39. Bramhall, *Castigations of Mr. Hobbes*, 41.

40. Hobbes, "Selections from Hobbes, *The Questions*," 81–82.

41. Ibid., 82.

42. Ibid., 72.

43. On agent causation, see Chisholm, "Human Freedom." On theories of intentionality, see Ginet, *On Action*. On indeterminate causation, see Kane, *Significance of Free Will*.

44. See, for example, Van Inwagen, *Essay on Free Will*. See also the "Danielle" example in McKenna, "Compatibilism."

45. It is always possible to cut against the grain of narrative's temporal orderliness by representing consciousness as a jumble of contradictory thoughts (e.g., the "Proteus" chapter of Joyce's *Ulysses*). But doing this precludes any coherent representation of what we might recognize as deliberate choice.

46. The finest recognition of this narrative effect still comes from Leslie Brisman, who undertakes a study of free will in *Paradise Lost* with the assumption that "choice is necessarily belied when it is written about" (*Milton's Poetry of Choice*, 55).

47. Dennett, "I Could Not Have Done Otherwise," 533–67.

48. Kane, "Responsibility, Luck, and Chance," 240.

49. John S. Tanner, in a brilliant discussion of Milton's representation of evil, notes that "absolute freedom does not lend itself to realistic narrative. . . . Human evil always emerges in the context of prior evil" ("'Say First What Cause,'" 55n7). This is quite right, except that the problem of

"absolute freedom" derives from the nature of narrative, not evil. In *Comus*, the Lady's virtuous choice to refuse her tempter's advances would likewise be rendered arbitrary if the story gave us no earlier indications of her character or her reflections on the danger surrounding her.

50. Bear in mind that this dichotomous effect occurs in narrative, not necessarily in reality. Libertarian philosophers would certainly deny that their perspective divides real human cognition in the manner that I describe below.

51. Danielson, *Milton's Good God*, 131–63; and Fallon, "'To Act or Not,'" 427–29. See also Fallon, *Milton among the Philosophers*, 30–41.

52. Danielson, *Milton's Good God*, 146.

53. For instance, in her otherwise informative discussion of the emblematics of free will in *Paradise Lost*, Mindele Anne Treip confuses reason's ability to "arbitrate over sensible images: to sift, *choose*, and discard"—a function that would clearly seem to determine the will—with reason's alleged status as "preeminently bound up with the act of *free choice*" (162, emphases in original). See "'Reason Is Also Choice,'" 147–77.

54. One can always respond, as I suspect many Milton critics would, that the chooser is free to ignore the promptings of reason and choose evil—as the example of the rebel angels demonstrates. Yes: insofar as we identify choice with power, one always has "free will and power to stand" (*PL* 4.66) and is likewise "free to fall" (3.99). Yet to say this necessarily cramps the poem's alternative formula that "reason also is choice" (3.108): if reason is the condition of choice, it is hard to understand how one chooses against that condition. Hobbes's question emerges: "And if a man determine himself, the question will still remain: what determined him to determine himself in that manner?"

55. For example, Harold Skulsky, in *Milton and the Death of Man*, argues that Eve's mistaken impression of the serpent's reasonableness "is something she's doing to herself" (48), insisting that Eve's poor reasoning as she prepares to eat the fruit derives not from error but rather from deliberate choice: "We are listening to a veteran in the art of lying (in this instance, to herself). Eve is already infected. Once again, the decisive act of will, if any, is well past" (50).

56. Anne Ferry argues that Milton deliberately confines Sin and Death, and allegory in general, to the world of fallen experience; see *Milton's Epic Voice*, 128–40. Maureen Quilligan, in *Milton's Spenser*, suggests that in birthing Sin Satan "has authored something less than pure *res*. He can't do the real thing" (126). Stephen Fallon ("Milton's Sin and Death,"

329–50) has influentially interpreted Sin and Death as allegorical examples of Augustine's claim that evil does not have independent existence but rather represents the absence of good.

57. P. Fletcher, *Locusts* 1.10, 1.11.1–5. Subsequent citations are given parenthetically in the text by canto, stanza, and line number.

58. Fletcher consults the same biblical source as Milton: "When lust hath conceived, it bringeth forth sin" (KJV, James 1:15).

59. John S. Tanner makes a similar point about Sin's birth in the context of discussing the representation of evil: "Milton's myth . . . acknowledges that, at the deepest level, complete self-determination begins to look more like compulsion than like free choice. . . . The evil to which Satan gives birth also possesses him; he does not appear so much to choose evil, rationally and deliberately, as to succumb to it in pain and lust" ("Say First What Cause," 49).

60. I derive this term in part from James Dougal Fleming's interpretation of the figure of Medusa, in *PL* 2.611–12, as a "semiotic radical," a figure who is curiously undetermined by the symbolic discourse of the story around her ("Meanwhile, Medusa").

61. Brisman, *Milton's Poetry of Choice*, 151.

62. I have thus far relied on the fine and dramatic translation of Noel Clark, but here I quote Watson Kirkconnell's less dramatic but more literal translation in his *Celestial Cycle*, 406.

63. *Contra* Stephen M. Fallon, who argues, without mentioning this line, that, unlike Satan, "it is inconceivable . . . that Sin and Death could be 'stupidly good' or 'abstracted from themselves'" ("Milton's Sin and Death," 345). Steven Knapp has argued that Sin's curious literalism "suggests that historical and allegorical agency are readily interchangeable—even in the career of a single agent—and that Milton has no consistent interest either in separating or reconciling the two" (*Personification and the Sublime*, 139). Yet this claim overlooks the fact that Milton has separated out allegorical and literal versions of the same event in books 2 and 5 of his poem.

64. V. Kahn, "Allegory, the Sublime," 143.

65. Calvin, *Institutes*, 152.

Epilogue

1. Shannon, *Accommodated Animal*. See also Boehrer, *Animal Characters*.

2. Puttenham, *Arte of English Poesie*, 246.

3. Boethius, *Treatise against Eutyches*, sec. 3, trans. Stewart and Rand, 84–85.

4. Haraway, "Cyborg Manifesto"; Hayles, *How We Became Posthuman*.

5. Morton, *Hyperobjects*, 84.

6. Hamilton, *Impersonations*, 7.

7. Ibid., 12.

8. Moore, *Ecology and Literature*.

9. Latour, *Reassembling the Social*, 53–58.

10. Ibid., 218, 230.

11. Yates, "Accidental Shakespeare," 96.

12. Yates, "Counting Sheep," para. 2.

13. Yates, "Accidental Shakespeare," 97. Yates makes a similar appeal for a "reverse-*prosopopeia*" in "What Are 'Things' Saying," 1004.

14. Yates, "Counting Sheep," para 3.

15. Wolfe, *What Is Posthumanism*, xvii.

16. Agamben, *Open*, 16.

17. Ibid., 77, my emphasis.

BIBLIOGRAPHY

Adams, Marilyn McCord. "Ockham on Will, Nature, and Morality." In *The Cambridge Companion to Ockham*, ed. Paul Vincent Spade, 245–72. Cambridge: Cambridge University Press, 1999.

Aers, David. *"Piers Plowman" and Christian Allegory*. London: Edward Arnold, 1975.

———. *Salvation and Sin: Augustine, Langland, and Fourteenth-Century Theology*. Notre Dame, IN: University of Notre Dame Press, 2009.

Agamben, Giorgio. *The Open: Man and Animal*. Trans. Kevin Attell. Stanford, CA: Stanford University Press, 2004.

Alexander, Gavin. "Prosopopoeia: The Speaking Figure." In *Renaissance Figures of Speech*, ed. Sylvia Adamson, Gavin Alexander, and Katrin Ettenhuber, 97–114. Cambridge: Cambridge University Press, 2007.

Anderson, Daniel E. *The Masks of Dionysos: A Commentary on Plato's "Symposium."* Albany: State University of New York Press, 1993.

Anderson, Judith. *Reading the Allegorical Intertext: Chaucer, Spenser, Shakespeare, Milton*. New York: Fordham University Press, 2008.

———. "What I Really Teach When I'm Teaching Spenser." *Pedagogy* 3, no. 2 (2003): 177–83.

Anscombe, G. E. M. *Intention*. 2nd ed. Ithaca, NY: Cornell University Press, 1963.

Anselm. *De casu diaboli*. In vol. 2 of *Anselm of Canterbury*, trans. Jasper Hopkins and Herbert Richardson. Toronto: Edwin Mellen Press, 1975.

Apuleius. *The God of Socrates [De Deo Socratis]*. In *Apuleius: Rhetorical Works*, trans. Stephen Harrison, 195–216. Oxford: Oxford University Press, 2001.

Aquinas, Thomas. *The Summa theologica of St. Thomas Aquinas*. Trans. Fathers of the English Dominican Province. New York: Benziger Brothers, 1948.

Arendt, Hannah. *The Human Condition*, 2nd ed. Chicago: University of Chicago Press, 1998.

———. *The Life of the Mind*. Vol. 2. *Willing*. New York: Harcourt, 1978.

Aristotle. *Nicomachean Ethics*. Trans. Roger Crisp. Cambridge: Cambridge University Press, 2000.

———. *Nicomachean Ethics*. Trans. H. Rackham. Loeb Classical Library. Cambridge, MA: Harvard University Press, 2003.

———. *Poetics*. Trans. Stephen Halliwell. Loeb Classical Library. Cambridge, MA: Harvard University Press, 1995.

———. *Physics*. In *The Basic Works of Aristotle*, ed. Richard McKeon, 218–397. New York: Random House, 1941.

Ashman, Ian, and Diana Winstanley. "For or against Corporate Identity? Personification and the Problem of Moral Agency." *Journal of Business Ethics* 76 (2007): 83–95.

Augustine. *City of God*. Trans. Henry Bettenson. New York: Penguin, 2003.

———. *Confessions*. Trans. R. S. Pine-Coffin. New York: Penguin, 1961.

———. *De libero arbitrio libri tres*. Ed. William M. Green. Vienna: Hoelder-Pinchler-Tempsky, 1956.

———. *On the Free Choice of the Will*. Trans. Anna S. Benjamin and L. H. Hackstaff. New York: Macmillan, 1964.

Baker, Denise N. "The Priesthood of Genius: A Study of the Medieval Tradition." *Speculum* 51, no. 2 (1976): 277–91.

Baker, Richard. *An Apology for Laymen's Writing in Divinity, with a Short Meditation upon the Fall of Lucifer*. London, 1691.

Baldwin, Geoff. "Individual and Self in the Late Renaissance." *Historical Journal* 44, no. 2 (2001): 341–64.

Barash, Moshe. "Despair in the Medieval Imagination." *Social Research* 66, no. 2 (1999): 566–76.

Barney, Stephen. *Allegories of History, Allegories of Love*. Hamden, CT: Archon, 1979.

Bataille, George. *Erotism: Death and Sensuality*. Trans. Mary Dalwood. San Francisco: City Lights, 1986.

Bean, John C. "Making the Daimonic Personal: Britomart and Love's Assault in *The Faerie Queene*." *Modern Language Quarterly* 40, no. 3 (1979): 237–55.

Beard, Thomas. *The Theater of God's Judgements*. London, 1597.

Beckwith, Sarah. *Signifying God: Social Relation and Symbolic Act in the York Corpus Christi Plays*. Chicago: University of Chicago Press, 2001.

Bekker, Hugo. "Vondel's 'Lucifer': An Inquiry into Its Structure." *Modern Language Review* 59 (1964): 425–34.

Bembo, Pietro. *Gli Asolani.* Trans. Rudolf B. Gottfried. Bloomington: Indiana University Press, 1954.

Berger, Harry. *Revisionary Play: Studies in the Spenserian Dynamics.* Berkeley: University of California Press, 1990.

Bergson, Henri. *Time and Free Will: An Essay on the Immediate Data of Consciousness.* Trans. F. L. Pogson. New York: Harpers, 1960.

Berlin, Isaiah. "Two Concepts of Liberty." In *The Proper Study of Mankind: An Anthology of Essays,* ed. Henry Hardy and Roger Hausheer, 191–241. New York: Farrar, Straus and Giroux, 1997.

Bernardus Silvestris. *The Cosmographia of Bernardus Silvestris.* Trans. Winthrop Wetherbee. New York: Columbia University Press, 1973.

Bevington, David. "Christopher Marlowe's *Doctor Faustus* and Nathaniel Woodes's *The Conflict of Conscience.*" In *The Oxford Handbook of Tudor Literature, 1485–1603,* ed. Mike Pincombe and Cathy Shrank, 704–17. Oxford: Oxford University Press, 2009.

———. "Marlowe and God." *Explorations in Renaissance Culture* 17 (1991): 1–38.

Blackwell, Mark, ed. *The Secret Life of Things: Animals, Objects, and It-Narratives in Eighteenth Century England.* Lewisburg, PA: Bucknell University Press, 2007.

Bloomfield, Morton. "A Grammatical Approach to Personification Allegory." *Modern Philology* 60, no. 3 (1963): 161–71.

Boehrer, Bruce Thomas. *Animal Characters: Nonhuman Beings in Early Modern Literature.* Philadelphia: University of Pennsylvania Press, 2010.

Boethius. *A Treatise against Eutyches and Nestorius.* In *The Theological Tractates and The Consolation of Philosophy,* trans. H. F. Stewart and E. K. Rand, 73–130. Loeb Classical Library. Cambridge, MA: Harvard University Press, 1968.

Borris, Kenneth. *Allegory and Epic in English Renaissance Literature: Heroic Form in Sidney, Spenser, and Milton.* Cambridge: Cambridge University Press, 2000.

———. "(H)eroic Disarmament: Spenser's Unarmed Cupid, Platonized Heroism, and *The Faerie Queene*'s Poetics." *Spenser Studies,* forthcoming.

Bos, Jacque. "Individuality and Inwardness in Literary Character Sketches of the Seventeenth Century." *Journal of the Warburg and Courtauld Institutes* 61 (1998): 142–57.

Bowers, John M. *The Crisis of Will in "Piers Plowman."* Washington, DC: Catholic University of America Press, 1986.

Braden, Gordon. *Renaissance Tragedy and the Senecan Tradition: Anger's Privilege.* New Haven, CT: Yale University Press, 1985.

Bramhall, John. "Bramhall's Discourse of Liberty and Necessity." In *Hobbes and Bramhall on Liberty and Necessity*, ed. Vere Chapell, 1–14. Cambridge: Cambridge University Press, 1999.

——. *Castigations of Mr. Hobbes his Animadversions.* London, 1657.

——. "A Defence of True Liberty." In *Hobbes and Bramhall on Liberty and Necessity*, ed. Vere Chapell, 43–68. Cambridge: Cambridge University Press, 1999.

Brisman, Leslie. *Milton's Poetry of Choice and Its Romantic Heirs.* Ithaca, NY: Cornell University Press, 1973.

Brown, Jane. *The Persistence of Allegory: Drama and Neoclassicism from Shakespeare to Wagner.* Philadelphia: University of Pennsylvania Press, 2006.

Bunyan, John. *The Pilgrim's Progress.* Ed. Roger Sharrock. New York: Penguin, 1986.

Burckhardt, Jacob. *The Civilisation of the Renaissance in Italy.* Trans. S. G. Middlemore. London, 1878.

Burton, Robert. *The Anatomy of Melancholy.* Ed. Holbrook Jackson. New York: E. P. Dutton, 1932.

Bynum, Caroline Walker. *Metamorphosis and Identity.* New York: Zone Books, 2001.

Calvin, John. *Calvin's New Testament Commentaries.* Ed. David W. Torrance and Thomas F. Torrance. 12 vols. Grand Rapids, MI: Eerdmans, 1959–72.

——. *Institutes of the Christian Religion.* Trans. Henry Beveridge. Grand Rapids, MI: Eerdmans, 1989.

Campana, Joseph. *The Pain of Reformation: Spenser, Vulnerability, and the Ethics of Masculinity.* New York: Fordham University Press, 2012.

Carey, John. "Milton's Satan." In *The Cambridge Companion to Milton*, ed. Dennis Danielson, 160–74. Cambridge: Cambridge University Press, 1989.

Cassirer, Ernst. *The Individual and the Cosmos in Renaissance Philosophy.* Trans. M. Domandi. Oxford: Basil Blackwell, 1963.

Castiglione, Baldassare. *The Book of the Courtier.* Trans. Charles S. Singleton. New York: Anchor Books, 1959.

Charron, Pierre. *Of Wisdome Three Bookes, Written in French by Peter Charron.* Trans. Samson Lennard. London, 1608.

Cheney, Patrick. "'And Doubted Her to Deeme an Earthly Wight': Male Neoplatonic 'Magic' and the Problem of Female Identity in Spenser's Allegory of the Two Florimells." *Studies in Philology* 86 (1989): 310–40.

Cheung, King-Kok. "The Dialectic of Despair in *Doctor Faustus.*" In *"A Poet and a filthy Play-Maker": New Essays on Christopher Marlowe,* ed. Kenneth Friedenreich, Roma Gill, and Constance Brown Kuriyama, 193–201. New York: AMS, 1988.

Chisholm, Roderick. "Human Freedom and the Self." In *Free Will,* 2nd ed., ed. Gary Watson, 26–37. Oxford: Oxford University Press, 2003.

Cicero. *De fato.* Trans. H. Rackman. Loeb Classical Library. Cambridge, MA: Harvard University Press, 1968.

———. *Nature of the Gods.* Trans. H. Rackman. Loeb Classical Library. Cambridge, MA: Harvard University Press, 2005.

Cole, Douglas. "*Doctor Faustus* and the Morality Tradition." In *Suffering and Evil in the Plays of Christopher Marlowe,* 231–46. Princeton, NJ: Princeton University Press, 1962.

Coleridge, Samuel. *The Collected Works of Samuel Taylor Coleridge.* Ed. R. J. White. 23 vols. Bollingen 75. Princeton, NJ: Princeton University Press, 1972.

Conti, Natale. *Mythologiae.* New York: Garland, 1976.

Cummings, Brian. *Literary Culture of the Reformation: Grammar and Grace.* Oxford: Oxford University Press, 2002.

Curran, John E., Jr. *Character and the Individual Personality in English Renaissance Drama: Tragedy, History, Tragicomedy.* Newark: University of Delaware Press, 2014.

Dandas, Judith. "The Masks of Cupid and Death." *Comparative Drama* 29, no. 1 (1995): 38–60.

Danielson, Dennis. *Milton's Good God: A Study in Literary Theodicy.* Cambridge: Cambridge University Press, 1982.

Dante. *Vita nuova.* Trans. Mark Musa. Bloomington: Indiana University Press, 1973.

Davidson, Clifford, and Peter Happe, eds. *The World and the Chylde.* Kalamazoo, MI: Medieval Institute Publications, Western Michigan University, 1999.

Deats, Sara Munson. "From Chapbook to Tragedy." *Essays in Literature* 3 (1976): 3–16.

De Man, Paul. "Autobiography as De-facement." In *The Rhetoric of Romanticism*, 67–82. New York: Columbia University Press, 1984.

———. "The Epistemology of Metaphor." In *On Metaphor*, ed. Sheldon Sacks, 11–28. Chicago: University of Chicago Press, 1979.

———. "Hypogram and Inscription." In *The Resistance to Theory*, 27–53. Manchester: Manchester University Press, 1986.

Demetrius. *On Style*. Trans. Doreen C. Innes. Loeb Classical Library. Cambridge, MA: Harvard University Press, 1995.

Dempsey, Joanne T. "Angel, Guyon's." In *The Spenser Encyclopedia*, ed. A. C. Hamilton. Toronto: University of Toronto Press, 1997.

Deneef, A. Leigh. *Spenser and the Motives of Metaphor*. Durham, NC: Duke University Press, 1982.

———. "Spenser's *Amor Fuggitivo* and the Transfixed Heart." *ELH* 46, no. 1 (1979): 1–20.

Dennett, Daniel. "I Could Not Have Done Otherwise—So What?" *Journal of Philosophy* 81 (1984): 533–67.

Descartes, René. *Meditations*. In *Descartes: Philosophical Writings*, ed. and trans. Elizabeth Anscombe and Peter Thomas Geach. Indianapolis: Bobbs-Merrill, 1971.

———. *Passions of the Soul*. In *The Philosophical Writings of Descartes*, ed. J. Cottingham, R. Stoothoof, and D. Murdoch, 1:325–404. Cambridge: Cambridge University Press, 1984.

Dihle, Albrecht. *The Theory of the Will in Classical Antiquity*. Berkeley: University of California Press, 1982.

Dixon, Michael. *The Polliticke Courtier: Spenser's "The Faerie Queene" as a Rhetoric of Justice*. Montreal: McGill-Queen's University Press, 1996.

Dolven, Jeff. "Spenser's Sense of Poetic Justice." *Raritan* 21, no. 1 (2001): 127–40.

Donno, Elizabeth Story. "The Triumph of Cupid: Spenser's Legend of Chastity." *Yearbook of English Studies* 4 (1974): 37–48.

Dubos, Jean-Baptiste. *Critical Reflections on Poetry, Painting and Music*. Trans. Thomas Nugent. 3 vols. London, 1748.

Dubrow, Heather. *Echoes of Desire: English Petrarchanism and Its Counterdiscourses*. Ithaca, NY: Cornell University Press, 1995.

Duns Scotus. *Duns Scotus on the Will and Morality.* Ed. and trans. Alan B. Wolter. Washington, DC: Catholic University of America Press, 1986.

Dykes, Anthony. *Reading Sin in the World: The "Hamartigenia" of Prudentius and the Vocation of the Responsible Reader.* Cambridge: Cambridge University Press, 2011.

Eggert, Katherine. "Spenser's Ravishment: Rape and Rapture in *The Faerie Queene*." *Representations* 70 (2000): 1–26.

Ellrodt, Robert. *Neoplatonism in the Poetry of Edmund Spenser.* Geneva: E. Droz, 1960.

Epictetus. *Discourses and Selected Writings.* Trans. Robert Dobbin. New York: Penguin, 2008.

Erasmus, Desiderius. *De copia verborum ac rerum.* Vol. 17 of *Opera omnia,* ed. Betty I. Knott. Amsterdam: Elsevier, 1988.

———. *On Copia of Words and Ideas.* Trans. Herbert David Rix and Donald B. King. Milwaukee, WI: Marquette University Press, 1999.

Escobedo, Andrew. "Despair and the Proportion of the Self." *Spenser Studies* 17 (2003): 75–90.

———. "The Sincerity of Rapture." *Spenser Studies* 24 (2009): 185–208.

Euripides. *The Complete Greek Tragedies.* Ed. David Grene and Richard Lattimore. 4 vols. Chicago: University of Chicago Press, 1959.

Evans, Maurice. "Platonic Allegory in *The Faerie Queene*." *Review of English Studies* 12, no. 46 (1961): 132–43.

Fallon, Stephen M. *Milton among the Philosophers: Poetry and Materialism in Seventeenth-Century England.* Ithaca, NY: Cornell University Press, 1991.

———. "Milton's Sin and Death: The Ontology of Allegory in *Paradise Lost*." *ELR* 17 (1987): 329–50.

———. "'To Act or Not': Milton's Conception of Divine Freedom." *Journal of the History of Ideas* 49 (1988): 425–49.

Ferry, Anne. *Milton's Epic Voice: The Narrator in "Paradise Lost."* Cambridge, MA: Harvard University Press, 1963.

Ficino, Marsilio. *Commentary on Plato's "Symposium."* Trans. Sears Reynolds Jayne. Columbia: University of Missouri, 1944.

———. *The Letters of Marsilio Ficino.* Trans. members of the Language Department of the School of Economic Science. London: Shepheard-Walwyn, 1975.

———. *Marsilio Ficino and the Phaedran Charioteer.* Ed. and trans. Michael J. B. Allen. Berkeley: University of California Press, 1981.

Fisher, Philip. *The Vehement Passions*. Princeton, NJ: Princeton University Press, 2002.

Fleming, James Dougal. "Meanwhile, Medusa in *Paradise Lost*." *ELH* 69 (2002): 1009–28.

———. *Milton's Secrecy and Philosophical Hermeneutics*. Burlington, VT: Ashgate, 2008.

Fletcher, Angus (1930–2016). *Allegory: Theory of a Symbolic Mode*. Ithaca, NY: Cornell University Press, 1964.

———. "Allegory without Ideas." In *Thinking Allegory Otherwise*, ed. Brenda Machosky, 9–36. Stanford, CA: Stanford University Press, 2009.

Fletcher, Angus (1976–). "*Doctor Faustus* and the Lutheran Aesthetic." *ELR* 35, no. 2 (2005): 187–209.

Fletcher, Phineas. *The Locusts, or Apollyonists*. In *The Poetical Works of Giles and Phineas Fletcher*, ed. Frederick S. Boas, 1:125–86. Cambridge: Cambridge University Press, 1909.

———. *The Purple Island*. In *The Poetical Works of Giles and Phineas Fletcher*, ed. Frederick S. Boas, 2:1–172. Cambridge: Cambridge University Press, 1909.

Foucault, Michel. *The Use of Pleasure*. Trans. Robert Hurley. New York: Vintage, 1986.

Fowler, Elizabeth. *Literary Character: The Human Figure in Early English Writing*. Ithaca, NY: Cornell University Press, 2003.

Frank, Robert Worth, Jr. "The Art of Reading Medieval Personification-Allegory." *ELH* 20, no. 4 (1953): 237–43.

Frankfurt, Harry G. "Freedom of the Will and the Concept of a Person." *Journal of Philosophy* 68, no. 1 (1971): 5–20.

Fraunce, Abraham. *The Arcadian Rhetorike*. London, 1588.

Frede, Michael. *A Free Will: Origins of the Notion in Ancient Thought*. Ed. A. A. Long. Berkeley: University of California Press, 2011.

Freeman, Lisa. *Character's Theater: Genre and Identity on the Eighteenth-Century English Stage*. Philadelphia: University of Pennsylvania Press, 2002.

Freinkel, Lisa. *Reading Shakespeare's Will: The Theology of Figure from Augustine to the Sonnets*. New York: Columbia University Press, 2002.

Fulwell, Ulpian. *Like Will to Like*. London, 1568.

Furley, David. "Self-Movers." In *Aristotle on Mind and the Senses*, ed. G. E. R. Lloyd and G. E. L. Owen, 165–79. Cambridge: Cambridge University Press, 2007.

Gallagher, Lowell. *Medusa's Gaze: Casuistry and Conscience in the Renaissance*. Stanford, CA: Stanford University Press, 1991.

Gallaher, Philip J. *Milton, the Bible, and Misogyny*. Columbia: University of Missouri Press, 1990.

Garber, Margery. "Hamlet: Giving Up the Ghost." In *Shakespeare's Ghost Writers: Literature as Uncanny Casualty*, 124–76. New York: Methuen, 1987.

Gillespie, Michael Allen. *The Theological Origins of Modernity*. Chicago: University of Chicago Press, 2008.

Ginet, Carl. *On Action*. Cambridge: Cambridge University Press, 1990.

Ginzberg, Carlo. *The Cheese and the Worms: The Cosmos of a Sixteenth-Century Miller*. Trans. John Tedeschi and Anne Tedeschi. Baltimore: Johns Hopkins University Press, 1980.

Gless, Darryl J. *Interpretation and Theology in Spenser*. Cambridge: Cambridge University Press, 1994.

Goeglein, Tamara A. "Utterances of the Protestant Soul in *The Faerie Queene*: The Allegory of Holiness and the Humanist Discourse of Reason." *Criticism* 36, no. 1 (1994): 1–19.

Goethe, Johann Wolfgang von. *Maxims and Reflections*. Trans. Thomas Bailey Saunders. New York: Macmillan, 1908.

Gombrich, E. H. "Personification." In *Classical Influences on European Culture, A.D. 500–1500*, ed. R. R. Bolgar, 247–57. Cambridge: Cambridge University Press, 1971.

Goodman, Nelson. *The Languages of Art: An Approach to a Theory of Symbols*. Indianapolis: Bobbs-Merrill, 1968.

Googe, Barnabe. *Eclogues, Epitaphs, and Sonnets*. Ed. Judith M. Kennedy. Toronto: University of Toronto Press, 1989.

Grantley, Darryll. *English Dramatic Interludes, 1300–1580: A Reference Guide*. Cambridge: Cambridge University Press, 2004.

Griffiths, Jane. "Counterfeit Countenaunce: (Mis)representation and the Challenge to Allegory in Sixteenth-Century Morality Plays." *Yearbook of English Studies* 38, nos. 1/2 (2008): 17–33.

Griffiths, Lavinia. *Personification in "Piers Plowman."* Cambridge: D. S. Brewer, 1985.

Grotius, Hugo. *Adamus exul.* In *The Celestial Cycle: The Theme of Paradise Lost in World Literature*, ed. Watson Kirkconnell, 96–220. Toronto: University of Toronto Press, 1952.

Guenther, Genevieve. "Spenser's Magic, or Instrumental Aesthetics in the 1590 *Faerie Queene.*" *ELR* 36, no. 1 (2006): 194–226.

Guillaume de Lorris. *Romance of the Rose.* Trans. Charles Dahlberg. Princeton, NJ: Princeton University Press, 1995.

Halperin, David. "Love's Irony: Six Remarks on Platonic Eros." In *Erotikon: Essays on Eros, Ancient and Modern*, ed. Shadi Bartsch and Thomas Bartscherer, 48–58. Chicago: University of Chicago Press, 2005.

Hamilton, Sheryl. *Impersonations: Troubling the Person in Law and Culture.* Toronto: University of Toronto Press, 2009.

Hamlin, William M. "Casting Doubt in Marlowe's *Doctor Faustus.*" *Studies in English Literature 1500–1900* 41, no. 2 (2001): 257–75.

Hanna, Robert. "Persons and Personation in Hobbes's *Leviathan.*" *Southern Journal of Philosophy* 21, no. 2 (1983): 177–91.

Haraway, Donna. "Cyborg Manifesto." In *Simians, Cyborgs and Women: The Reinvention of Nature*, 149–81. New York: Routledge, 1991.

Harington, John. *A New Discourse of a Stale Subiect, Called the Metamorphosis of Aiax.* London, 1596.

Harris, W. S. *Mr. World and Miss Church-Member: A Twentieth Century Allegory.* Harrisburg, PA: Minter, 1903.

Harsnett, Samuel. "A Sermon Preached at Saint Paul's Cross" [October 27, 1584]. In Richard Stewart, *Three sermons . . . To which is added . . . a fourth sermon . . . by . . . Samuel Harsnett.* London, 1656.

Hayles, K. Katherine. *How We Became Posthuman: Virtual Bodies in Cybernetics, Literature, and Informatics.* Chicago: University of Chicago Press, 1999.

Hebreo, Leone. *The Philosophy of Love.* Trans. F. Friedberg-Seeley and Jean H. Barnes. London: Soncino Press, 1937.

Hendrix, Laurel L. "'Mother of Laughter, and Wellspring of Blisse': Spenser's Venus and the Poetics of Mirth." *ELR* 23, no. 1 (1993): 113–33.

Henry of Ghent. *Quodlibetal Questions on Free Will.* Trans. Roland J. Teske. Milwaukee, WI: Marquette University Press, 1993.

Herdt, Jennifer A. *Putting on Virtue: The Legacy of the Splendid Vices.* Chicago: University of Chicago Press, 2008.

Herodotus. *The History*. Ed. David Grene. Chicago: University of Chicago Press, 1988.

Heywood, Thomas. *The Hierarchy of the Blessed Angels*. London, 1635.

Hieatt, A. Kent. "Room of One's Own for Decisions: Chaucer and *The Faerie Queene*." In *Refiguring Chaucer in the Middle Ages*, ed. Theresa M. Krier. Gainesville: University Press of Florida, 1998.

Higgins, John. *The First Part of the Mirour for Magistrates*. London, 1574.

Hinks, Roger. *Myth and Allegory of Ancient Art*. London: Warburg Institute, 1939.

The Historie of the Damnable Life and Deserved Death of Doctor John Faustus. Trans. A. P., Gent. London, 1592.

Hobart, R. E. "Free Will as Involving Determinism and Inconceivable without It." *Mind* 43, no. 169 (1934): 1–27.

Hobbes, Thomas. "Hobbes' Treatise *Of Liberty and Necessity*." In *Hobbes and Bramhall on Liberty and Necessity*, ed. Vere Chapell, 15–42. Cambridge: Cambridge University Press, 1999.

———. *Leviathan*. Ed. Edwin Curley. Indianapolis: Hackett, 1994.

———. "Selections from Hobbes, *The Questions Concerning Liberty, Necessity, and Chance*." In *Hobbes and Bramhall on Liberty and Necessity*, ed. Vere Chapell, 69–90. Cambridge: Cambridge University Press, 1999.

Home, Henry (Lord Kames). *Elements of Criticism*. 6th ed. 1785. Reprint, New York: Garland, 1972.

Hooker, Richard. *A learned and comfortable sermon of the certaintie and perpetuitie of faith in the elect*. Oxford, 1612.

———. *Of the Laws of Ecclesiastical Polity*. Ed. Arthur Stephen McGrade. 3 vols. Oxford: Oxford University Press, 2013.

Hoskyns, John. "Direccions for Speech and Style." In *The Life, Letters, and Writings of John Hoskyns, 1566–1638*, ed. Louise Brown Osborn. New Haven, CT: Yale University Press, 1937.

Hyde, Thomas. *The Poetic Theology of Love: Cupid in the Renaissance*. Newark: University of Delaware Press, 1986.

Imbrie, Ann E. "'Playing Legerdemaine with Scripture': Parodic Sermons in *The Faerie Queene*." *ELR* 17 (1987): 142–55.

James, Susan. *Passion and Action: The Emotions in Seventeenth-Century Philosophy*. Oxford: Oxford University Press, 1999.

Jefferson, Thomas. *The Papers of Thomas Jefferson: Retirement Series*. Ed. J. Jefferson Looney. 8 vols. Princeton, NJ: Princeton University Press.

Jewett, William. "*The Fall of Robespierre* and the Sublime Machine of Agency." *ELH* 63 (1996): 423–52.

Johnson, Samuel. *The Lives of the Most Eminent English Poets; with Critical Observations on Their Works.* Ed. Roger Lonsdale. Oxford: Clarendon Press, 2006.

Junker, William. "Spenser's Unarmed Cupid and the Experience of the 1590 *Faerie Queene.*" *ELH* 79 (2012): 59–83.

Kahn, Charles H. "Discovering the Will, from Aristotle to Augustine." In *The Question of "Eclecticism": Studies in Later Greek Philosophy*, ed. John Dillon and A. A. Long, 243–60. Berkeley: University of California Press, 1988.

Kahn, Victoria. "Allegory, the Sublime, and the Rhetoric of Things Indifferent in *Paradise Lost.*" In *Creative Imitation: New Essays on Renaissance Literature in Honor of Thomas M. Greene*, ed. David Quint et al., 127–52. Binghamton, NY: Medieval and Renaissance Text Studies, 1992.

———. "Revising the History of Machiavellianism: English Machiavellianism and the Doctrine of Things Indifferent." *Renaissance Quarterly* 46, no. 3 (1993): 526–61.

Kane, Robert. "Responsibility, Luck, and Chance: Reflections on Free Will and Determinism." *Journal of Philosophy* 96 (1999): 217–40.

———. *The Significance of Free Will.* Oxford: Oxford University Press, 1996.

Kant, Immanuel. *Anthropology from a Pragmatic Point of View.* Ed. Robert B. Louden. Cambridge: Cambridge University Press, 2006.

———. *Critique of Judgment.* Trans. Werner S. Pluhar. Indianapolis: Hackett, 1987.

———. *Critique of Pure Reason.* Trans. Norman Kemp Smith. 2nd ed. New York: Palgrave Macmillan, 2003.

———. *Groundwork of the Metaphysics of Morals.* Ed. Mary Gregor. Cambridge: Cambridge University Press, 1997.

Kaske, Carol, ed. *The Faerie Queene: Book One.* By Edmund Spenser. New York: Hackett, 2006.

Keenleyside, Heather. "Personification for the People: On James Thomson's *The Seasons.*" *ELH* 76 (2009): 447–72.

Kenny, Anthony. *Aristotle's Theory of Will.* New Haven, CT: Yale University Press, 1979.

Kent, Bonnie. *Virtues of the Will: The Transformation of Ethics in the Late Thirteenth Century.* Washington, DC: Catholic University of America Press, 1995.

Kessler, Samuel R. "An Analogue for Spenser's Despair Episode: Perkins's 'Dialogue . . . between Sathan and the Christian.'" *Notes and Queries* 47, no. 1 (2000): 31–34.

Kierkegaard, Søren. *The Sickness unto Death: A Christian Psychological Exposition for Upbuilding and Awakening.* Ed. and trans. Howard V. Hong and Edna H. Hong. Princeton, NJ: Princeton University Press, 1980.

Kiessling, Nicolas. "*Doctor Faustus* and the Sin of Demoniality." *Studies in English Literature* 15, no. 2 (1975): 205–11.

Kingsley-Smith, Jane. *Cupid in Early Modern Literature and Culture.* Cambridge: Cambridge University Press, 2010.

Knapp, Steven. *Personification and the Sublime: Milton to Coleridge.* Cambridge, MA: Harvard University Press, 1985.

Korolec, J. B. "Free Will and Free Choice." In *The Cambridge History of Later Medieval Philosophy*, ed. Norman Kretzmann et al., 629–41. Cambridge: Cambridge University Press, 1982.

Krier, Theresa. "Daemonic Allegory: The Elements in Late Spenser, Late Shakespeare, and Irigaray." *Spenser Studies* 18 (2003): 315–42.

———. "Psychic Deadness in Allegory: Spenser's House of Mammon and Attacks on Linking." In *Imagining Death in Spenser and Milton*, ed. Elizabeth Bellamy, Patrick Cheney, and Michael Schoenfeldt, 46–64. Basingstoke: Palgrave Macmillan, 2003.

Lakoff, George, and Mark Turner. *More Than Cool Reason: A Field Guide to Poetic Metaphor.* Chicago: University of Chicago Press, 1989.

Lancashire, Ian, ed. *Two Tudor Interludes.* Manchester: Manchester University Press, 1980.

Langland, William. *Piers Plowman: A Parallel-Text Edition of the A, B, C, and Z Versions.* Ed. A. V. C. Schmidt. New York: Longman, 1995.

La Primaudaye, Pierre de. *The Second Part of the French Academie.* London, 1594.

Latour, Bruno. *Reassembling the Social: An Introduction to Actor-Network-Theory.* Oxford: Oxford University Press, 2005.

———. *We Have Never Been Modern.* Trans. Catherine Porter. Cambridge, MA: Harvard University Press, 1993.

Leonard, John. *Naming in Paradise: Milton and the Language of Adam and Eve.* Oxford: Clarendon Press, 1990.

Lewis, C. S. *The Allegory of Love: A Study in Medieval Tradition.* Oxford: Clarendon Press, 1936.

———. *Spenser's Images of Life.* Cambridge: Cambridge University Press, 1967.

Loewenstein, Joseph. "Echo's Ring: Orpheus and Spenser's Career." *ELR* 16 (1986): 287–302.

Lombard, Peter. *The Sentences, Books 1–4.* Toronto: Institute of Medieval Studies, 2007–10.

Long, A. A. "Freedom and Determinism in the Stoic Theory of Human Action." In *Problems in Stoicism,* ed. A. A. Long, 175–92. London: Athlone Press,1971.

Lowe, Dunstan M. "Personification Allegory in the *Aeneid* and Ovid's *Metamorphoses.*" *Mnemosyne* 61 (2008): 414–35.

Lucan, Marcus Annaeus. *Pharsalia.* Trans. J. D. Duff. Loeb Classical Library. Cambridge, MA: Harvard University Press, 1969.

Lucretius. *De rerum natura.* Trans. W. H. D. Rouse and Martin Ferguston Smith. Loeb Classical Library. Cambridge, MA: Harvard University Press, 2002.

Lukacher, Ned. *Daemonic Figures: Shakespeare and the Question of Conscience.* Ithaca, NY: Cornell University Press, 1994.

Lupton, Christina. *Knowing Books: The Consciousness of Mediation in Eighteenth-Century Britain.* Philadelphia: University of Pennsylvania Press, 2012.

Lupton, Thomas. *A Moral and Pitieful Comedie, intituled, All for Money.* London, 1578.

Luther, Martin. *A Commentarie of M. Doctor Martin Luther upon the Epistle of S. Paul to the Galathians.* Trans. anonymous. London, 1575.

———. *On the Bondage of the Will.* In *Luther and Erasmus: Free Will and Salvation.* Trans. Phillip S. Watson. Philadelphia: Westminster Press, 1969.

MacCaffrey, Isabel G. *Spenser's Allegory: The Anatomy of the Imagination.* Princeton, NJ: Princeton University Press, 1976.

Magnusson, Lynne. "A Play of Modals: Grammar and Potential Action in Early Shakespeare." *Shakespeare Survey* 62 (2009): 69–80.

Mâle, Émile. *Religious Art in France, XIII Century.* Trans. Dora Nussey. London: J. M. Dent, 1913.

Mankind. In *Everyman and Mankind,* ed. Douglas Bruster and Eric Rasmussen. London: Arden Shakespeare, 2015.

Maresca, Thomas. "Saying and Meaning: Allegory and the Indefinable." *Bulletin of Research in the Humanities* 83 (1980): 248–61.

Marlowe, Christopher. *Doctor Faustus: The A- and B-Texts (1604, 1616).* Ed. David Bevington and Eric Rasmussen. Manchester: Manchester University Press, 2014.

Marvell, Andrew. *The Complete Poems.* Ed. Elizabeth Story Donno. New York: Penguin, 2005.

McKenna, Michael. "Compatibilism." In *The Stanford Encyclopedia of Philosophy*, online ed., ed. Edward N. Zalta. October 5, 2009. http://plato.stanford.edu/entries/compatibilism/.

Mill, John Stuart. "On the Freedom of the Will." In *An Examination of William Hamilton's Philosophy and of the Principal Philosophical Questions Discussed in His Writings*, vol. 9 of *The Collected Works of John Stuart Mill*, ed. John M. Robson, 437–69. Toronto: University of Toronto Press; London: Routledge and Kegan Paul, 1979.

Miller, David Lee. "*Fowre Hymnes* and *Prothalamion* (1596)." In *Oxford Handbook of Edmund Spenser*, ed. Richard A. McCabe, 293–313. Oxford: Oxford University Press, 2010.

———. *The Poem's Two Bodies: The Poetics of the 1590 "Faerie Queene."* Princeton, NJ: Princeton University Press, 1988.

Miller, J. Hillis. *Versions of Pygmalion.* Cambridge, MA: Harvard University Press, 1990.

Milton, John. *Complete Prose Works of John Milton.* New Haven, CT: Yale University Press, 1973.

———. *Paradise Lost.* 2nd ed. Ed. Alistair Fowler. London: Longman, 1998.

Monta, Susannah Brietz, and Lisi Oliver. "Spenser, Wolfram, and the Reformation of Despair." *Journal of Literary Onomastics*, forthcoming.

Moore, Bryan L. *Ecology and Literature: Ecocentric Personification from Antiquity to the Twenty-First Century.* New York: Palgrave, 2008.

Morton, Timothy. *Hyperobjects: Philosophy and Ecology after the End of the World.* Minneapolis: University of Minnesota Press, 2013.

Moss, Daniel. "Spenser's Despair and God's Grace." *Spenser Studies* 23 (2008): 73–102.

Murrin, Michael. *The Veil of Allegory: Some Notes toward a Theory of Allegorical Rhetoric in the English Renaissance.* Chicago: University of Chicago Press, 1969.

Nehamas, Alexander. *Only a Promise of Happiness: The Place of Beauty in a World of Art.* Princeton, NJ: Princeton University Press, 2007.

Nestrick, William. "Spenser and the Renaissance Mythology of Love." In

Medieval and Renaissance Literature, ed. Eric Rothstein and Joseph Anthony Wittreich Jr. Literary Monographs 6. Madison: University of Wisconsin Press, 1975.

Newman, Barbara. *God and the Goddesses: Vision, Poetry, and Belief in the Middle Ages*. Philadelphia: University of Pennsylvania Press, 2003.

Nice Wanton. Ed. Leonard Tennenhouse. New York: Garland, 1984.

Nietzsche, Friedrich. *Beyond Good and Evil*. Trans. Walter Kaufman. New York: Vintage, 1966.

Nishimura, Satoshi. "Personification: Its Functions and Boundaries." *Papers on Language and Literature* 50, no. 1 (2014): 90–107.

Nitzsche, Jane Chance. *The Genius Figure in Antiquity and the Middle Ages*. New York: Columbia University Press, 1975.

Norland, Howard D. *Drama in Early Tudor Britain, 1485–1558*. Lincoln: University of Nebraska Press, 1995.

Normore, Calvin G. "Ockham, Self-Motion, and the Will." In *Self-Motion: From Aristotle to Newton*, ed. Mary Louise Gill and James G. Lennox, 291–303. Princeton, NJ: Princeton University Press, 1994.

Nuttall, A. D. *The Alternative Trinity: Gnostic Heresy in Marlowe, Milton, and Blake*. Oxford: Clarendon Press, 1998.

———. *Two Concepts of Allegory: A Study of Shakespeare's "The Tempest" and the Logic of Allegorical Expression*. New York: Barnes and Noble, 1967.

Olympiodorus. *Commentary on the First Alcibiades of Plato*. Ed. L. G. Westerink. Amsterdam: North-Holland, 1956.

Oram, William A. "Characterization and Spenser's Allegory." In *Spenser at Kalamazoo, 1984: Proceedings of the Nineteenth International Congress on Medieval Studies*, ed. Francis G. Greco, 91–122. Clarion, PA: Clarion University Press, 1984.

———. "Spenser's Crowd of Cupids and the Language of Pleasure." In *Rhetorics of Bodily Health in Medieval and Early Modern England*, ed. Jennifer C. Vaught, 87–104. New York: Ashgate, 2010.

O'Reilly, Jennifer. *Studies in the Iconography of the Virtues and the Vices in the Middle Ages*. New York: Garland, 1988.

Ornstein, Robert. "Marlowe and God: The Tragic Theology of *Dr. Faustus*." *PMLA* 83, no. 5 (1968): 1378–85.

Padel, Ruth. *In and Out of Mind: Greek Images of the Tragic Self*. Princeton, NJ: Princeton University Press, 1992.

Parsons, Robert. *A Booke of Christian exercise apperteining to Resolution*. Oxford, 1585.

Paster, Gail Kern. *Humoring the Body: Emotions and the Shakespearean Stage.* Chicago: University of Chicago Press, 2004.

Paster, Gail Kern, Katherine Rowe, and Mary Floyd-Wilson. Introduction to *Reading the Early Modern Passions: Essays in the History of Emotion,* ed. Gail Kern Paster, Katherine Rowe, and Mary Floyd-Wilson, 1–20. Philadelphia: University of Pennsylvania Press, 2004.

Paxson, James J. *The Poetics of Personification.* Cambridge: Cambridge University Press, 1994.

———. "Queering 'Piers Plowman': The Copula(tion)s of Figures in Medieval Allegory." *Rhetoric Society Quarterly* 29, no. 3 (1999): 21–29.

Peacham, Henry. *The Garden of Eloquence.* 2nd ed. London, 1593.

Perkins, William. *A Discourse of Conscience.* London, 1596.

———. *The Golden Chaine.* London, 1600.

———. *A Reformed Catholike.* London, 1598.

———. *Treatise tending unto a declaration whether a man be in the estate of damnation or in the estate of grace.* London, 1590.

———. *The Works of that Famous and Worthy Minister of Christ in the University of Cambridge, Mr. William Perkins. The First Volume: Newly Corrected. . . .* 2 vols. London, 1626.

Petrarca, Francesco. *Rime, trionfi, e poesie latine.* Ed. F. Neri. Milan: Ricciardi, 1951.

———. *The Triumphs of Petrarch.* Trans. Ernest Hatch Wilkins. Chicago: University of Chicago Press, 1962.

Pfau, Thomas. *Minding the Modern: Human Agency, Intellectual Traditions, and Responsible Knowledge.* Notre Dame, IN: University of Notre Dame Press, 2013.

Pheifer, J. D. "Errour and Echidna in *The Faerie Queene*: A Study of Literary Tradition." In *Literature and Learning in Medieval and Renaissance England,* ed. John Scattergood, 127–74. Blackrock, Dublin: Irish Academic Press, 1984.

Pieper, Josef. *Enthusiasm and Divine Madness: On the Platonic Dialogue "Phaedrus."* Trans. Richard and Clara Winston. South Bend, IN: St. Augustine's Press, 2000.

Pierce, C. A. *Conscience in the New Testament.* London: SCM Press, 1955.

Pittock, Malcolm. "God's Mercy Is Infinite: Faustus's Last Soliloquy." *English Studies* 4 (1984): 302–11.

Plato. *The Collected Dialogues of Plato.* Ed. Edith Hamilton and Huntington Cairns. Princeton, NJ: Princeton University Press, 1961.

———. *Platonis opera.* Ed. John Burnet. Oxford: Oxford University Press, 1901.

Platt, Peter G. *Reason Diminished: Shakespeare and the Marvelous.* Lincoln: University of Nebraska Press, 1997.

Plotinus. *Enneads.* 6 vols. Trans. A. H. Armstrong. Loeb Classical Library. Cambridge, MA: Harvard University Press, 1966–67.

Plutarch. *Obsolescence of the Oracles.* Trans. Frank Cole Babbit. Loeb Classical Library. Cambridge, MA: Harvard University Press, 1993.

Pomponazzi, Pietro. *Libri quinque de fato, de libero arbitrio et de praedestinatione.* Ed. Richard Lemay. Lucani: Thesaurus Mundi, 1957.

Poole, William. *Milton and the Idea of the Fall.* Cambridge: Cambridge University Press, 2005.

Poppi, Antonino. "Fate, Fortune, Providence, and Human Freedom." In *The Cambridge History of Renaissance Philosophy*, ed. Quentin Skinner and Eckhard Kesser, 641–67. Cambridge: Cambridge University Press, 1998.

Porphyry. *On Abstinence from Killing Animals.* Trans. Gillian Clark. Ithaca, NY: Cornell University Press, 2000.

Prieto-Pablos, Juan A. "'What Art Thou Faustus? Self-Reference and Strategies of Identification in Marlowe's *Doctor Faustus.*" *English Studies* 74 (1993): 66–83.

Prudentius Clemens, Aurelius. *Works: English and Latin.* Trans. H. J. Thomson. 2 vols. Loeb Classical Library. Cambridge, MA: Harvard University Press, 2006.

Puttenham, George. *The Arte of English Poesie.* London, 1589.

Quilligan, Maureen. *The Language of Allegory: Defining the Genre.* Ithaca, NY: Cornell University Press, 1979.

———. *Milton's Spenser: The Politics of Reading.* Ithaca, NY: Cornell University Press, 1983.

Quintillian. *Institutio oratoria.* Trans. Doland A. Russell. 5 vols. Cambridge, MA: Harvard University Press, 1999.

Quitslund, Beth. "Despair and the Composition of the Self." *Spenser Studies* 17 (2003): 91–106.

Quitslund, Jon. *Spenser's Supreme Fiction: Platonic Natural Philosophy and "The Faerie Queene."* Toronto: University of Toronto Press, 2001.

Raskolnikov, Masha. *Body against Soul: Gender and Sowlehele in Middle English Allegory.* Columbus: Ohio State University Press, 2009.

Reiss, Timothy. *Mirages of the Selfe: Patterns of Personhood in Ancient and Early Modern Europe.* Stanford, CA: Stanford University Press, 2003.

Revard, Stella Purce. *The War in Heaven: "Paradise Lost" and the Tradition of Satan's Rebellion.* Ithaca, NY: Cornell University Press, 1980.

Reynolds, Edward. *A Treatise of the Passions and Faculties of the Soul of Man.* London, 1640.

Riffaterre, Michael. "Prosopopeia." *Yale French Studies* 69 (1985): 107–23.

Roche, Thomas P. *The Kindly Flame: A Study of the Third and Fourth Books of Spenser's "Faerie Queene."* Princeton, NJ: Princeton University Press, 1964.

———. "The Menace of Despair and Arthur's Vision, *Faerie Queene, I.9.*" *Spenser Studies* 4 (1984): 71–92.

Ryle, Gilbert. *The Concept of Mind.* Harmondsworth: Penguin, 1973.

Sanchez, Melissa E. *Erotic Subjects: The Sexuality of Politics in Early Modern English Literature.* Philadelphia: University of Pennsylvania Press, 2011.

Sander, Nicholas. *The Supper of Our Lord.* English Recusant Literature 199. Menston: Scolar Press, 1974.

Sanders, Wilbur. *The Dramatist and the Received Idea.* Cambridge: Cambridge University Press, 1968.

Sartre, Jean-Paul. *Existentialism Is a Humanism.* Trans. Carol Macomber. New Haven, CT: Yale University Press, 2007.

Saul, Jennifer. "On Treating Things as People: Objectification, Pornography, and the History of the Vibrator." *Hypatia* 21, no. 2 (2006): 45–61.

Schoenfeldt, Michael. *Bodies and Selves in Early Modern England: Physiology and Inwardness in Spenser, Shakespeare, Herbert, and Milton.* Cambridge: Cambridge University Press, 1999.

Schwarz, Kathryn. *What You Will: Gender, Contract, and Shakespearean Social Space.* Philadelphia: University of Pennsylvania Press, 2011.

Seneca. *Moral Essays.* Trans. John W. Basore. 2 vols. Loeb Classical Library. Cambridge, MA: Harvard University Press, 1998.

Shakespeare, William. *The Riverside Shakespeare.* Ed. Harry Levin. Boston: Houghton Mifflin, 1974.

Shannon, Laurie. *The Accommodated Animal: Cosmopolity in Shakespearean Locales.* Chicago: University of Chicago Press, 2013.

Sheffield, Frisbee C. *Plato's "Symposium": The Ethics of Desire.* Oxford: Oxford University Press, 2006.

Shuger, Debora. *The Renaissance Bible: Scholarship, Sacrifice, Subjectivity.* Berkeley: University of California Press, 1995.

Sidney, Philip. *An Apology for Poetry.* Ed. Forrest G. Robinson. New York: Macmillan, 1985.

Silberman, Lauren. *Transforming Desire: Erotic Knowledge in Books III and IV of "The Faerie Queene."* Berkeley: University of California Press, 1995.

Simpson, James. "The Power of Impropriety: Authorial Naming in *Piers Plowman.*" In *William Langland's "Piers Plowman": A Book of Essays,* ed. Kathleen M. Hewett-Smith, 145–65. New York: Routledge, 2001.

———. *Sciences and the Self in Medieval Poetry: Alan of Lille's "Anticlaudianus" and John Gower's "Confessio amantis."* Cambridge: Cambridge University Press, 1995.

Sitter, John. *The Cambridge Introduction to Eighteenth-Century Poetry.* Cambridge: Cambridge University Press, 2011.

Skelton, John. *Magnificence.* Ed. Paula Neuss. Baltimore: Johns Hopkins University Press, 1980.

Skulsky, Harold. *Milton and the Death of Man: Humanism on Trial in "Paradise Lost."* Newark: University of Delaware Press, 2000.

———. "Spenser's Despair Episode and the Theology of Doubt." *Modern Philology* 78, no. 3 (1981): 227–42.

Slights, Camille Wells. *The Casuistical Tradition in Shakespeare, Donne, Herbert, and Milton.* Princeton, NJ: Princeton University Press, 1991.

Smith, Bruce. "Premodern Sexualities." *PMLA* 115 (2000): 318–29.

Snow, Edward. "Marlowe's *Doctor Faustus* and the Ends of Desire." In *Two Renaissance Mythmakers: Christopher Marlowe and Ben Jonson,* ed. Alvin Kernan, 70–110. Baltimore: Johns Hopkins University Press, 1977.

Snyder, Susan. "The Left Hand of God: Despair in Medieval and Renaissance Tradition." *Studies in the Renaissance* 12 (1965): 18–59.

Spaemann, Robert. *Persons: The Difference between "Someone" and "Something."* Trans. Oliver O'Donovan. Oxford: Oxford University Press, 2006.

Spenser, Edmund. *The Faerie Queene.* Ed. A. C. Hamilton. New York: Longman, 2001.

———. *The Works of Edmund Spenser: A Variorum Edition.* Ed. Edwin Greenlaw, Charles Grosvenor Osgood, and Fredrick Morgan Padelford. Baltimore: Johns Hopkins University Press, 1934.

———. *The Yale Edition of the Shorter Poems of Edmund Spenser.* Ed. William Oram. New Haven, CT: Yale University Press, 1989.

Spivak, Bernard. *Shakespeare and the Allegory of Evil: The History of a Metaphor in Relation to His Major Villains.* New York: Columbia University Press, 1958.

Spruyt, Joke. "Duns Scotus's Criticism of Henry of Ghent's Notion of Free Will." In *John Duns Scotus: Renewal of Philosophy*, ed. E. P. Bos, 139–54. Amsterdam: Rodopi Press, 1998.

Stachniewski, John. *The Persecutory Imagination: English Puritanism and the Literature of Religious Despair.* Oxford: Clarendon Press, 1991.

Stafford, Emma. *Worshipping Virtues: Personification and the Divine in Ancient Greece.* Swansea: Duckworth and the Classical Press of Wales, 2001.

Stafford, Emma, and Judith Herrin, eds. *Personification in the Greek World: From Antiquity to Byzantium.* Aldershot: Ashgate, 2005.

Stephens, Dorothy. *The Limits of Eroticism in Post-Petrarchan Narrative.* Cambridge: Cambridge University Press, 1998.

Strier, Richard. "Milton's Fetters, or, Why Eden Is Better Than Heaven." *Milton Studies* 38 (2000): 169–97.

Stump, Eleonore. "Augustine on Free Will." In *The Cambridge Companion to Augustine*, ed. Eleonore Stump and Norman Kretzmann, 124–47. Cambridge: Cambridge University Press, 2001.

Sutcliffe, Matthew. *A Ful and Round Answer to N.D., Alias Robert Parsons, the Noddie his Foolish and Rude Warne-Word.* London, 1604.

Tanner, John S. "'Say First What Cause': Ricoeur and the Etiology of Evil in *Paradise Lost*." *PLMA* 103 (1988): 45–56.

Taylor, Charles. *A Secular Age.* Cambridge, MA: Harvard University Press, 2007.

Tertullian. *De anima.* Ed. J. H. Waszink. Leiden: Brill, 2010.

Teskey, Gordon. "Allegory." In *The Spenser Encyclopedia*, ed. A. C. Hamilton, 43–59. Toronto: University of Toronto Press, 1990.

———. *Allegory and Violence.* Ithaca, NY: Cornell University Press, 1996.

———. "Death in an Allegory." In *Imagining Death in Spenser and Milton*, ed. Elizabeth Jane Bellamy, Patrick Cheney, and Michael Schoenfeldt, 65–77. Basingstoke: Palgrave, 2003.

———. "From Allegory to Dialectic: Imagining Error in Spenser and Milton." *PMLA* 101 (1986): 9–23.

Treip, Mindele Anne. "'Reason Is Also Choice': The Emblematics of Free Will in *Paradise Lost*." *Studies in English Literature, 1500–1900* 31 (1991): 147–77.

Trevor, Douglas. *The Poetics of Melancholy in Early Modern England.* Cambridge: Cambridge University Press, 2004.

Tuckney, Anthony. *Thanatoktasia, or, Death disarmed: and the grave swallowed up in victory.* London, 1653.

Turner, Henry S. "Corporate Persons, between Law and Literature." In *The Oxford Handbook of English Law and Literature, 1500–1700*, ed. Bradin Cormack and Lorna Hutson. Oxford: Oxford University Press, forthcoming.

Valla, Lorenzo. *Dialectical Disputations.* Trans. Brian P. Coperhaver and Lodi Nauta. 2 vols. Cambridge, MA: Harvard University Press, 2012.

———. *Dialogue on Free Will.* Trans. Charles Edward Trinkaus. In *The Renaissance Philosophy of Man*, ed. Ernst Cassirer, Paul Oskar Kristeller, and John Herman Randall Jr., 155–82. Chicago: University of Chicago Press, 1948.

Van Dyke, Carolynn. *The Fiction of Truth: Structures of Meaning in Narrative and Dramatic Allegory.* Ithaca, NY: Cornell University Press, 1985.

Van Inwagen, Peter. *An Essay on Free Will.* Oxford: Clarendon Press, 1983.

Vondel, Joost van den. *Lucifer.* Trans. Noel Clark. Bath: Absolute Classics, 1990.

———. *Lucifer.* Trans. Watson Kirkconnell. In *The Celestial Cycle: The Theme of Paradise Lost in World Literature*, ed. Watson Kirkconnell, 361–421. Toronto: University of Toronto Press, 1952.

Wager, Lewis. *The Life and Repentance of Mary Magdalene.* London, 1566.

Wager, William. *The Longer Thou Livest and Enough Is as Good as a Feast.* Lincoln: University of Nebraska Press, 1967.

Wapull, George. *The Tide Tarryeth No Man.* London, 1576.

Watson, Gary. *Agency and Answerability.* Oxford: Clarendon Press, 2004.

Wever, Richard. *Lusty Juventus.* Ed. Helen Scarborough Thomas. New York: Garland, 1982.

Whitman, Jon. *Allegory: The Dynamics of an Ancient and Medieval Technique.* Cambridge, MA: Harvard University Press, 1987.

Wilks, John S. *The Idea of Conscience in Renaissance Tragedy.* New York: Routledge, 1990.

William of Ockham. *Quodlibetal Questions.* Trans. Alfred J. Freddoso and Francis E. Kelley. New Haven, CT: Yale University Press, 1991.

Willymat, William. *Physic to Cure the Most Dangerous Disease of Desperation.* London, 1605.

Wilson, Luke. *Theaters of Intention: Drama and the Law in Early Modern England.* Stanford, CA: Stanford University Press, 2000.

Wofford, Susanne. *The Choice of Achilles.* Stanford, CA: Stanford University Press, 1992.

Wojciehowski, Dolora A. *Old Masters, New Subjects: Early Modern and Poststructuralist Theories of the Will.* Stanford, CA: Stanford University Press, 1995.

Wolfe, Cary. *What Is Posthumanism?* Minneapolis: University of Minnesota Press, 2010.

Woodes, Nathaniel. *The Conflict of Conscience.* Oxford: Malone Society, 1952.

Wordsworth, William. "Preface to the *Lyrical Ballads.*" In *Lyrical Ballads,* ed. R. L. Brett and A. R. Jones. London: Methuen, 1965.

Wright, Thomas. *The Passions of the Minde in General.* Ed. Thomas O. Sloan. Urbana: University of Illinois Press, 1971.

Yachnin, Paul, and Jessica Slights, eds. *Shakespeare and Character: Theory, History, Performance, and Theatrical Persons.* New York: Palgrave, 2009.

Yates, Julian. "Accidental Shakespeare." *Shakespeare Studies* 34 (2006): 90–122.

———. "Counting Sheep: Dolly Does Utopia (Again)." *Rhizomes* 8 (2004): paras. 1–42.

———. "What Are 'Things' Saying in Renaissance Studies?" *Literature Compass* 3, no. 5 (2006): 992–1010.

Zackman, Randall C. *The Assurance of the Faith: Conscience in the Theology of Martin Luther and John Calvin.* Minneapolis: Fortress Press, 1993.

Zagzebsky, Linda. "The Uniqueness of Persons." *Journal of Religious Ethics* 29, no. 3 (2001): 401–23.

Karenina, Anna (character), 231
Kaske, Carol, 275n44
Keenleyside, Heather, 2
Kenny, Anthony, 262n5
Kierkegaard, Søren, 136, 147–48,
    272n3, 273n32
Kingsley-Smith, Jane, 176, 278n18
Knapp, Steven, 5, 41, 288n63
Krier, Theresa, 25, 41, 240, 259n91

Lakoff, George, 8
landscape
    in ancient and Christian
        literature, 52, 260n100
    barrier between mind and, 246–47
    human agent and, 251
    transactional, 20–21
Langland, William, 104
La Primaudaye, Pierre de, 89
Latour, Bruno, 2, 248
Leonard, John, 221
Leone Hebreo, 53–54, 175, 190, 199,
    255n20
Leviathan (Hobbes), 86
Lewis, C. S., 55, 179, 261n107
*Life and Repentance of Mary
    Magdalene, The* (Wager), 53,
    121–22, 123, 271n72
Like Will to Like (Fulwell), 121
Lille, Alain de, 28
liminal beings, 247, 248
literal character, 33, 48, 236
literary prosopopoeia, 4, 8, 12–13,
    86, 92
    See also personification
Locusts, The (P. Fletcher), 210, 237
Loewenstein, Joseph, 197
Lorris, Guillaume de, 39, 46–47
love
    ambiguity of, 175–76
    cruelty of, 278n11

as daemonic agent, 13, 175
disparate qualities of, 179–80
as divine madness, 189
dual function of, 177
free decision making about,
    198–99
as god and poetic figure, 173
iconographic depiction of, *172*
inspiration and, 194
personifications of, 35–36,
    173–74, 183, 245
in Platonic dialogues, 174–75
Plotinus's essay on, 175
reason and, 280n46
Renaissance interpretations of,
    175, 189–91
suffering and, 190
virtue and, 206
Lucifer
    fall of, 216–17, 218, 238–39
    sinful choice of, 226
    transformation to Satan, 223
    volition of, 238
Lucifer (Vondel), 220, 284nn24–25
Lukacher, Ned, 101, 103
Lupton, Thomas, 209
Lust (character), 36
Lusty Juventus (Wever), 122, 127
Luther, Martin
    on act of will, 266n85, 266n87
    on agent causation, 81–82
    break with Rome, 230
    commentary on Galatians, 17
    on daemonic conscience, 111
    on free choice, 269n35
    on Judas's betrayal of Christ,
        81–82
    moral choice of, 230
    notion of providence, 80
    on "royal freedom," 117
    on sin, 266n82

ANDREW ESCOBEDO is professor of English at Ohio State University and co-editor of *Spenser Studies*.